COGNITIVE STRUCTURE:

THEORY AND MEASUREMENT OF INDIVIDUAL DIFFERENCES

SCRIPTA SERIES IN PERSONALITY AND SOCIAL PSYCHOLOGY

Siegfried Streufert and Peter Suedfeld · *Consulting Editors*

King, Streufert, and Fiedler · Managerial Control and Organizational Democracy, 1978

Streufert and Streufert · Behavior in the Complex Environment, 1978

Gullahorn · Psychology and Women: In Transition, 1979

Scott, Osgood, and Peterson · Cognitive Structure, 1979

COGNITIVE STRUCTURE:

THEORY AND MEASUREMENT OF INDIVIDUAL DIFFERENCES

William A. Scott
The Australian National University

D. Wayne Osgood
Behavioral Research Institute
Boulder, Colorado

Christopher Peterson
Hamilton College

with the collaboration of
Ruth Scott
The Australian National University

1979

V. H. WINSTON & SONS
Washington, D.C.

A HALSTED PRESS BOOK

JOHN WILEY & SONS

New York   Toronto   London   Sydney

V. H. Winston & Sons, a Division of Scripta Technica, Inc.,
Publishers
1511 K Street, N.W., Washington, D.C.   20005

Distributed solely by Halsted Press, a Division of John Wiley
& Sons, Inc.

Library of Congress Cataloging in Publication Data:

Scott, William Abbott, 1926–
   Cognitive structure, theory and measurement of individual
differences.

   (Scripta series in personality and social psychology)
   Bibliography: p.
   1. Cognition.   2. Cognitive styles.   3. Personality.
I. Osgood, D. Wayne, joint author.   II. Peterson,
Christopher, joint author.   III. Title.
BF311.S39   153.4   79-12876
ISBN 0-470-26734-8 (Halsted)

Composition by Marie A. Maddalena, Scripta Technica, Inc.

To Victor Raimy, who made it all possible

CONTENTS

PREFACE

This book has three main objectives: to consider together several rather different perspectives on cognitive structure, within the framework of personality theory; to present in detail measures of several structural properties of cognition, so that they can be used directly by interested investigators; and to evaluate those measures critically, using data on their reliabilities and theoretically relevant correlates, collected in four different cultures.

We have drawn our ideas from many sources, including Gestalt psychology, theories of Lewin and Freud, of developmental epistemology, personal constructs, person perception, cognitive complexity, social judgment, and information integration. Segments of these theories are merged into a structural model of cognition from which we develop quantitative measures of several variable properties such as differentiation and integration, utilizing questionnaire-based descriptions from respondents of meaningful events in their lives. The questionnaires are presented in full, together with the formulae by which responses are combined to yield the structural measures. In addition, we describe procedures and indices developed by other investigators to assess related constructs.

As this is a relatively new and complicated area of psychological research, the measures are often inadequate, and we devote considerable attention to examining their strengths and weaknesses, drawing, where possible, on published data and on some original cross-cultural investigations in four countries—the United States, New Zealand, Australia, and Japan. In addition, we report data from these studies on the relations which the structural measures bear to such variables as information, intelligence, political ideology, and interpersonal adjustment. We hope that these results will serve to encourage improvements in both the conceptualization and measurement of cognitive structure as a central aspect of personality. One might even look forward to future efforts at measuring structural variables of personality processes not directly represented in the subjects' own cognitions.

All three authors are committed to better integration among the various fields of psychology and only regret that most of the progress in this direction has taken place at a conceptual, rather than an empirical, level. It seems that our subdisciplines are both advanced and divided by their specialized technologies. It has been a matter of some concern to us that the very title, cognitive structure, will have quite different meanings for psychologists reared within different traditions; hence, the special pains we have taken to specify our own focus so that other readers will feel neither lost nor offended. Nevertheless, in stating our definite preference for an objective, quantified approach to assessment, we run the risk of alienating some nearby investigators who prefer more global, judgmental approaches. This would be unfortunate, for we would rather hope that scholars with such preferences might learn as much from us as we have from them.

Our work on these problems began as long ago as the summer of 1958, when the first author attended a Behavioral Sciences Conference at the University of New Mexico, affording an opportunity to think about the relation between cognitive structure and social structure. Subsequently, over a number of years, development of measures was aided by many students—most notably by Kay Blight, Ruth Brush, John Crabbe, Leandre Desjardins, Jerry Diller, Elizabeth Faguy-Coté, Lynella Grant, Barbara Havassy, Stanley Jones, George Kelling, James Kline, Julie LeBach, Leon Rappoport, Mania Seferi, Carl Shames, Carl Sternberg, Richard Swanson, Theodore Weissbach, Robert Wyer, and Michael Ziegler. The investigations were supported financially by the National Institute of Mental Health, the University of Colorado, and The Australian National University.

Cross-cultural replications in Japan and New Zealand were made possible mainly by the imaginative contributions of Shigeo Imamura and Laurence Brown. Several chapters of this book have benefitted from critical reading by Rachelle Canter, Siegfried Streufert, and Peter Suedfeld. Typing of the final manuscript and earlier drafts was ably performed by Pat Macindoe, Phyllis O'Meara, and Gail Kern.

Our kind of work is slow and, in many ways, tedious. It depends on a politically tranquil, intellectually lively, and interpersonally supportive atmosphere in which scholars can concentrate primarily on seeking bright insights out of the gray welter of data. For a long time Victor Raimy helped foster that kind of atmosphere at the University of Colorado, so we gratefully dedicate this book to him.

William A. Scott

Chapter 1

INTRODUCTION

There are many perspectives on personality, each of which offers a different view of the ways people differ from one another. In this book we present an approach to studying personality in terms of cognitive structure. Our interest is in certain features of the way people view the world around them and in how these features relate to adaptation. Our conceptualization is defined in terms of a geometric model of cognitive representation.

The research presented spans well over a decade. The primary goal of this program of research has been to develop a set of procedures for measuring structural properties of cognition. It is in the area of assessment that research on individual differences in cognition has particularly fallen short. There has been a general failure to develop measures which are conceptually appropriate and methodologically sound. Instead, different investigators employ different measures for the same construct; the few attempts to compare measures typically show that they have little in common. Our ultimate objective is to help accomplish for cognitive structure what Alfred Binet, Lewis Terman, and others did for the concept of intelligence, namely to fix it in the psychologist's theoretical repertory by providing adequate measuring instruments which any investigator can use with minimal reliance on subjective judgment.

Of course, from the vantage of today one may recognize deficiencies associated with the concept of intelligence, many of which stem from years of reliance on a few standard measures. It seems almost impossible to root out of the popular culture the notion that capacity for adaptation is unitary, fixed, and inherited. It is even difficult to expose an assumption behind measures of intelligence that success in school is equivalent to successful human adaptation. There is little danger that the present effort will have an ultimately stultifying effect on psychological theory comparable to that charged by the critics of intelligence testing. Ours is only a modest beginning; it entails no single criterion of performance (like grades in school) and embodies no simple assumptions about what features of cognitive structure are likely to be adaptive or maladaptive. Our approach to the assessment of cognitive structure is more a strategy than a specific test, yet it offers a clear advantage over many other approaches by suggesting how to develop a variety of structural measures for any topic of interest. It is this modest contribution toward a technology that may help gain acceptance for the conceptual model we propose.

There are three general psychological terms which pervade this book: cognition, structure, and personality. Unfortunately, all three are used widely and variously, with the result that they have no specific meanings. This is not to say that the terms are meaningless; more likely, they take a variety of meanings because they are central to many psychological theories.

Cognition, in particular, has received increasing attention in recent years. Cognitive psychology has now taken a wide variety of forms, many having very little in common. For that reason, it is important for the reader to understand that the present book is based on only one approach to cognitive psychology. Our works falls within the tradition of cognitive social and personality psychology, as exemplified by the work of Kurt Lewin, Fritz Heider, Solomon Asch, and George Kelly. Since 1950, this approach to such topics as attitudes and attitude change, social influence, and person perception has been dominant in American social psychology.

The reader whose background is in other fields of cognitive psychology may be surprised to see how unfamiliar our approach is. In recent years, books bearing the title "cognitive psychology" have been devoted almost exclusively to experimental psychology, covering such topics as attention, pattern recognition, and memory. Though our use of the term cognitive structure is different from theirs, it is not capricious. There are both a coherent logic and a tradition of research behind our approach. We hope that cognitive psychologists from other areas find the view we offer an interesting alternative.

This book is divided into three sections. First is a section of theoretical chapters. One purpose of that section is to review certain uses of the terms cognition, structure, and personality and to make clear just what we will mean by them. We attempt to clarify the relation between personality and cognition, review certain conceptual issues from the field of personality which are relevant to our own work, and then consider research on cognitive structure leading to a presentation of our own model.

The second section presents a detailed description of assessment procedures, not only those implied by our own model, but also some that have gained currency through prior research by others. There are two major steps in assessing structural properties: the first, instrumentation, is aimed at eliciting responses from which a particular property can be inferred; the second, indexing, is aimed at scoring the responses so as to reflect the intended property accurately. We present examples of instruments for eliciting verbal responses and formulas for combining the responses into indices. The casual reader may wish to skip over these sections, using them for later reference when the time comes to apply the concepts and measures to a particular research project. In actual practice, most of the scoring is done by computer programs operating on data from rating forms, checklists, or free descriptions. The particular programs used are not included in this section because of their length and dependence upon specific techniques (punchcard input/output and **FORTRAN** IV compiler), but they are available from the authors on request.

The third section presents some findings on correlates of the structural properties. These represent only the beginning of programmatic research and cover a range of independent and dependent variables dictated more by the circumstances of study than by the demands of theory. They serve to illustrate ways in which structural concepts can illuminate processes of adaptation to complex environments. The section concludes with a suggestion for future research and a consideration of unsolved problems.

SECTION I

THEORIES OF COGNITIVE STRUCTURE

The next four chapters develop a perspective on cognitive structure which has grown out of the works of recent personality theorists. Chapter 2 is concerned with the meaning of cognition, Chapter 3 with the meaning of personality, and Chapter 4 with conceptions of cognitive structure offered by other investigators. Our own formulation, presented in Chapter 5, incorporates many of these ideas into a systematic model, which provides a basis for measuring procedures to be presented in the following section.

COGNITION:
CONTENT AND PROCESS

The concept of cognition may be traced to Plato and Aristotle's division of the mind into three faculties: cognition or knowing, affect or feeling, and conation or willing. As the term is generally used in modern psychology, cognition concerns that which is known by an individual. Our interest is in knowledge in a subjective rather than an objective sense, the ideas a person holds about the self and world.

To speak of "the world as one knows it" is to speak of one's awareness of reality. Cognition is the representation of reality that the person experiences as reality itself. It is from the point of view of an external observer, the psychologist, that cognition is regarded as representation. An individual may report, "That is a bad man," with all the conviction attached to the statement, "That is a cat." Taking the position of an external observer, one would say that the former cognition entails evaluative and attitudinal components as well as perceptual ones, but the individual holding the beliefs might consider the two equally objective. Likewise, the memory, "He has harmed me," is a present cognition, presumably derived from past experience, but not necessarily as a true record. Thus, while cognitions are typically seen by the holder as facts about reality, they may or may not have some factual basis in the eyes of an external observer.

Our use of the term requires a distinction between the contents of cognition—a person's ideas about the world—and cognitive processes—the mechanisms by which ideas arise, are maintained and transformed. Other psychologists might subsume both contents and processes under a single category called simply "cognition." In his influential book, Neisser (1967) uses the term cognition for what is here considered cognitive processes, "all the processes by which sensory input is transformed, reduced, elaborated, stored, recovered, and used" (p. 4).

Though cognitive contents and cognitive processes are in some ways a single field of study, there are good reasons for using separate terms to refer to them. Because their subject matter is the individual's own experience, a person can, in principle, give accurate reports about the contents of cognitions. The investigator's ability to choose the right questions and the person's cooperation and linguistic fluency set the only limits on the adequacy of such reports. Cognitive processes, on the other hand, are not typically available to awareness (see Nisbett & Wilson, 1977). If an investigator asked a respondent, "Do you think that your friend, Charles, is intelligent?", it is reasonable to assert that the answer accurately reflects the content of cognitions. A question concerning cognitive processes, such as "By what process of reasoning did you come to the conclusion that Charles is intelligent?", is another matter. The respondent is not likely to know how he or she came to that opinion. We are often aware that we are weighing information in the process of coming to a judgment, and when our beliefs are challenged we can usually offer a line of reasoning to justify them. Nevertheless, we have arrived at most of our ideas about the surrounding world without ever being aware of going through such processes, and there is no guarantee that our occasional interpretations of the processes are accurate or complete.

The task of studying cognitive content is essentially different from that of studying cognitive processes. To describe the contents of cognition is to describe a representation of reality, and thus to describe the facts from some person's point of view. Though a subject's cognitive contents are not directly known to an observing psychologist, they are known to the subject. Cognitive processes, on the other hand, involve not beliefs but mechanisms, structures, and states. Neither the observing psychologist nor the subject can know these processes directly; they must be inferred from behavior and reports.

It is also necessary to distinguish psychological concepts which describe, or refer to, cognition from the contents of cognition itself. That a psychological construct describes a person's views does not imply that the construct itself will be represented among those views. For example, the concept of internal locus of control is defined as the generalized belief that one is in control of one's destiny. It would not be reasonable, however, to assess this variable by asking a respondent, "Is your locus of control internal?", or, "Are you in control of your own destiny?" More likely than not, the first question would be meaningless. The person might be more comfortable answering the second question, but most investigators would be reluctant to accept the answer as an adequate measure of internal locus of control. To accept such a measure would be to agree that whatever the respondent means by "I feel in control of my destiny," expresses the essence of what is meant by internal locus of control. The researcher interested in a more complex conception of the variable will require a procedure that captures it in more detail. An adequate measure would require a series of questions about the respondent's views, each of which can be answered meaningfully, and which taken together will approach the full meaning of the concept.

VARIETIES OF COGNITIVE PSYCHOLOGY

An enormous range of research is being conducted today under the rubric of cognitive psychology. Though the cognitive psychology of experimental psychologists has little in common with the cognitive psychology of social psychologists, both use the label with good reason. To gain a feeling of what is meant by cognitive content and processes, it is worth considering some illustrations of both as studied in different areas of psychology.

Experimental Cognitive Psychology

There has been a virtual explosion of cognitive psychology within experimental psychology during the past two decades. Though many prominent experimental psychologists of the late 19th century studied topics that would now be recognized as cognitive psychology, their work was all but lost during the domination of behaviorism. Experimental psychologists turned away from the "study of the mind" in despair over the fruitlessness of the methods of introspection employed by Wundt and Titchener. Modern day experimentalists have discovered, however, that there are much sounder and more productive methods for studying mental processes, that rigorous science does not demand that the organism be regarded as unthinking.

A wide variety of current experimental research is generally classified as cognitive, including such topics as visual memory, attention, pattern recognition, concept formation, short-term memory, and long-term memory. An excellent review of these may be found in the handbooks edited by Estes (1975-1978). A few examples of research paradigms will give some of the flavor of experimental cognitive psychology:

Sperling (1960) developed a technique which established the existence of visual memory, using a tachistoscope to display an array of letters for 50 milliseconds. Under such circumstances, subjects were able to report about 4.5 items from a display that contained 6 or more items. After showing the letters, Sperling projected a circle where one of them had been, and asked the subject to identify that letter. The accuracy of reports depended on the amount of time between the display of the letter and the appearance of the circle. When the elapsed time was very short, subjects were quite accurate; if a second or more passed, accuracy decreased markedly. Thus, for a very brief period, there is a visual memory of the display. When attention is directed to a particular portion of it, the subject is able to "inspect" that memory and recall the item.

A study by Peterson and Peterson (1959) illustrates the manner in which psychologists study short-term memory. The task set for their subjects was to remember nonsense syllables of three consonants. The investigators' interest was in seeing how long items could be remembered when subjects were prevented from rehearsing them. Between the time subjects saw a nonsense syllable and the time they were asked to recall it, they were required to count backwards by threes or fours. Given this distracting task, recall declined to about 10% after only 15 seconds. From this finding, Peterson and Peterson deduced that perceived events enter short-term memory, which decays very rapidly unless the events can be mentally rehearsed. If there is opportunity for rehearsal, short-term memory can be maintained much longer, and events may enter long-term memory, where they can be stored indefinitely.

A different topic within experimental cognitive psychology is concept formation. Bruner, Goodnow, and Austin (1956) established the basic paradigm of research on this process. Their method was to present subjects with a series of objects (these may be physical objects, pictures, or descriptions) each of which is identified as a positive or negative instance of a concept. The subject must use this minimal information to discover the basis of classification which comprises the concept. In this study, university students were shown a succession of 6 cards that differed in several ways, such as number of figures (1, 2, or 3), kind of figures (square, circle, or cross), and color of figures (red, blue, or green). Half the cards were identified by the experimenter as instances of "*X*," and subjects were asked to determine the basis of classification—for example, red squares or three crosses. This was a rather difficult task, because there were barely enough instances offered to allow a correct answer. These investigators were interested in the sorts of hypotheses and strategies of confirmation used by their subjects.

It is usually the case in such experimental studies that subjects, rather than acquiring novel concepts, learn to choose, from a preestablished repertory, the concepts required by an experimenter. For this reason, some investigators prefer to call these studies of concept attainment, rather than of concept formation. However designated, studies of this type have been useful for increasing our understanding of reasoning and problem solving.

Developmental Cognitive Psychology

While many experimental and social psychologists study cognitive problems from a developmental perspective, certain topics are particularly identified with developmental psychology. Two of these are intelligence and stages of mental development.

Few psychological concepts have received as much attention as intelligence. Beginning with the first standardized tests of Binet, intelligence tests have been developed with the primary goal of predicting academic achievement. The methods of testing are far more advanced than the conceptualization of their meaning; hence we are better able to predict academic achievement than to explain these predictions. Nevertheless, it is clear that the skills involved are primarily cognitive, for they concern the acquisition and retention of knowledge.

Over the past several decades, Piaget (1927, 1932, 1952) has extensively studied principles of cognitive development, and his theories have recently gained worldwide popularity. The main tenets of Piaget's theory are that there are discrete stages of mental development and that each of these stages is characterized by a different form of reasoning. Piaget distinguishes four stages of intellectual development: sensorimotor, preoperational, concrete operations, and formal operations. One may contrast the middle stages, e.g.: In the preoperational stage, which usually extends approximately from age 2 to 7, symbolic functioning begins; that is, the ability to use words or objects to represent something else. During this stage the child maintains an egocentric view of the world and tends to attribute animate characteristics to inanimate objects. From the age of about 7 to 12, children are said to be in the concrete operational stage because they are able to conduct mental operations on concrete objects, grouping objects into classes and ordering them on the basis of relations such as size. Features of the preoperational phase disappear; for instance, through the performance of mental operations on objects, the child learns that they will appear different to someone standing in another position. Thus, egocentric thinking gradually gives way to the understanding that there are other valid points of view.

Social Cognitive Psychology

Because the approach to studying personality which is presented later in this book is derived largely from the social psychological study of cognition, and Chapter 4 is devoted to background in that field, only the study of attitudes will be discussed here as an example to compare with those from experimental and developmental psychology. Attitudes have been studied in various ways within disciplines ranging from experimental psychology to political science, but they have undoubtedly received the most attention from social psychologists. There have, of course, been many definitions of attitudes. The one offered by Krech and Crutchfield (1948) will be useful for present purposes because it shares a great deal with other prominent definitions. These authors proposed that an attitude is "an enduring organization of motivational, emotional, perceptual, and cognitive processes with respect to some aspect of the individual's world" (p. 152).

Most definitions refer not only to cognitive components, but to affective (emotional) and conative (motivational) components as well. Operationally, however, most measures are derived from verbal report, hence are "cognitive" in this sense. Rarely is there any physiological measure of an emotional state or any behavioral measure of a motivational tendency. Instead, attitudes are typically inferred from affectively oriented beliefs about the attitudinal object. For example, Woodmansee and Cook (1967) assessed attitudes towards Blacks from statements like these: "I think Negroes have a kind of quiet courage which few Whites have." "Although social equality of the races may be the democratic way, a good many Negroes are not yet ready to practice the self-control that goes along with it."

These researchers chose a set of 100 items on the basis of correlations among a larger set of trial items, so that there was a tendency among people to answer items consistently pro- or anti-Black. The statements include a mixture of cognitive, affective, and conative beliefs. Agreement with the second statement indicates the belief that Blacks lack self-control (a question of "fact" which is cognitive), often used to justify the opinion that Blacks should be denied social equality (a preference for action which is conative), both of which imply a negative evaluation of Blacks (a feeling of dislike which is affective). As with most attitude scales, emphasis is on the affective component, cognitively assessed. In scoring the Woodmansee and Cook measure, one simply counts the number of favorable statements endorsed and the number of unfavorable statements rejected.

A COMPARISON OF EXPERIMENTAL, DEVELOPMENTAL, AND SOCIAL PSYCHOLOGICAL APPROACHES

The three approaches to cognitive psychology illustrated above differ substantially in focus. The study of attitudes deals mainly with ideas already held, and presumably of substantial importance to the person, while studies in the experimental tradition focus on new combinations of ideas that result from scanning and restructuring presented stimuli. In attitude assessment, the required task is expressive, while the subject's task in studies of concept formation is to solve a problem. Studies of cognitive development in the Piagetian tradition are concerned with the way in which a child's successive views of the world each depend on those which preceded it, while the social psychological approach is generally ahistorical, in that the nature of the present view is considered independently of its antecedents. In the developmental tradition, only certain types of ideas are expected at any one stage or level of intelligence, while in the experimental tradition, ideas are assumed to depend largely on individual experience.

What all three approaches have in common is a focus on the subject's phenomenology. A person's reported ideas are taken as valid indicators of what they actually are. Of course, it is recognized that some people may misreport what they think, or misunderstand the task and therefore give misleading evidence about their ideas, but all investigations of cognitive contents and cognitive processes imply that subjects themselves are potentially the most accurate reporters of their ideas, once their cooperation has been enlisted.

Cognitive Content and Cognitive Processes

The distinction between cognitive content and cognitive processes will prove useful for contrasting the three approaches to cognitive psychology.

Any study of cognitive processes specifies certain contents on which those processes operate. Research within the experimental tradition is notable for complex, detailed elaboration of cognitive processes. Through systems and computer analogies, sophisticated models of human information processing have been developed. These have often dealt with very narrow contents. For instance, the representations of reality involved in the three experimental research paradigms considered on p. 9 would amount to: "The letter at that location was H," "That nonsense syllable was NTL," and "The Xs are red squares." More complicated problems can be tackled, however, e.g., in the study of how short prose passages are remembered and how chess games are played.

Broader conceptions of cognitive content typically arise within developmental approaches to cognitive psychology. The study of intelligence is an interesting case in that it seems to presume very broad conceptions of cognitive process and content, though neither is specified. Since intelligence predicts scholastic performance, it must presuppose the diverse and complicated cognitive processes which give rise to academic learning. Furthermore, the cognitive contents (ideas about the world) resulting from these processes potentially include all human knowledge. On the other hand, those who study intelligence have yet to provide persuasive theories of cognitive contents and processes to elaborate these implications.

Piaget's theory of developmental stages includes useful notions of cognitive contents and processes, capturing in both cases a very meaningful portion of the child's world view. Concepts such as egotism and animism refer primarily to contents, the substance of the ideas: A young child does not hold opinions about what others think which are distinct from what the child thinks; inanimate objects such as clouds and trees are imbued with animate characteristics such as thoughts and desires. Piaget's theory refers to cognitive processes as types of reasoning in which children engage. During the period of concrete operations the child is able to reason by certain operations on concrete objects, but is unable to engage in abstract reasoning. These processes determine in a very general way the manner in which children are able to comprehend the world around them.

Social psychological approaches to cognition tend to emphasize cognitive contents more than processes. Attitudes are a particular variety of cognitive content: favorable and unfavorable beliefs about an object. Processes such as learning, forgetting, and enhancement of contrast are often studied in an experimental way, as is attitude change, a process of transformation from one attitude to another. For example, social judgment theory (Sherif & Hovland, 1961) proposes that attitude change is a function of the original attitudinal position of the person in relation to the position advocated by a persuasive communication. Most such studies refer to contents that are real and meaningful to the subject—such as war, politics, and sex—rather than to deliberately meaningless contents, such as nonsense syllables that have been traditionally used by experimental psychologists to avoid confusing their view of the process by contents that have different meanings for different subjects.

Our own approach to cognitive structure falls within the social psychological tradition, in its reliance on specific, meaningful content, rather than on content constructed specifically for the occasion of study. Consonant with the experimental tradition, however, we conceive of structural properties as content-free in the sense that they can be applied to any cognitive contents that a person may possess, just as the processes of learning and memory are assumed to apply to any content that is introduced by an investigator.

There is another way in which our approach follows the social psychological, more than the experimental, tradition. That is in treating the contents and structure of cognition as parts of a relatively enduring personality system, rather than as transient events that are made and unmade by changing circumstances. The next chapter elaborates this view.

Chapter 3

COGNITION AS AN ASPECT OF PERSONALITY

Differences among the various branches of psychology arise not only in the kinds of behavior chosen for the study, but, more fundamentally, in the manner by which behavior is explained. The personality psychologist seeks to interpret diverse behaviors as due to consistent differences among people. Such an explanation might be proposed for any behavior; all that is necessary is that the behavior be seen as part of some larger pattern of what a person does. The task of the personality psychologist is to identify within-individual regularities in behavior and between-individual differences.

INDIVIDUAL DIFFERENCES

The mark of personality research is a concern with variables describing individual differences, commonly called personality traits. Whether they are defined as behavioral tendencies or as hypothetical structures and processes, certain features characterize personality traits: They are typically nonmaterial, nonbiological variables which are general, distinctive, and enduring. Generality refers to the range of behavior to which the trait applies. Though intelligence, the global capacity to acquire new information, would make a reasonable personality trait, the ability to perform specific acts, such as tight-rope walking, would not, even though such an ability is both distinctive and enduring.

Personality traits distinguish among people by dividing them into categories. Features which are not distinctive, those which all people have in common, do not qualify as personality traits. Though the term personality is often associated with the uniqueness of individuals, it is not necessary that a personality trait, or a set of traits embodied in a theory, differentiate all people from each other. Not only would that be impossible, given our current measurement techniques, but it would also make generalizations across people impossible.

The enduring quality of personality traits is only relative; any property that characterizes a person at one moment may be inapplicable at another. Nevertheless, ephemeral features are of little interest since the goal is to find regularities in behavior. Though any trait is potentially subject to change, the study of personality is most concerned with those which are typically more constant. Stabilities are, however, rarely as great as trait language implies; one can only discern tendencies to behave in a certain way, not the certainty of recurrence. A personality trait as measured is but an event—fixed as in a photograph—which may be transient or enduring, depending on the aspects to which one attends. The flushed face vanishes, while the vulnerability to hurt remains.

Personality is often spoken of as an entity which people possess. Just as one's body possesses various features, so, according to this view, does one's personality. From this perspective, the purpose of personality research is to explain the nature of that entity and determine its effects on behavior. A major problem arises, however, when one seeks a definition of personality as entity. There are definitions aplenty (most personality theorists have offered one), but they have remarkably little in common. A review of prominent definitions reveals that they constitute policy statements as to what will be included in the writer's theory rather than criteria for distinguishing personality from other phenomena (Levy, 1970).

As can be seen from this disagreement, there is no basis for concluding that there is a thing called personality possessed by individuals. We assert instead that personality is a set of characteristics imputed to the individual by an outside observer utilizing a frame of reference provided by a theory. This perspective constitutes a nominalist position, within which personality is considered a hypothetical construct, postulated by an observer to account for stabilities in behavior. In highly developed sciences, there is typically agreement among observers on the meaning of important constructs, but such is not the case in today's psychology. Psychologists' conceptions of personality are typically more sophisticated and complex than those of laymen, but they are probably just as diverse. Diversity is not necessarily undesirable. Both the wave and particle theories of light are useful, and it is likely that a variety of perspectives on personality would encompass a great deal of truth. On the other hand, there is scant evidence to support the complexities of most available personality theories.

THE NATURE OF PERSONALITY THEORY

More than any other branch of psychology, personality has been known for its theories; it is the one branch in which theories have been more prominent than research. What has been most notable about personality theories is their scope. As Hall and Lindzey (1970) put it, "Theories of personality . . . have generally accepted the challenge of accounting for or incorporating events of the most varied nature so long as they possess demonstrated functional significance for the individual" (p. 18). Though there have been complex theories in all areas of psychology, none have addressed as many facets of human behavior as the personality theories of Freud, Jung, Murray, and Lewin.

It appears, however, that the days of grand theorizing have passed. In the last two decades it is hard to identify any new theories of grand scope; the most recent efforts which qualify are probably those of Julian Rotter (1954) and George Kelly (1955). This is not to say that personality psychologists have lost their penchant for theorizing. As with all of psychology, the last two decades have been the busiest for personality. Along with an enormous increase in empirical work, there have also been many new theoretical developments. In comparison to their predecessors, however, modern theorists have limited their attention to more circumscribed problems. They have not sought, as did Freud, the wellsprings of all human activity; they have focused instead on more narrow aspects of the individual such as dogmatism, cognitive complexity, self-disclosure, and locus of control.

Levy (1970) points out that grand theories still play an important role in the study of personality because they offer broad conceptions of human behavior, suggesting questions to be asked and the form which answers might take. Nevertheless, it must be remembered that most of these theories were originally proposed by clinical psychologists, whose primary goal was to construct a framework to guide psychotherapy. Their theories operate at a level of generality that presents difficulties for empirical research; often they are founded on analogy where the researcher requires analysis. Grand theories have paved the way for modern research by providing a forum in which basic conceptual issues in the study of personality were defined. More circumscribed theories now seem to meet the needs of researchers better and, as the reader will discover in later chapters, the present offering is of that variety.

The grand theorists typically sought a complete description of personality. Adopting such a goal implies a definition of personality as an entity which people possess. From the nominalist perspective which we have chosen, complete description of personality is an impossibility; there is nothing to describe, only recurrent behaviors to explain. It is meaningless to ask whether or not a construct such as dogmatism is a part of personality, because personality is a hypothetical construct. That dogmatism is a personality trait often used to describe people is all that need to be said concerning its relation to personality. Our attention turns instead to the value of the concept: What is important is whether or not it is useful for systematizing and better understanding diverse behavioral phenomena and ultimately for predicting behavior.

Thus, it is overt behavior which gives rise to theories and explanatory constructs, and it is overt behavior against which the utility of the constructs should be appraised. A feature which has characterized the field of personality is its focus on complex behavior. (This may be due more to historical circumstances than to the nature of the subject matter.) Instead of attempting to explain left and right turns in a maze or speed of running, which are unequivocal dependent variables, personality research has generally been aimed at accounting for complex achievements such as adjustment, occupational success, marital stability, and juvenile delinquency. Such socially significant behaviors are overt acts or accomplishments in terms of which individuals differ and on which a given person changes over time and circumstances. They are usually operations or transformations on the person's environment; they are ways in which a person is known to others. The social significance of these behaviors makes personality research both important and interesting, but their complexity has made personality a difficult domain in which to conduct research of the highest scientific standards.

Descriptive and Explanatory Concepts

Though theories arise out of an attempt to account for observed events, they sometimes take on lives of their own, defining a new reality and posing additional problems for solution. So it has been with personality theories. Psychoanalytic theory, for example, was born in an attempt to account for neuroses, and did so (at least in part) through a structural model which includes the mental domains of id, ego, and superego. Subsequently, theoretical effort was directed toward accounting for postulated or inferred relationships among these domains, such as how the ego handles stresses arising out of conflict between the id and superego. In other words, hypothetical constructs have been substituted for the behaviors they were designed to explain, and they have become foci of inquiry in their own right.

The line between hypothetical and descriptive concepts is often fuzzy; in fact, some notions have made a transition from one status to the other. At the time it was first proposed, the idea of electricity was a hypothetical construct, an unobservable entity which would account for a variety of previously unexplained phenomena. Evidence gradually accumulated to demonstrate the usefulness of the construct; it served to organize so much knowledge that means were developed for measuring electricity directly. One can now observe its presence through instruments whose operation is based on scientifically established principles.

Hypothetical concepts in personality theory have yet to attain this status. As an example, consider Allport's (1961) concept of trait, defined as a "neuropsychic structure having the capacity to render many stimuli functionally equivalent and to initiate and guide equivalent (meaningfully consistent) forms of adaptive and expressive behavior" (p. 347). Traits, as defined by Allport, are hypothetical constructs. We have no way of directly knowing whether or not such neuropsychic structures exist; certainly, physiological psychology has not revealed any structures of that coherence and comprehensiveness. If we wish to measure a trait such as generosity, we must do so indirectly. There is no means of measuring neuropsychic structures, so the trait must be inferred from other indicators. One practical means would be to assess the tendency to act in a generous manner across a series of circumstances which would call for such behavior. If a neuropsychic structure guiding generous actions were present, it would result in that behavior.

Instead of postulating an underlying neural entity, one might simply define a trait as a behavior tendency; generosity is a tendency to behave in a generous manner. Given such a definition, generosity could be assessed directly, by observing the behavior which defines the trait; we need no other evidence to support the concept.

There are advantages and disadvantages to both approaches. The primary advantage of hypothetical constructs is the predictive power they lend. By speculating about something that is not itself observable, the theorist may be able to connect logically, and thereby explain, many observable phenomena which would otherwise seem unrelated. The scope of behavior explained through the mental domains hypothesized by psychoanalytic theory suggests the comprehensiveness of this approach. Nevertheless, such logical edifices do not extend knowledge unless they lead to testable propositions. The value of including hypothetical constructs is that questions are raised which can later be answered. Unless testable propositions are forthcoming, hypothetical constructs serve only to obscure.

Instead of providing fruitful sources of testable propositions, hypothetical constructs in personality theory have often just superimposed analogy or speculation on the observed facts. Defining traits as neuropsychic structures does not help relate traits to other variables. No testable hypotheses follow from this definition that would not also follow from defining a trait as a behavioral tendency. The role of neuropsychic structure in Allport's definition is only to assert that all behavior has a neurological basis. Regardless of the validity of that assumption, including it in the definition serves only to obscure the concept of trait and to make the derivation of testable propositions more difficult.

While descriptive concepts are more restrictive for the theorist, they are much more straightforward for the researcher. Propositions involving descriptive concepts are necessarily testable because they provide a forum for discourse which does not include speculations about the unobservable.

The problem which introduced this discussion, the replacement of behavior by hypothetical constructs as the things to be explained, demonstrates a confusion of hypothetical and descriptive concepts. Since descriptive concepts are themselves observable, they may legitimately serve as either explanatory variables or as the subject matter to be explained. This is not the case for hypothetical constructs; they are appropriate only in an explanatory role. To treat hypothetical constructs as dependent variables is to seek explanations for things which may not even exist. Certainly, higher-order explanations have their role in science, as exemplified in contemporary physics, but only when these "explanations of explanations" clarify further the original observations of interest.

Independent Variables

Theories differ principally in the kinds of explanatory variables they include. A single dependent variable, such as proximity of a newly married couple's residence to the residence of their parents, may be investigated from a variety of perspectives. Within psychoanalytic theory, it might be seen as depending on the maintenance or resolution of oedipal conflicts. Within Lewinian field theory, it might be interpreted in terms of the new couple's valences for parents in relation to their valences for a state of independence. An anthropologist might expand the perspective to a cross-cultural explanation in terms of neolocal vs. patrilocal rules of residence prevailing within the society. Each of these sets of independent variables provides a satisfactory explanation in terms of the particular theory by relating a new event to familiar concepts.

Considering only psychological theories of behavior, three major classes of independent variables can be identified, dealing respectively with characteristics of the stimulus events, with individual predispositions, and with changes in individuals over time. Propositions about the impact of stimuli are most common in theories of perception—for example, Fechner's law and the Gestalt principle of Prägnanz, both of which describe typical effects of stimuli on most humans. Propositions about individual dispositions abound in trait and type theories—for example, Sheldon's theories concerning the relation of physique to temperament and the theory of the authoritarian personality. Propositions about the way people change are found both in theories of child development, such as Piaget's, and in learning theories which explain the acquisition of skills and dispositions.

The more extensive a theory, the more likely it is to cover all three classes of independent variables and their interactions. In a single theory, reactions to stimuli might be explained by the characteristics of perceivers, and changes in these characteristics might be attributed to experiences with stimuli. Comprehensive personality theories of the past usually included all three classes of independent variables. Most current personality theories concentrate on individual differences with some consideration of their origins in personal experiences. Theories from experimental psychology have emphasized common responses to stimuli and their origins in typical characteristics of the nervous system.

Nomothetic and Idiographic Propositions

It is commonplace to contrast psychology, the study of individuals, with sociology, the study of groups. Yet it is doubtful whether any science, including psychology, is concerned with an individual per se. Instead, the particular case is seen as manifesting a general principle which presumably applies to a larger set of comparable cases. The misunderstanding probably arises out of confusion over the use of the terms "person" and "individual." The person is the focus of personality theories; most constructs are ascribed to "the person" or "the individual." Nevertheless, this locus is to be understood, not as a neurophysiological organism, but as an abstract and generalized fiction which represents many individuals.

A personality theory may include a proposition like "people with high need for achievement tend to prefer moderate levels of risk." Such a proposition refers to a class of people every bit as much as does a sociological proposition like "lower class members of a society are more likely than upper class members to advocate change in the status quo." The main difference is that the independent variables found in most psychological theories, the psychologist's bases for classifying people, depend for their assessment on responses of specific people, while the independent variables of most sociological theories are appraised from external circumstances. Status on an independent variable like level of achievement motivation must be assessed from the person's test behavior, while socioeconomic status is typically ascertained from characteristics of the person's environment. Thus, psychological theories are no more individual in their focus than sociological theories; they simply employ a different way of classifying people into groups for which differential predictions are to be made. The individual is the unit of analysis, a carrier of variables, rather than the final object of study.

Our interest throughout this book lies in nomothetic propositions. A nomothetic proposition is one which applies across a population of persons, in contrast to an idiographic proposition, which applies to a single individual. It has often been said that clinical study of the individual demands idiographic propositions of the type, "John Jones is likely to react anxiously to displays of affection from women." A science of the individual would, in principle, be possible through observation of one's behavior as it fluctuates systematically over time and circumstances. But such idiographic propositions would have little utility for understanding other people. Even John Jones' behavior has meaning only in relation to implicit nomothetic variables that apply to other people as well. His therapist would be interested in his anxiety only because most men do not react that way to displays of affection from women.

Traits vs. States

Traits refer to enduring individual differences, while states arise out of changing circumstances. The concept of trait is ancient, antedating systematic psychology by many centuries. The definition of the term adopted here derives from Allport's definition, previously discussed, but without any neurological referents. A trait is any psychological variable that is general, distinctive, and enduring. Thus, the term encompasses such varied concepts as attitudes, motives, abilities, knowledge, habits, defense mechanisms, intelligence, and mental health.

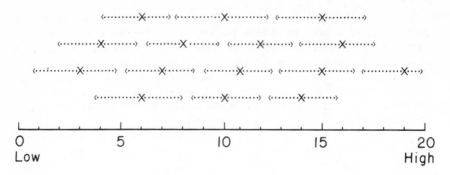

Fig. 1. Hypothetical distribution of 15 people on the trait, achievement motivation. *X*s represent "typical" locations of individuals; lines represent individual fluctuations in the trait over time.

It is useful to distinguish a trait from a characteristic: A trait is a dimension, continuum, or other basis of classification consisting of two or more categories, each of which represents a distinguishable characteristic. A person is assigned to only one of the categories; thus, characteristics are mutually exclusive and, together, represent all possible positions on a trait. To say that a trait is distinctive implies that people are distributed over two or more categories. To say that a trait is enduring implies that individual locations are fairly constant and that people are usually found in the same category on repeated observations.

A trait may be schematically represented as in Figure 1, which illustrates a hypothetical distribution of 15 people (indicated by *X*s) along a continuum representing the trait, achievement motivation. The trait is measured by a test with 20 dichotomously scored items, so the possible range of scores is from 0 to 20. Extending from each *X* are arrows indicating typical fluctuations of the individual from one time to another. To the extent that such fluctuations are small, on the average, the trait is stable; to the extent that they are large, the trait is variable, and approaches the character of a state. What constitutes a large or small fluctuation might be specified by considering the theoretical scale limits (0 to 20); but a more useful standard of comparison is the range of inter-individual variability typically encountered. Test-retest reliability indicates consistency across assessments in this way. The concept of a trait as a relatively enduring quality has meaning only if the average intra-individual variability is less than the typical inter-individual variability

If most individuals fluctuate so much over time that their average locations are almost the same, there is no point in calling the variable a trait. The term "state" is used to designate a psychological variable on which all individuals are expected to fluctuate over time, with no typical, enduring location. The line of demarcation between trait and state is not precise; in fact, many psychological constructs partake of both qualities. Moods and emotions are usually considered states, but motives too may show wide intra-individual fluctuations. A person may have an average level of achievement motivation, with a varying level of activation; the motive is aroused or sated depending on recent behaviors, on the conditions to which the person has been exposed, and on the strength of competing motives. There are no a priori grounds for distinguishing traits from states. Instead, the researcher must consider the relative amounts of inter- and intra-individual variation in scores over time to determine the degree to which a variable displays both trait-like and state-like qualities.

Interaction of Personality and Situation

Because the traits of individuals are so central to the study of personality, it is tempting to treat them as adequate explanations for all action. This "organism error" has plagued the psychology of personality. Generality across a variety of behaviors is one of the defining qualities of traits, but it is a problematic one, for consistency across behavior in different circumstances is often difficult to demonstrate. The statements "John is intelligent" and "Jane has a strong drive to succeed" are not likely to predict most of the acts in which John and Jane engage.

The validity of personality traits has both methodological and theoretical limitations. Most personality traits are inferred from very restricted samples of behavior, such as paper-and-pencil tests or content analysis of imaginative stories. Even though the psychometrician may aim to construct a test that samples widely from typical behavior repertoires, this can be accomplished only to a limited degree without overtaxing the respondent's patience. Furthermore, the only sources of information available are likely to be verbal responses and very limited observations of action. Thus, measures of traits are ordinarily based on samples of behavior that are too small and too unrepresentative to justify the generalizations made from them.

Even if a test sample were ideal, it could only predict behavior outside the test situation to the extent that the respondent's behavior is consistent from one circumstance to another. A moment's reflection will indicate that this is rarely the case, if only because most circumstances do not afford a ready opportunity to display all of one's personality traits. It is rather difficult to be achievement-oriented while watching a movie or to display superior intellect while swimming or eating. The situations ideally suited for displaying one trait are not particularly appropriate for displaying others.

The situational limitation on displaying personality traits is likely to be overlooked by a committed personologist, who may single out the few instances when a trait of interest is most clearly manifest. More realistically, one must recognize that the determination of behavior is only in part personality-based; it is also dependent on the situation and on the interaction between personality and situation. Figure 2 depicts this notion schematically. The cells of the matrix represent observed behavior of a particular individual in a particular situation. The rows represent individuals and the columns situations. One can abstract commonalities across the several situations in a

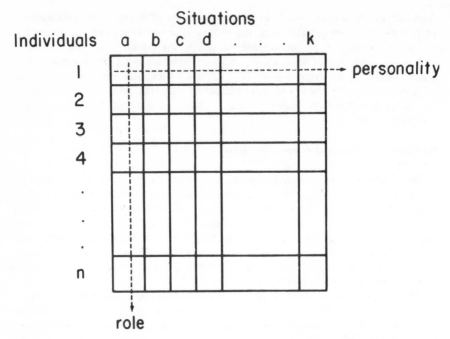

Fig. 2. A personality-role interaction matrix (after Newcomb, 1950a).

particular row to infer a personality trait like "laziness" or "ambition." Alternatively, one can abstract commonalities over the several individuals in a particular column to infer a role-demand imposed on all participants, such as "attentive respect for authority."

It is likely that, except for unusual situations or unusual individuals, the degree of consistency in either direction is not very great. Yet the psychologist typically infers a rather general trait, and the sociologist typically infers a rather strong role demand. A psychologist interested in abstracting the trait "intelligence" from a given row is likely to pay special attention to those situations presenting novel stimuli to the individual. A sociologist interested in the role "attentive respect for authority" would pay special attention to those persons who know how to be deferential and who are aware of their inferior status in the circumstances.

There may be a main effect of a personality trait across situations, and a main effect of a role demand over individuals, but these are likely to be weak in comparison with the interactions between person and situation. The circumstances in which one individual displays a trait are not the same as those in which the same trait is displayed by a different individual; some people do not show a trait under conditions that would be optimal for others. Applying this reasoning to a testing situation, it is quite conceivable that some people will not display in the test itself the very trait that is being measured, even though they display it amply in other circumstances.

Recognizing the full implications of this complex interaction among trait, role, person, and situation had led some psychologists to abandon the fundamental postulate of traditional personality theory; they simply assert that behavior is not consistent over situations. This is a step forward only if one has something more definite to substitute than the general recognition that the effect of personality is largely interactive. We do not have a useful set of abstract variables by which to represent the effects of situations. Aside from a few efforts like that of Parsons and Shils (1951), which never yielded a measuring technology, one is left with no systematic basis for distinguishing among situations.

Although we recognize that situations play an important role in determining behavior, the model of cognitive structure developed in subsequent chapters is limited to main effects in the tradition of classical personality theories. One of the most pressing needs of psychology is to develop a theoretically coherent scheme for elaborating situational variables and a technology of assessing them that approaches the sophistication attained in some current psychometric methods. Until this is done, it will not help simply to abandon the "organism error" inherent in present personality theory for a helpless recognition that there are so many unspecified sources of situational variance that the proportion of behavior explainable by the main effects of personality is small.

PERSONALITY STRUCTURE

The approach to studying personality which is developed in later chapters is a structural one. Though this approach uses structural concepts in a way that has not been common, consideration of the place which structure has occupied in personality psychology will be valuable background to what follows. This section begins with a brief description of structural concepts from Freud's psychoanalytic theory and Lewin's field theory; they will serve as examples in the discussion which follows. Attention is then focused on the relation of personality structure to personality dynamics and development, a relation which demonstrates the role of structure in explanations of behavior. Though many personality traits are considered structural, that which makes them structural has rarely been articulated. Three primary ways in which traits might qualify as structural will be distinguished.

Psychoanalytic Theory

Among the most important structural principles in psychoanalytic theory are the overlapping distinctions between conscious and unconscious, and among id, ego, and superego. The second distinction is more important, in that it is relatively permanent and forms the basis for dynamic principles of personality growth and change. For Freud, the id stood for the innate drives and sources of mental energy which operate unconsciously throughout the person's life, directing behavior in ways which conflict with similar drives in other people and with societal norms. The superego represented the internalization of societal prohibitions, largely unconscious, that counteract the id impulses and prevent their direct expression. The ego was conceived as a set of adjustive processes, both conscious and unconscious, whereby the person comprehends the external world and shapes id impulses to the demands of the superego and external reality.

For Freud, the bulk of mental life was unconscious. Even the main workings of the ego, the mechanisms of defense, were seen as going on outside the person's awareness. Through introspection, psychoanalysis, or instruction, one could become aware of many of the previously unconscious ego and superego processes and recognize some distorted derivatives of id impulses, but the main workings of all mental processes were believed to lie beyond awareness.

Field Theory

Kurt Lewin's formulation of psychic structure was more phenomenological than Freud's. Although Lewin did not make use of the distinction between conscious and unconscious, his writings imply that his notion of the "life space," the psychological reality which determines a person's behavior, was intended to reflect the person's own ideas about the self and the surrounding world. The term "field theory" reflects Lewin's contention that the determinants of behavior are to be found in the field of forces operating on a person at the time of action. The field of forces is represented by positive and

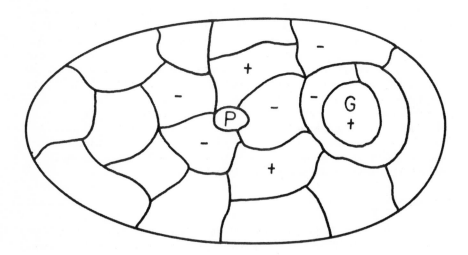

Fig. 3. Topological representation of "life space" (after Lewin).

negative *valences* attached to *regions* of the life space, and giving rise to *vectors*, or pressures toward locomotion. Some regions are illustrated in the topological diagram of Figure 3. Each region represents the person's ideas about an activity, goal, or aversive condition. The arrangement of the regions represents their psychological proximity and connections. The region includes a valence (positive, negative, or neutral), which implies a force, or vector, acting on the person. Generally, psychological locomotion is determined by the vectors, but barriers between the person (P) and goal region (G) may impede direct movement, causing detours or substitute activity.

Personality Structure, Dynamics, and Development

Though the term "dynamics" has many meanings in psychological theory, most meanings derive from the physical concept of forces acting on a body. Motives are prominent among the personality constructs conceived as forces; in fact, "personality dynamics" is often synonymous with the study of motivation. Vectors and valences serve as contemporaneous motivational forces in field theory. The relations among id, ego, and superego in psychoanalytic theory are dynamic as well since they are primarily conceived in terms of conflicting forces such as impulse, repression, and distortion.

More generally, personality dynamics refers to those aspects of a theory which describe or explain changes in states. Structure, in contrast, designates static patterns or arrangements. Concepts such as the proximity of regions in the life space or the availability of impulses to awareness are structural because they refer to relatively constant states. Processes directed toward changing the current state, through striving, pressure, growth, or regression, can be classified as dynamic.

Structure and dynamics bear an intimate relation to one another. Structure represents the current situation in which the dynamic forces operate, while dynamic forces are pressures toward altering the steady state. The view that repressive forces act from the superego on the id, for example, implies both the structural principle that the mind is divided into the mental regions of id, ego, and superego and the dynamic principle that the superego acts to limit id expression.

Change due to internal dynamics. Personality development and change can be viewed from a variety of perspectives, all of which presuppose both structural and dynamic concepts. One perspective uses only concepts of dynamic processes to explain long-term changes in the structure of personality, without any implication that change moves toward ever more advanced states. In Lewinian terms, for example, vectors in the life space produce locomotion toward goals, resulting in a reorganized life space with a new set of valences and vectors. This alternation between state, movement, and state applies to both short- and long-term change; hence, principles of personality development are implicit in the principles of personality dynamics. Structural notions are necessary to describe the states reached in the course of development, and the principles of change from one state to another are by definition dynamic.

Change as improved adaptation. Other perspectives emphasize the generally superior adaptive value of each subsequent stage, although regression and maladaptive growth are recognized as possibilities. One such perspective is embodied in theories of learning. These theories assume that, in order to maximize reinforcement within a relatively stable environment, personality traits are altered in the direction of adaptive requirements. The individual comes to behave in whatever way is forced, suggested, or encouraged. Reinforced responses become part of a new behavior repertory, and personality is thereby altered. Personality is conceived as the accumulation of acquired dispositions to engage in behavior that is rewarded in the interpersonal surround. Change is interpreted as "growth" or "improvement," implying that environmental requirements are appropriate.

Change as maturation. The notion of gradual unfolding or epigenetic growth provides another perspective within which personality is seen as developing toward greater maturity. This is the approach taken in the theories of Freud, Eriksen, and Piaget. Psychoanalytic theory postulates the development of mental processes in yoke with physical development, particularly with the shifting locus of sexual gratification. Thus, stages in psychosexual development affect the way in which sexual energy (libido) is manifest and thereby the way in which id forces drive the rest of the psychic system. An interpersonal, nonsexual variant of psychoanalytic theory was proposed by Eriksen (1955), who held that the outcome of each stage of development depends importantly on the kinds of relations the person has with significant others.

Piaget's theory is based on a comparable epigenetic principle applied to cognition. To the notions of structure and dynamics, epigenetic theories add conceptions of the changing capabilities of human beings which result from physical growth and experience. Just as one must walk before one can run, one must think in a simple way before one can reason with sophistication. The features common to epigenetic theories are the designation of stages in a certain order of maturity and the assertion that progress to any higher stage depends upon passage through the immediately preceding stage. In addition to distinguishing stages, psychoanalytic theory specifies satisfactory and unsatisfactory outcomes at each stage. An unsatisfactory experience in a given stage—e.g., too little or too much oral gratification—results in fixation at that stage. Fixation is displayed as a subsequent tendency to return to that stage under frustration. This is regression, which provides an interpretation for many childlike characteristics of adults. In psychoanalytic theory, maturation is temporarily or permanently reversible and need not display constant progress toward ever more adaptive forms.

Uses of Structural Concepts in Personality Psychology

Structures as entities. Personality theories often include structures which are distinct entities analogous to physical structures such as buildings and mountains. Freud's mental domains of id, ego, and superego illustrate structures as entities. Each includes a set of similar processes operating under common principles. Common to the processes which comprise the ego is the function of adjusting libidinal desires to the requirements of the superego and external reality. By designating the ego as a structure, one points out the interrelations among its processes, thereby suggesting unity among disparate events.

Structural relations. The second use of structural concepts in personality psychology is to specify relations among particular elements. Since structure concerns patterning or arrangement of an enduring state, many relations among components of a personality theory are structural. Lewin's life space represents relations among its elements, as well as suggesting a total structural entity: The arrangement of regions reflects their associations in the person's views about the world; connections or barriers between regions represent possibilities for movement. There are also structural relations in psychoanalytic theory: The dynamic notion that the superego acts to limit id expression presupposes some structural relation by which the two regions are in contact. In general, structural relations provide means for theorists to propose dynamic connections among the constructs they posit.

Structural traits. Though structural concepts abound in personality theory, very few personality traits represent individual differences in structure. Structures as entities and standard structural relations among elements are used by theorists in building logical frameworks of explanation. These structures include the same processes, related in the same fashion for all people. In distinguishing id, ego, and superego Freud did not postulate structures which differ from person to person. Instead he postulated a common structure, with principles of operation that could explain how differing experiences result in differing personality traits.

Alternatively, it would be possible to use the logic of the relations explicated in a theoretical structure as a basis for defining personality traits. Lewin proposed such traits, structural variables defined in terms of the relations included in the life space. These features vary from person to person according to differences in psychological realities represented in the life space. One trait defined by Lewin is differentiation, the degree to which the life space is subdivided into many distinct regions. Integration was seen as the opposite of differentiation, the degree to which previously distinct regions are merged. The structural trait of connectedness among regions represents the person's perception of freedom of movement and range of choices in action.

THE RELATION BETWEEN PERSONALITY AND COGNITION

Theories of personality and cognition have developed within quite different traditions, the former stemming largely from clinical experience with deviants and the latter deriving from academic research with various normal populations. It is not surprising that their concepts show little overlap and that their relations are not readily apparent. One of the first systematic efforts at integration appeared in the "new look" school of perception in the late 1940s and early 1950s. Its major theme was that personality traits—specifically, the needs of an individual—influence perception by affecting the availability of interpretive categories. Thus, poor children were found to "see" a 5¢ coin as larger than rich children; analyses of language showed that Eskimos distinguished more kinds of snow than residents of temperate climes; and hostile people were said to recognize more acquaintances as dangerous than people who are benignly disposed toward the world. A dispute arose between traditionalists and modernists over the use of the term "perception" to describe these differences. Traditionalists preferred to reserve this term for immediate interpretation of sensory data, and to substitute the vaguer term "cognition" for higher-order interpretations conditioned by the person's needs, language, and experience.

Subsequent research made it quite clear that the observed differences in judgment were due not to differences in sensory acuity, but to differences in cognitive elaboration of the sensory data. This change in terminology from "personality affects perception" to "personality affects cognition" did not alter the fundamental implication that personality was more basic and cognition more superficial. Enduring needs within the person were said to influence transient judgments about events. The cognitions could be corrected or altered by additional sensory input, while the predisposing personality traits could not. This is still the prevailing view among most psychologists concerning the relation between personality and cognition.

Let us consider another possibility, one which we believe will be more reasonable and more productive: that neither personality nor cognition is more basic than the other. To say that personality affects cognition means that there are personality traits (general, distinct, and enduring individual differences) which affect people's ideas about themselves and the world around them. Like personality traits, both cognitive contents and cognitive processes are attributed to the person by an outside observer. In addition, however, the contents of cognition are directly apprehended by the person as well (though the person's and the observer's attributions of content may differ in detail). If people can be characterized in terms of cognitive contents and processes that are general, distinctive, and enduring, these characterizations can provide bases for personality traits; we shall call them personality traits of cognition or, for short, cognitive traits.

Most cognitive contents do not generate personality traits. A single idea is unlikely to be general enough to qualify; individual ideas do not typically guide a wide variety of behavior. At the same time, just as any behavior may be potentially subsumed under some personality trait, so may any cognition. The task is to develop higher order cognitive concepts that qualify as personality traits by grouping together a constellation of cognitive phenomena which is general, distinctive, and enduring.

SUMMARY

This chapter depicts a view of personality as a context within which to present some theory and research on cognitive structure. The psychology of personality is concerned with how people differ consistently from each other. Personality theories may be seen as explanations for individual differences in tendencies to behave. The ultimate concern of personality psychology is therefore behavior.

Personality theories specify structural and dynamic concepts. Structures may be seen as entities, relations, or variable traits; dynamics are the forces which operate within, and thereby change, structures. Cognitive contents and processes may reasonably be included as components of personality, provided they are represented in ways that are general, distinctive, and enduring.

Chapter 4

COGNITIVE STRUCTURE

Although cognitive structure is a term widely used in psychology, it has no single meaning which is generally accepted. Rather, cognitive structure includes the application to cognitive contents and cognitive processes of the entire range of structural concepts from personality theories, as discussed in Chapter 3.

Interest in cognitive structure follows from the presumption that behavior is guided by one's understanding of the world and that there is organization, meaning, and coherence to the understanding that one develops. Chapters 4 and 5 are devoted to developing a model of cognitive structure. The purpose of this model is to provide a structural framework for describing cognition which will serve as a basis for defining personality traits. This endeavor has its roots in Lewin's (1935, 1936) field theory. Like Lewin's life space, the model represents psychological reality for the individual, and structural personality traits are defined in terms of that representation. The present model, however, is much less ambitious than Lewin's; it includes none of the dynamic, goal-oriented features of the life space. These sacrifices were deliberate. Because no one has ever developed methods for assessing the life space, the value of Lewin's formulation for empirical research has been severely limited (at least by contrast with its theoretical implications). The present model, presented in Chapter 5, leads to empirical measures. It draws on major themes of research in social and personality psychology and some structural notions from developmental psychology.

INTELLECTUAL ROOTS

The prominent role of cognitive constructs in American social psychology can be attributed to the influence of European Gestalt psychologists, particularly Kurt Lewin and Fritz Heider, who migrated to the United States around the time of World War II. The role of cognitive constructs in Lewin's work was somewhat ambiguous. He stated that, in the life space, ". . . the situation must be represented as it is 'real' for the individual in question, that is, as it affects him" (1936, p. 25). Lewin was rather vague about the nature of this psychological reality, other than to say that it was not the reality of physics or biology. At one point he also rejected the idea that the phenomenally given is necessarily psychologically real because it may not qualify as the essential cause of behavior. In most of his descriptions of the psychological environment, however, it is apparent that Lewin was concerned with the phenomenally given environment. While rarely used in the original expositions of this theory, the term "cognitive" appears more frequently in Lewin's later writings. He was, in fact, one of the first to refer to "cognitive structure," equating it to "the way (the person) sees the physical and social worlds, including all his facts, concepts, beliefs, and expectations" (1948, p. 59). This usage is akin to "structure as entity" (see p. 28); it designates the representational aspect of a persons' life space as distinct from the dynamic aspect. It is a very broad usage and, unfortunately, does not specify the kinds of relations by which these elements form a structure.

There was a strong emphasis on the role of cognition in prominent social psychology textbooks by Asch (1952) and Krech and Crutchfield (1948). Both works were influenced by the phenomenological aspects of Gestalt psychology and sought to apply them to social psychology. Krech and Crutchfield attempted to define their social psychological concepts by phenomenological analysis, in accord with the recommendations of MacLeod (1947). Both they and Asch used the term cognitive structure quite frequently; nevertheless, it was left undefined, and was used for a variety of purposes. Nowhere did these authors offer a specific designation of just what was structured.

Zajonc (1960) elaborated several higher-order structural variables from Lewin's theory; these included differentiation, complexity, unity, and organization. These variables refer to relations among dichotomous attributes assigned to a single object. Zajonc was able to operationalize these concepts because he forsook Lewin's geometric model in favor of an algebraic model.

Another application of Lewin's structural ideas arose in Kounin's (1941) brilliant analysis of cognitive processes in mental retardates. He concluded that there is in these persons a "rigidity" of boundaries between adjacent regions of the life space, which results in resistance to "cosatiation." This accounted for their lowered susceptibility to fatigue and boredom, when one activity was repeatedly performed. However, these structural properties were simply postulated, without any attempt to assess them directly.

Another line of social psychological research on cognition originated in the analysis of the relation between perception and the environment by Heider (1959) and Brunswik (1934). In the 1950s both applied their conceptions of perception to problems of social cognition (Brunswik, 1956; Heider, 1958). The social judgment theory of Hammond (1972), which is distinct from that of Sherif and Hovland (1961), derives from Brunswik's lens model. It is discussed later in this chapter as an example of one method for assessing structural relations. Heider's work led to two of the most influential theories in recent social psychology, cognitive balance and attribution theory.

Heider's concept of balance referred to "a situation in which the relations among the entities fit together harmoniously"—more specifically, to the similar valence of objects seen as "belonging together." This concept is structural at both a simple and a complex level. The judgment "belong together" is a simple way of relating objects; the proposition that objects seen as belonging together will be similarly liked is a complex principle of cognitive organization that relates two lower-order relationships. This illustrates the manner in which a structure at one level can itself be utilized as an element in some higher-order structure. In Chapter 5 we take this process of abstraction one step further by suggesting that individuals differ in the degree to which their cognitions are balanced in Heider's sense.

Festinger's (1957) theory of cognitive dissonance has probably received more attention than any other social psychological approach to cognition. Dissonance was defined in structural terms: Two concepts are dissonant when the opposite of one follows from the other. The magnitude of dissonance depends on the ratio of dissonant concepts to the total number of concepts, both consonant and dissonant, maintained by the individual. As in the case of Kounin's concepts of rigidity and satiation, Festinger made no attempt to assess dissonance directly, but instead utilized this construct to explain changes in expressed attitudes. In some ways dissonance might better be regarded as a dynamic rather than a structural concept, since the dissonant state never lasts for long; the theory predicts that it will be reduced by one method or another as soon as it arises.

Much of social psychological research on cognition has been devoted to the study of person perception. Early investigations on this subject were concerned with the correlates of accuracy in making judgments about others. In their review of research on person perception, Bruner and Tagiuri (1954) suggested that less attention be paid to accuracy and more be given to the means by which people learn about each other. This position was further encouraged by Cronbach (1955), who demonstrated that serious statistical artifacts pervade the study of accuracy. In addition, Cronbach proposed a method for studying implicit personality theories, which will be considered later in this chapter. Other useful methods for studying people's views about each other arose in Asch's (1946) analysis of the formation of impressions and in Bruner, Shapiro, and Tagiuri's (1958) trait-implication method. These methods have become the basic tools of research in person perception, while the study of accuracy has all but disappeared.

George Kelly's (1955) personal construct theory also emerged about this time. Kelly's theory was a very important development because it used structural notions of cognition as the basis for a general theory of personality. From this work and the refinements by Bieri (1955, 1966) came a more precise meaning of cognitive differentiation and a way of measuring it systematically.

Structural personality variables also developed from the "new look" school of perception (Blake & Ramsey, 1951; Tajfel, 1969), which was concerned broadly with the influence of needs on perception, including the person's openness to new information and experience. Relevant variables included rigidity, speed of closure, intolerance for ambiguity, and field dependence. Rigidity may be seen as a relation among concepts (or regions of the life space) that makes them highly resistant to change from appropriate inputs (see Scott, 1966a). Premature closure (Frenkel-Brunswik, 1949) refers to the readiness of a person to draw inferences from partial information. Field dependence (Witkin, 1962) may be viewed in our terms as the tendency to judge objects on the basis of explicitly presented information, rather than on the basis of internal standards maintained by the individual. While the structural bases of these variables have generally not been explicitly formulated, they all suggest ways of processing and utilizing information.

COGNITION AS THE ASCRIPTION OF ATTRIBUTES TO OBJECTS

One view of cognition taken by many social and personality psychologists describes people's beliefs about themselves and the world as the ascription of attributes to objects and events. As the term is used here, an attribute is any basis a person uses to distinguish or group objects and events. An attribute may be an objective feature such as color or a subjective feature such as attractiveness. This object-attribute formulation is implicit in a great deal of research. Investigators have used many terms for the concept of attribute, such as "personal construct" (Kelly, 1955), "trait" (Bruner et al., 1958), "cue variable" and "judgment variable" (Hammond, 1972), and "item of information" and "dimension of judgment" (Anderson, 1971).

It is possible to treat attributes as dichotomous variables—for instance, whether or not an object is red; as multicategory nominal-scale variables, such as color; or as ordinal or higher-order scale variables—for example, the wave-length of a visual stimulus. It is doubtful whether many people can comprehend most attributes in scales more precise than ordinal. Though a skilled musician may display "absolute pitch," or at least be able to tune an instrument by distinguishing slight differences in pitch, the average listener can only distinguish varying degrees of high and low notes. For the average viewer, wave-length of light is reported as red, orange, yellow, etc., and height of objects is translated into tall, medium, and short.

The principle advantage of an object-attribute analysis of cognitive content is that it provides a basis for structurally representing a person's views which is readily translated into objective measuring procedures. The respondent need only assign an object to an attribute by describing the object, rating it, or comparing it with some other object; the investigator may then analyze these assignments in ways that permit the inference of structural properties.

The convenience of the object-attribute conception for empirical study should not blind one to the fact that it is only one of many possible ways of characterizing an individual's view of the world. It is an appropriate formulation for many kinds of cognition, but quite awkward for others. For example, it would be difficult to describe a person's knowledge of the rules of chess as a set of objects and attributes. These rules could only be very clumsily translated into attributes of pieces, and the formulation would be of little use for describing a person's knowledge of the object of the game or of when to take one's turn.

Lewin's (1936) topological psychology illustrates an alternative approach to describing cognition. Lewin sought to represent the individual's psychological world with a spatial representation stressing the psychological proximity of objects and events to the individual and to each other. His approach appears more useful than the object-attribute formulation for describing people's ideas about means for achieving goals. Different purposes require different approaches to the study of cognition. The reason we focus attention on theories employing the object-attribute formulation is that this conception has yielded objective methods for characterizing cognitive structure. Objective methods pertaining to other aspects of cognition are badly needed.

Using the object-attribute formulation as our starting point, we can define structural relations among concepts. Objects may be similar or dissimilar; this is a rudimentary relationship. One object may be included within another (as a species of animal is included within a genus). Two attributes may be similar, as mass and weight, or dissimilar, as mass and volume. Attributes may be opposite, as kindness and cruelty, or orthogonal, as kindness and intelligence. All these are instances of structural relations in the sense that one element of content is related to another. Note that it is the relationship as it exists in the persons' view that is of concern, not the relationship in some external sense, such as physical reality or social norms. Designating structural relations among cognitive representations does not imply that some corresponding neurological structure exists within the person. Instead, these notions should be regarded merely as constructs used by an observer to systematize phenomena; they serve their purpose if they lead to useful predictions about behavior.

Personal Construct Theory

George Kelly's (1955) personal construct theory deserves special attention as an application of the object-attribute formulation. The thrust of the theory is that behavior is guided by one's personal construct system. This system provides a means of understanding, anticipating, and predicting events. The personal construct system is a structural representation of cognition; it consists of a set of attributes (called personal constructs) in terms of which reality is interpreted. Thus, an actor is portrayed as a construer of events who gives meaning to the world and acts on the basis of that meaning. Kelly contrasted this to the view of man at the mercy of external forces, which he thought unduly prevalent in American psychology of the time.

Kelly's concept of personal constructs is more narrowly defined than the usual concept of attributes, though it serves the same function in his theory (i.e., a basis for representing and differentiating among objects and events). A personal construct is a dichotomous distinction such as tall-vs.-short. It provides a basis for comparing objects and, if systematically applied, leads to an ordering of objects on a dimension (in this case, height). Kelly emphasized the dichotomous nature of personal constructs because he believed that both sides of the construct are necessary to specify the meaning of the dimension. This emphasis is somewhat arbitrary, however, for there is no reason to consider a bipolar distinction more fundamental or meaningful than its underlying concept. The contrast between tall and short is nothing more nor less than the concept of height. Furthermore, due to the ambiguities and complexities of language, an attempt to define both poles of attributes in psychological research may lead to a combination of two attributes which are distinct for some persons. That this is not just a hypothetical problem is demonstrated by Green and Goldfried's (1965) finding that correlations between ratings on scales with semantically opposite labels were often not highly negative and were occasionally positive.

It is difficult to assess Kelly's contribution to the study of cognition. Unlike most authors in this field, Kelly was a practicing clinician. His greatest contribution is probably that he used the clinician's perspective to give a much fuller exposition of the consequences of viewing people as construers of events than has ever been offered elsewhere. While Kelly was certainly not the first psychologist concerned with the individual's construction of reality, there has been no one more committed to this position, and his work is notable for his application of the concept of cognitive structure to problems of psychotherapy, emotion, and language and for his clarification of the relation of cognition to motivation.

On the other hand, Kelly's positions on many issues seem more idiosyncratic than necessary. He gave interesting arguments for considering personal constructs bipolar, but no evidence. Furthermore, Kelly was quite out of touch with the work of other psychologists studying the same issues. His characterizations of American psychology seem to imply that he was the only psychologist who wasn't a radical behaviorist. There is some indication that he did not know what cognitive psychology was, for he rejected the label of cognitive for his own theory (Kelly, 1970). One of Kelly's followers, Holland (1970), criticized him on this count, stating ". . . in his use of the term cognitive, I believe he is giving it a narrow meaning so that it refers primarily to studies of perceptual mechanisms" (p. 119). Nevertheless, Kelly's students have made greater use of the work of other cognitive psychologists (e.g., Bannister, 1977; Bannister & Mair, 1968), and personal construct theory has had considerable influence on cognitive research in social and personality psychology.

RELATIONS AMONG ATTRIBUTES

A great deal of research has been devoted to relations among attributes; in fact, most research on person perception is of this sort. We shall devote considerable attention to this type of structural relation because it is the backbone of the model of cognitive structure to be presented in Chapter 5 and of the variables defined from that model. Within an object-attribute formulation, the relation between two attributes may be either of two types: a relation of association or a relation of implication. This distinction refers to the method by which relevant data are obtained, and there is reason to interpret the results of the different methods as implying different things about the organization of cognitions.

RELATIONS OF ASSOCIATION

One major tradition in studying cognition focuses on associations among attributes as inferred from expressed views about objects. Because most of this research is in the field of person perception, the objects studied are usually people and the attributes are usually dispositional labels. In principle, however, these relations can be assessed for any domain of objects that can be sensibly described in terms of attributes.

Relations of association are illustrated in Cronbach's (1955) proposal of a method for studying implicit personality theories. An implicit personality theory is a structural characterization of a person's appraisals of people. Cronbach suggested that the observer be required to describe several people on a set of attributes, and that the means, variances, and correlations of those attributes be taken as this respondent's implicit personality theory. Using the attribute "friendliness" as an example, this method yields the following information: (a) The mean indicates the average amount of friendliness a respondent attributes to people; (b) the variance indicates the extent to which a respondent distinguishes degrees of friendliness among the people he describes; and (c) the correlation of friendliness with some other attribute, such as generosity, indicates the extent to which friendliness and generosity are associated with one another in this observer's views of people. Only the last of these is a structural characteristic.

Kelly's (1955) method for assessing personal construct systems, the *Role Constructs Repertory Test*, also focuses on relations of association. In this test, constructs are elicited by having the respondent consider a number of person-objects, and pick out successive triads consisting of two persons who seem alike, and different from the third, in some way. This process may be continued until the meaningful distinctions among persons are exhausted or until a specified number of triads have been selected. Next, the respondent describes every person on the list on every one of the dichotomous attributes, assigning each person to one or the other pole of the attribute. Relations of association are then determined by the similarity of assignments between a pair of attributes. This procedure may be varied to allow continuous, rather than dichotomous, attribute ratings. Hypothetical ratings using a 7-point rating scale are presented in Table 1. These show an individual respondent's ratings of 15 people on 4 attributes—friendliness, generosity, intelligence, and ruthlessness. The 7-point scales were defined like this:

In comparison to most people, how friendly is this person?

1	2	3	4	5	6	7
Very much less	Much less friendly	Somewhat less friendly	About as friendly as most	Somewhat more friendly	Much more friendly	Very much more friendly

From the bottom of Table 1, we may note that the strongest relations are a positive correlation between friendliness and generosity (.78) and a negative correlation between friendliness and ruthlessness (−.82). There is also a fairly strong negative relation between generosity and ruthlessness (−.60). Thus, it appears that friendliness and generosity go together in this hypothetical observer's view of people, and both are associated with a lack of ruthlessness. Intelligence is somewhat more independent of the other attributes. It is moderately correlated with friendliness (.48) and generosity (.46), and slightly correlated (−.28) with ruthlessness.

Interpreting Relations of Association

It is important that the meaning of relations of association be clearly understood, for it is easy to assume that they provide information which they do not or that they may be assessed by methods which are, in fact, inappropriate. This structural relation reflects the association of a pair of attributes across objects seen by the person. Thus, in the case of the strong relation between generosity and friendliness, it can be said that for the respondent the world contains many people who are both friendly and generous and many people who are neither friendly nor generous, but few people who are friendly but not generous or generous but not friendly.

Although the basis of association is the person's views about objects, it cannot be presumed that the person can express the association in abstract terms. Computed correlations will not necessarily coincide with the respondent's introspections about relations among the attributes. It is quite possible for a person to believe that friendliness and intelligence are not correlated, yet at the same time show a strong relation between the two traits in describing actual acquaintances. More will be said about this matter below when we discuss relations of implication.

Relations of association do not yield any information about how the views of objects arise. Although it might be tempting to do so, one cannot interpret a strong relation between friendliness and generosity as indicating

Table 1. Ratings of 15 Hypothetical People on 4 Attributes

Person	Attribute			
	Friendly	Generous	Intelligent	Ruthless
A	4	2	4	2
B	1	3	1	5
C	7	5	2	2
D	2	1	4	7
E	7	5	2	2
F	6	7	3	2
G	1	2	3	7
H	2	1	1	6
I	6	4	7	1
J	5	5	5	3
K	3	4	5	4
L	4	3	4	4
M	3	2	2	3
N	5	6	7	4
O	4	4	6	6

Correlations Among the Attributes				
	Friendliness	Generosity	Intelligence	Ruthlessness
Friendliness	–	.78	.48	−.82
Generosity	.78	–	.46	−.60
Intelligence	.48	.46	–	−.28
Ruthlessness	−.82	−.60	−.28	–

that someone found to be friendly would consequently be judged generous. Though it is necessarily true that relations of association result from information processing, such relations provide little information about the processes themselves. The relation between friendliness and generosity might result from judging generosity on the basis of friendliness, from judging friendliness on the basis of generosity, or from judging both on the basis of one or more other attributes. A method for studying relations of implication is necessary for answering questions about how information is used to make judgments.

Associative Structures Derived From Mean Ratings

The *Role Constructs Repertory Test* and similar rating procedures are aimed at assessing relations of association for an individual. This use should not be confused with the analysis of mean ratings derived by pooling several people's descriptions of a set of objects. It is possible to apply similar techniques to mean ratings, but the resulting correlations don't necessarily have anything to do with an individual's cognitive structure.

For example, Norman (1963) attempted to study personality structure by analyzing mean ratings received by people from close acquaintances. He intercorrelated mean ratings on numerous personality traits and derived five major factors which he called extraversion, agreeableness, conscientiousness, emotional stability, and cultural refinement. As a check on whether these personality factors might be an artifact of the rating method, Passini and Norman (1966) repeated the study using raters who were barely acquainted with the people whom they rated. The same five factors emerged, leading the investigators to conclude that they were dealing, not with actual intercorrelations among personality traits, but with implicit personality theories, or conceptions, shared by raters concerning how various personality traits go together in strangers as well as in close friends.

There is reason to doubt, however, whether many or most of the raters in these studies were actually using these five factors as bases for judging the personalities of others. One may derive factors and correlational structures from mean ratings which represent only vaguely the implicit personality theories of individual raters. Kuusinen (1969) had 39 high school students rate each other on 33 personality attributes. He factor analyzed their mean ratings, and also chose 12 of the respondents for individual factor analysis. He concluded that there was sufficient correspondence between the individual and group factors to attribute differences among individuals to measurement error. However, Kuusinen's conclusions were challenged by Hamilton (1970), who noted that for several of Kuusinen's observers, fewer than half of the individual factors were held in common with the group. In many cases, pairs of students had only one or even none of the group factors in common. In Hamilton's own study, 7 college students rated 15 objects on 42 bipolar attributes. He then extracted 5 factors for each student and assessed the number of factors held in common by each of the 21 pairs of raters. The average was three, and very few of the factors were held in common by more than two students.

While these results are based on very few subjects and confuse the issue somewhat by comparing factors rather than relations of association, they at least caution one against concluding anything about the structure of trait associations in an individual rater from data based on pooled ratings. As conceived here, structural relations of cognition are a property of an individual, not of a group. Inferences about an individual are properly based on data obtained from that individual alone. Whether or not those structural relations are shared with some larger group is a matter that may be investigated, but should not be assumed.

RELATIONS OF IMPLICATION

In contrast to relations of association, relations of implication reflect the use of information in forming judgments. The relation of implication depends on the distinction between informational and judgmental roles of attributes. A relation of implication indicates the extent to which an informational attribute influences positions on the judgmental attribute. The differences between relations of association and relations of implication are analogous to those between correlational and experimental research. In correlational research, the investigator measures variables as they occur in natural events. The results are then informative about associations among those variables. The study of relations of association is similar to correlational research in that it focuses on views of the world as they already exist. Insofar as the objects sampled typify the person's world, that world will be portrayed by those relations. In experimental research, the investigator creates objects and events, manipulating the independent variables to test their effects on the dependent variables. Because of this control over the events, conclusions can go beyond statements that two variables are associated to statements that changes in one variable lead to changes in another. On the other hand, because the investigator has created artificial phenomena, the results do not necessarily describe relations among variables as they occur naturally.

Just as experimental research depends on the manipulation of independent variables in order to assess their impact on dependent variables, the study of relations of implication depends on the manipulation of information to assess its impact on judgments. Relations of implication are, therefore, informative about how information can be used in forming views of objects. Because the researcher has created the objects judged rather than sampled the person's own world, relations of implication do not directly reflect the world as the person sees it, but rather the formation of views under certain circumstances. We shall consider two methods for studying relations of implication.

The Trait-Implication Method

The trait-implication method assesses the degree to which one attribute implies another by posing the question, "If a person possesses trait A, how likely is it that he or she also possesses trait B?" This method has been used by Bruner et al. (1958), D'Andrade (1965), Hays (1958), and Wyer (1974). The observer responds on a rating scale of likelihood. As in the study of trait association (p. 40), the trait-implication method yields a matrix of relations among characteristics. This method, however, separately assesses the degree to which A implies B and the degree to which B implies A. Relations obtained by the trait-implication method do not simply refer to the association of two characteristics; they refer to the observer's use of one trait as a basis for making judgments about another.

Hypothetical data are presented in Table 2; the entries represent responses to questions of the form, "If a person is (information trait), how likely is it that he or she will also be (judgment trait)?" Responses are made on a 7-point rating scale ranging from 1, extremely unlikely, to 7, extremely likely. The structure of trait inference shown in Table 2 is quite similar to the structure of associated traits presented in Table 1 (p. 41): Friendliness and generosity

Table 2. Hypothetical Data for the Trait-Implication Method

Judgment	Information trait			
	Friendly	Generous	Intelligent	Ruthless
Friendly	–	7	6	1
Generous	6	–	5	1
Intelligent	4	5	–	5
Ruthless	3	2	3	–

are closely associated and both go with a lack of ruthlessness; intelligence is slightly associated with friendliness and generosity, and rather independent of ruthlessness. The distinction between informational and judgmental traits leads to some interesting differences in this hypothetical example, though. For instance, a person who is intelligent is considered somewhat unlikely to be ruthless, but a person who is ruthless is considered somewhat likely to be intelligent. We might interpret this as indicating that the respondent believes it isn't very smart to be ruthless, but to be truly ruthless one has to be fairly smart.

An example of this method appears in a study by Bruner et al. (1958), who investigated the implications of 4 information traits for a set of 59 judgment traits. The information traits were presented both singly and in combination, two or three at a time. It was found that the inferences drawn from trait combinations could be accurately predicted by averaging inferences from single traits.

Research using the trait-implication method has shown a certain predictability and consistency in implication judgments. These findings must be interpreted with caution, however, because the observers have been required to make abstract judgments about trait implications, not concrete judgments about real or even hypothetical objects. This procedure requires that respondents be capable of accurately describing their use of information. If someone doesn't realize that his or her judgments of intelligence are strongly influenced by the object-person's friendliness, the trait-implication method would inaccurately indicate that there is no such relation between the attributes. While this method provides a means of studying beliefs about the relations among attributes, a more thorough procedure is required to study the actual use of information in making judgments about objects.

Experimental Manipulation of Information

An experimental method for assessing relations of implication follows the paradigm of research on impression formation established by Asch (1946). The basic procedure consists of giving respondents verbal information about hypothetical objects and having them judge other characteristics of those objects. The investigator then determines the influence of the information on the judgments. This general method has been very widely applied, and many mathematical models about the formation of judgments have been developed. We shall discuss the approach of two investigators, Hammond and Anderson, whose work is somewhat broader than others in this field. More extensive reviews are provided by Slovic and Lichtenstein (1973) and by Wyer (1974).

Social judgment theory. Hammond's (1972) social judgment theory is an extension of Egon Brunswik's probabilistic functionalism from its original application, perceptual processes, to problems of social judgment. Brunswik was particularly concerned with perceptual constancy, the fact that objects are seen as having constant shapes, sizes, and colors despite a nonconstancy of their retinal image due to changes in position, distance, and lighting. His theory was greatly influenced by Heider's (1959, pp. 1–34) paper, "Thing and Medium." Originally published in 1926, this paper was a careful analysis of the manner in which the invariant properties of objects in the environment are related to perception indirectly through the variable properties of physical media. Brunswik (1934) extended this analysis, arguing that perception should be studied in terms of the relations among properties of distal objects, proximal cues, and perceptions of the distal objects. (The distal object is the actual object in the environment. Proximal cues are those physical events which contact the person, such as the retinal image.) Thus, he viewed perception as the interaction of two systems. The first is the environmental system of distal objects and the various effects they emit which are proximally available to the person. The second is the person system which includes the proximal variables together with the person's perception of the distal object. Brunswik referred to this conception of the perceptual process as the lens model in analogy to the focusing of light from a source (distal object)

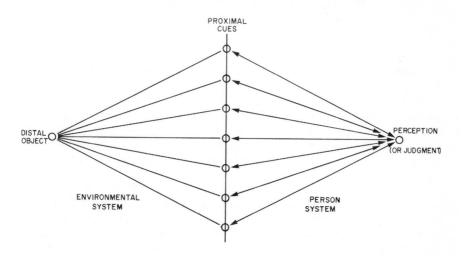

Fig. 4. The lens model (after Brunswik)

Table 3. Judgments of Liking for Hypothetical People

Object	Cue variables (X)				Observer's Judgment of liking (Y)
	Friendly	Generous	Intelligent	Ruthless	
A	4	2	4	2	3
B	1	3	1	5	2
C	7	5	2	2	6
D	2	1	4	7	1
E	7	5	2	2	6
F	6	7	3	2	7
G	1	2	3	7	1
H	2	1	1	6	2
I	6	4	7	·1	7
J	5	5	5	3	5
K	3	4	5	4	4
L	4	3	4	4	4
M	3	2	2	3	3
N	5	6	7	4	5
O	4	4	6	6	4

Regression model for judgments of liking (after Hammond)

Cue variable	Beta weight
Friendly (X_1)	.42
Generous (X_2)	.35
Intelligent (X_3)	.08
Ruthless (X_4)	−.27

$$z_Y = .42z_1 + .35z_2 + .08z_3 - .27z_4$$
Squared multiple correlation = .94

through a lens (proximal cues) to a focal point (the percept). Figure 4 depicts the lens model.

Hammond uses the same basic theory, but he is concerned with social judgment instead of perception. In problems of judgment, the proximal variables are whatever information the person uses in making judgments. The distal objects would be defined by whatever criteria of accuracy are available. In cases where there can be no right or wrong answers, the concept of distal object is irrelevant.

An example of the application of social judgment is illustrated in Table 3. Our hypothetical subject has been told the degree to which each of 15 people (A through O) are friendly, generous, intelligent, and ruthless. Judgments are given on a 7-point scale indicating the subject's liking for each person-object. The relations of implication are determined by a multiple regression analysis, treating the cue variables as predictors and the judgment variable as the criterion. Table 3 shows the beta weights (standardized regression weights) which indicate the degree of relation between each cue variable and the judgment variable. Friendliness and generosity are positively associated with liking for a person (weights of .42 and .35), while ruthlessness is negatively associated with liking (−.27). The relation of intelligence to judgments of liking is negligible (.08). The squared multiple correlation of the set of cues to the judgment variable reflects the proportion of the variance in judgments accounted for by the cues. In this case it is .94, indicating that the model accounts for a high proportion of the variance.

Information integration theory. Anderson's (1971) information integration theory is concerned with the manner in which people combine information about objects. In this approach dichotomous cue information is presented in various combinations, and the subject is required to judge the described object on some continuous attribute. For instance, the four traits—friendly, generous, intelligent, and ruthless—might be presented in their six possible pairs, and the respondent asked to indicate how much he or she would like a person who had that pair of characteristics. When enough different combinations are used and repeated judgments are obtained, one may estimate the relevance of each cue for the judgment, and the weight attached to the cue by a subject.

The relations of implication are specified by an equation which integrates the several cues according to a weighted average of their separate scale values in relation to the judgmental attribute. The scale value of a cue (informational stimulus) is "the location of the informational stimulus along the dimension of judgment. The weight represents the psychological importance of the information" (Anderson, 1971, p. 172). The distinctive feature of Anderson's theory is that the importance (effective weight) of any cue varies depending on what other cues it is associated with. Thus, "friendly" in combination with "intelligent" might have a different influence on a judgment (such as a subject's liking for the person) than would "friendly" in combination with "ruthlessness." Specifically, a subject's judgment, R, is predicted from the equation:

$$R = \sum_{i=1}^{n} w_i s_i$$

To predict liking for a person, one would multiply the scale value (likeableness) of each trait, s_i, by the effective weight of that trait in the present combination, w_i, and sum these products over all the specified traits. The effective weight of a trait (w_i) is calculated from its absolute weight (W_i) in relation to the absolute weights of all other traits in the combination, i.e.:

$$w_i = \frac{W_i}{\sum_{j=1}^{n} W_j}$$

Table 4. Predicted Judgments (R) From Combinations of Items (Anderson's Model)

Item	Friendly $s = 4, W = 2$	Generous $s = 3, W = 1$	Intelligent $s = 2, W = 1$	Ruthless $s = -4, W = 3$
Friendly	–	3.67	3.33	–.80
Generous	3.67	–	2.50	–2.25
Intelligent	3.33	2.50	–	–2.50
Ruthless	–.80	–2.25	–2.50	–

An example in Table 4 should help clarify the meaning of these equations. It is assumed there that "friendly" has a scale value (s) of 4 and an absolute weight (W) of 2. (In practice s and W for each stimulus are determined mathematically from the total set of judgments made by the particular subject for the various combinations of stimuli.) Similarly, each of the other traits has its own scale value and absolute weight, representing the subject's liking for that trait and its absolute importance, regardless of other traits in the combination.

When "friendly" is combined with "generous," its effective weight, w_i, is calculated as:

$$w_1 = \frac{W_1}{W_1 + W_2} = \frac{2}{2 + 1} = .67$$

Similarly, the effective weight of "generous," w_2, is $1(2+1)$, or .33. The liking for an object that is both "friendly" and "generous" is therefore predicted to be:

$$R_{12} = w_1 s_1 + w_2 s_2 = (.67)(4) + (.33)(3) = 3.67$$

Combining "friendly" with "ruthless" yields the effective weights, $w_1 = .40$ and $w_4 = .60$, which combine with their respective scale values to yield a predicted liking of $R_{14} = -.80$.

Anderson's model provides a very precise description of the formation of a judgment from a composite of information. The model has received considerable support in a variety of contexts, for example, in clinicians' judgments of the degree of psychological disturbance manifest in various composite descriptions of patients' ward behaviors (Anderson, 1972). The price paid for this precision, however, is extreme specificity of the models generated. Not only is a different effective weight generated each time a cue appears in a new combination, but a different absolute weight and scale value are required for each new judgmental variable to be predicted from any given cue. Thus, there may be as many different relations as there are judgments to be made and composites of stimuli from which to make them. Judgment may, indeed, be this complex and task-specific, but the psychologist seeking parsimonious explanations would rather hope not.

In spite of their complexities, the procedures for studying relations of implication developed by Hammond and Anderson are quite straightforward. One needs only an adequate sample of verbal stimuli representing a range of cue variables to ascertain the way in which any given subject will infer a variety of characteristics not immediately provided. These methods seem far preferable to the trait implication method for studying inference processes, because they assess how subjects actually deal with a sample of information, rather than requiring subjects to generalize abstractly about inferences. On the other hand, the experimental procedures are substantially more time-consuming, and there may be occasions when the quicker, introspective procedure is adequate.

CONSIDERATIONS IN DEFINING NOMOTHETIC VARIABLES OF COGNITIVE STRUCTURE

Structural relations such as association and implication provide bases for defining personality traits that reflect cognitive structure. A model for defining such variables is presented in the next chapter; subsequent chapters present variables and some methods for assessing them which have been developed by ourselves and other investigators. Before presenting these, we need to consider some issues pertaining to the definition of structural variables. These can be clarified by discussing the closely related approaches of Harvey, Hunt, and Schroder (1961) and Schroder, Driver, and Streufert (1967). The work of these authors is a developmentally based approach to studying individual differences in the structure of cognition, and is strongly influenced by developmental theorists such as Murphy (1947), Werner (1957), and Piaget (1971). The key concepts in this perspective on cognition are differentiation and integration. Drawing analogies with biological development, these theorists see cognitive growth as a process of increasing differentiation, whereby distinct ideas arise from a vague, homogeneous composite. As differentiation proceeds, it is usually, but need not be, accompanied by increasingly elaborate integrative processes. If integration develops apace with differentiation, it serves to maintain flexible interrelations among the various ideas; if it does not, the distinct ideas may be disconnected or become interrelated in rather stereotyped and inflexible ways.

The unit of concern here is not a particular set of beliefs, but rather the total ideational system of an individual. Thus, no particular elements are specified as entering into an integrated system. Instead, structural concepts are defined in rather vague terms. For Harvey et al. (1961), development typically consists of acquiring increasingly abstract concepts, abstractness being defined as "the how of differentiation and integration, how the ambiguous or undifferentiated is broken down or differentiated into parts and then integrated or interrelated into a conceptual pattern" (p. 22). Schroder et al. (1967) see adaptation to complex stimuli as requiring a high level of integrative complexity, which is their principal structural variable. They define integrative complexity as "the complexity of the schemata that determines the organization of several dimensions in a complex cognitive structure" (p. 165). They state elsewhere that a low integration index "is roughly synonymous with a hierarchical form of integration, in which rules or programs are fixed. Schemata for organizing alternate sets of rules are not present. Consequently, a hierarchical structure can have a small or large number of parts, rules or procedures, but the relationships between these parts are relatively static." By contrast, "high integration index structures have more connections between rules; that is, they have more schemata for forming new hierarchies, which are generated as alternate perceptions or further rules for comparing outcomes. High integration index structures contain more degrees of freedom, and are more subject to change as complex changes occur in the environment" (p. 8).

Confounding of Structure and Content

These conceptions are provocative and lead the investigators to a wide range of intriguing correlates—for example, that concrete persons are more rigid and authoritarian than abstract persons, that integratively complex persons cope with complex stimuli better than do integratively simple persons. But just as the precise formulations of Anderson pay the penalty of specificity, so the general formulations of these investigators suffer the handicap of vagueness and imprecision. Their writings specify no particular cognitive elements, so their structural concepts do not refer to relations among particular elements or types of elements. Therefore, the major variables of the theories cannot be assessed analytically but must be assessed judgmentally.

Harvey, Hunt, and Schroder's method for assessing level of abstractness-vs.-concreteness is the "This I Believe" Test, in which the subject completes sentences starting with "This I believe about . . . . " Included are such topics as religion, marriage, and the American way of life. Responses are coded into four levels of abstractness on the basis of such manifestations as absolutism, ethnocentrism, concern with interpersonal relations, and dependence on religion, external authority, and social norms. Coding criteria rely on the content of beliefs expressed more than on direct manifestations of differentiation and integration. As a consequence it becomes impossible to assess the relation between level of abstractness and cognitive contents such as authoritarianism, patriotism, affiliation, and religious ideology. These beliefs have already been embodied in the structural classification, and an obtained correlation would therefore be spurious. In fact, while the conception of abstractness is mainly structural, because it implies relations among ideas and the manner in which they are organized, the measure used by Harvey, Hunt, and Schroder does not appear to assess the relationships intended.

Schroder et al.'s (1967) method of assessment attempts to eliminate contamination between content and structure. In the *Paragraph Completion Test*, subjects write paragraphs about a variety of personal and interpersonal topics such as parents, doubt, and confusion. These responses are coded for integrative complexity according to a variety of criteria, such as whether they were generated by a single fixed rule, alternate rule structures, or the integration of conflicting rules. While an attempt is made to ignore the content of the beliefs expressed, and to focus instead on their logical structure, the judgments required are subtle and many-faceted. Coders must infer from a person's views the rules by which the views were formed. Even if high agreement is achieved, there is always a strong possibility that coders have relied on particular kinds of content for inferring the intended property, especially given the vagueness of the structural concepts.

Unit of Analysis

Another problem which confronts us in defining personality traits which reflect cognitive structure is the scope of the variables, the range of a person's beliefs to be included. Abstractness vs. concreteness and integrative complexity are very broad variables in this sense because they are intended to reflect the individual's beliefs on all issues; they concern types of reasoning that apply regardless of the topic. Personality traits that are this general have the potential of being related to a great variety of behavior. No matter what behavior is involved, these traits should have bearing on the person's understanding of reality, as a basis for action. On the other hand, defining variables of such generality presumes that there is, in fact, consistency across all of a person's ideas. If this is not the case, the trait as assessed may be meaningless over much of its assumed range of application.

Relations of association and implication refer to specific attributes named by the investigator. The objects may be only vaguely indicated (as in the trait-implication method) or presented as a sample from some larger, unspecified set (as in the *Role Constructs Repertory Test*). These methods assume that relationships between the attributes apply to some wider range of objects that is left unspecified. At its widest generality, the relation could apply to all objects embodying those particular attributes. This degree of generality was assumed by Osgood, Suci and Tannenbaum (1957) in developing their semantic differential scales. This assumption seems to us unwarranted; rather it seems plausible that many attributes are not meaningful, or change their meanings, when applied to different types of objects.

An opposite, very conservative, interpretation would be that these relations among attributes apply only to the specific objects for which they are assessed. Such a narrow interpretation would be of little help toward defining personality traits, which are supposed to aid prediction of behavior under a range of circumstances. As a compromise between extreme generality and extreme object-specificity, we propose to consider domains of cognition, within which people may be presumed to apply attributes with a consistent meaning; we then assess relations across a representative sample of objects and attributes from each domain.

Because relations of association concern pairs of attributes and relations of implication concern only small sets of attributes, they lack the generality required of personality traits. If we require traits general enough to aid in the understanding of complex behavior, we must combine these relations for several attributes to reflect more broadly the person's world views. So researchers who define personality traits in terms of an object-attribute formulation need to consider what range of attributes and cognitive domains will be represented in the traits. The problem in delimiting attributes and domains is that, as the unit becomes larger, the structural variables generated have increasing significance, but it becomes increasingly difficult to be explicit about the content being analyzed, to sample from it in a representative way, and to demonstrate that the descriptions and principles apply equally to all parts of the unit.

Elements of Cognitive Structure

Although some earlier writers were not consistent on this point, there is little argument today that cognitive structure means something different from cognitive content. The problem arises primarily at the level of operations, where structure is occasionally inferred primarily from the content of beliefs, rather than relations among them.

When the elements of cognitive content are specified, as in the experimental assessment of relations of implication, there is no difficulty in defining structure precisely in terms of a linear composite of cue weights. Ambiguities arise with regard to large cognitive units, such as the "total set of ideas entertained by a person," in which particular elements are not specified. This need not be a problem intrinsically associated with size of the unit, for it is possible to sample elements from a unit of whatever size and construct precise relations among them to represent structural parameters or variables. The impediment seems rather to lie in the imprecise language employed by those theorists who deal with the largest cognitive units. They tend to express their structural ideas by poetic analogy, rather than by equations. Of course, it is possible that equations are as inappropriate as poetry to our present understanding of such large units, but unless one can specify the elements to which a structural concept applies, it is difficult to develop measuring operations that are clearly appropriate to the concept.

Analytical vs. Judgmental Assessment

There is another typical, and by no means coincidental, association between the detail with which structural variables are specified and the degree to which measures depend on coder judgment. Those theorists concerned with generally defined variables are likely to assess them judgmentally, while theorists concerned with precisely defined variables employ analytical scoring of specific responses, typically by computer. The limitations of analytical assessment are severe; one needs to elicit specific responses, such as checks or numerical ratings, which are then combined according to precise rules that are often complex but rarely subtle. Many conceptions of structural properties—such as integrative complexity—are so broad that only a subject's free responses give enough scope for inferring them. Nevertheless, the limitations of judgmental measures are perhaps even more pronounced than their advantages. Besides the length of time and level of sophistication required for valid coding, the limited control over coders' inference processes leaves room for irrelevant considerations to affect their scoring. If structural variables are conceived as distinct from content, then there must be substantial assurance that content does not enter into the measurement of structure. It is difficult to offer such assurance when human judgment is involved in the scoring of each individual's responses.

Inter-measure Agreement: Convergent Validity

Analytical rigor is no substitute for validity, and one would have to prefer a valid judgmental measure to an invalid analytical measure. If the history of measurement in other areas is any guide, however, the choice is unlikely to be so stark as this. When it comes to measuring cognitive structure, the state of the art is such that we can hardly tell a valid instrument from an invalid one. It is rare for investigators to employ more than one measure of a particular structural property. If they do, the several measures are likely to require the same task of respondents, so that any convergence among them may be due to common response sets rather than to a common underlying construct. When the level of abstractness or integrative complexity can only be assessed from the way a person writes about the topics specified in "This I Believe" or the *Paragraph Completion Test*, how is one to know that the scores reflect more than particular styles of written expression, rather than cognitive processes that would be similarly manifest in other ways as well?

These are perhaps unfair challenges to workers in a relatively new and complicated area. It is hard enough to develop one compelling test or experimental paradigm, let alone several. The typical course of careful research on cognitive structure is for the investigator to try a range of measuring procedures until one is found that seems to yield the expected results with reasonable efficiency. The investigator then proceeds to refine the measure and standardize it for all subsequent studies, and other investigators adopt this preferred measure without question. This is perhaps all that can be expected of one careful investigator. Yet it is apparently not enough, for subsequent attempts to reconcile results from different measures are too often frustrated by the belated recognition that they do not measure the same thing after all.

We shall try to improve on the current state of affairs in two ways: First, while dealing with fairly large units of analysis, we propose measures that are quite analytic and independent of coder judgment. Second, we propose at least two, and usually several, measures of every structural property defined, so that their degree of correspondence may be assessed before they are used to assess relations with other variables. The minimal requirement of convergent validity must first be achieved; it is pointless to test hypotheses regarding variables for which we have invalid measures.

SUMMARY

The concepts of cognitive structure may be derived from the theories of Lewin and Heider, among others. Subsequent investigators have built on this work in various, rather different, ways—by defining more precisely the elements of structure and manners in which they are interrelated, by elaborating independent and dependent variables to which structural concepts may be related, or by developing some reasonably precise measures of certain structural properties.

Most of the empirically fruitful work on cognitive structure may be formulated within an object-attribute view of concepts. Relations among attributes have been assessed in various ways—by direct reports, by comparing descriptions of objects, and by experimental manipulation of information about novel objects. Although logical considerations lead to certain preferences, there is almost no research available on the degree to which these different methods yield similar or differing descriptions of cognitive structures.

A number of methodological choices face the investigator, including the size of the cognitive set to be treated as the unit of analysis, the way elements of the structure are to be identified, and the relative reliance to be placed on subjective report, as opposed to experimental manipulation. It is generally conceded that cognitive structure should be defined and measured independently of cognitive content; it is also unarguable that multiple measures are required to define structural concepts operationally. It is almost equally clear that these desirable objectives have not been attained in most research to date.

Chapter 5

A STRUCTURAL MODEL
OF COGNITION

Here we shall present a model of cognition which incorporates many of the ideas discussed in the preceding chapter and extends them in the direction of measuring procedures for structural personality traits. The model is essentially a geometric display of cognitive elements. It functions as a conceptual framework for describing a person's cognitions, but should not be understood as referring to any unobservable features of the person such as psychic mechanisms or predicted neurological structures. The only cognitions portrayed in the model are those available to the individual's awareness. Because the model applies to a single person, it yields an idiographic description. Its principal utility, however, lies in providing a framework within which nomothetic, inter-individual variables can be clearly defined. The value of the model, of course, depends on the extent to which it indicates relations among phenomena that would not otherwise be apparent.

COGNITIVE DOMAINS

Central to the model is the concept of a cognitive domain. The model is intended to represent only a single set of cognitions, rather than the totality of ideas entertained by a person. Separate structures are required for each domain of interest. Choosing the domain as the unit of analysis avoids the assumption that there is consistency across a person's concepts about all types of objects. Comparisons among measures from different domains will empirically establish the degree of inter-domain consistency.

For an individual, a cognitive domain consists of the set of phenomenal objects treated as functionally equivalent in the sense that a common set of attributes can be meaningfully used to appraise them. Though a particular set of objects may constitute an identifiable domain for one person, for someone else the same objects may be scattered over several domains, or be included as a subset of some larger domain, or not enter into a cognitive domain at all. Furthermore, any given object may be considered as belonging to several domains, depending on the basis of classification employed. For some purposes a particular set of objects may be viewed as functionally equivalent but for other purposes as divided into distinct subsets. As an example, consider the rather obscure domain of the self. For one person this might refer to aspects of physical appearance while for another it may include interests and values or occupational and familial ties.

The fluidity and hierarchization of domains presents considerable difficulty for assessment and research. While we recognize the idiosyncrasy of cognitive domains, in actual practice we adopt a more standardized approach. One way of circumventing undue complexity is to accept standard cultural definitions of domains. From a cultural perspective, a cognitive domain is the set of objects ordinarily classified as similar by linguistic conventions. For some purposes nations may constitute a domain; for other purposes all geopolitical units (nations, states, countries, cities, etc.) may be identified as a more inclusive domain; modern industrial nations might be identified as a distinct domain within the first set.

Cultural definitions are most straightforward when there is a clearly delineated set of objects available to all viewers. Though not all people are aware of the same objects, a standard subset which nearly all members of the population recognize may be specified for study. Even if objects are not identical across observers, it is often possible to identify a common domain by designating objects according to commonly understood categories. For example, the domain of acquaintances may be designated in fairly standard fashion by reference to spouse, best friend, a high school chum, etc. The domain of self may be standardized to some extent by referring to subclasses of appearance, talents, attitudes, and roles.

Cognitive domains identified by linguistic convention may have only limited meaning for some individuals, and this poses a theoretical as well as a methodological problem. The theoretical problem may be confronted by conceiving a culturally defined domain as having a variable degree of coherence across individuals; nations may constitute a clear domain for some observers, not for others. The problem of transiency and hierarchization may be approached by treating any cognitive domain, individually or culturally defined, as varying in centrality across observers. The centrality of a domain may be identified psychologically with the amount of time the person spends thinking about it, its importance, one's degree of commitment to it, etc. Nations may be a central, enduring concern for a geographer or foreign affairs specialist but only a transient focus for a student required to pass a history exam.

A GEOMETRIC MODEL

The elements in our model of cognition are objects and attributes. A cognitive domain is defined by the objects contained in it and attributes by which objects are appraised. Objects are represented geometrically as points in multidimensional space and attributes as lines. These lines are divided into segments representing the different levels or categories of attributes which the person distinguishes. The objects are phenomenological objects, i.e., objects as seen by the person, including all of the characteristics the person uses to conceive of them. The points representing the objects are located in the space according to the characteristics the person ascribes to them.

For example, within the domain of nations the Soviet Union might be viewed by one observer as a large, cold country, ethnically heterogeneous, with a totalitarian government and a communist economic system. Each of these characteristics is represented within the geometrical model as a segment of a line that includes one or more segments standing for the way the person sees objects as differing along the particular attribute. The characteristic, large, is represented as a segment of the attribute, size, which presumably contains other segments (characteristics) identified subjectively as small and medium, for example. The characteristic, totalitarian, is treated as a segment of an attribute which may have different meanings, and different complementary segments, depending on the observer. For one person, the inclusive attribute might be the degree of individual freedom—containing just two categories, totalitarian and free. For another observer the inclusive attribute might be the degree to which competition for political power is open and organized by different legal parties, and the categories of this attribute might be totalitarian, two-party, and multi-party. In practice, the categories of an attribute, and hence its meaning, are inferred by a coder from the subject's free descriptions, or they are specified on a multiple-response questionnaire. In theory, however, the meaning of an attribute, and its distinctiveness from other related attributes, could be taken as a problem for extensive investigation rather than simply settled by a coder or question writer.

Figure 5 displays in simplified geometric form the multidimensional arrangement of cognitive elements. It contains just three objects, labelled O_1, O_2, and O_3, projected onto segments of three attributes, A_1, A_2, and A_3. Not all points project onto all lines; this reflects the psychological reality that people do not ordinarily conceive of every object in terms of all the attributes they recognize as potentially applicable to other objects in the domain.

Continuing the previous example, China might be conceived by the person as a large country, ethnically homogeneous, agrarian, and poor. Only two of these characteristics represent segments of the same attributes employed to describe the Soviet Union, namely the attributes of size and ethnic diversity.

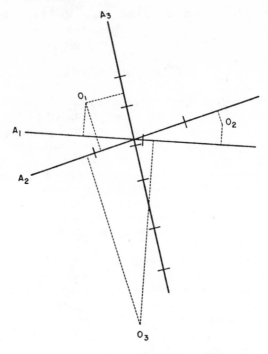

Fig. 5. Two-dimensional display of a simplified cognitive structure.

The last two characteristics are segments of different attributes (perhaps dominant occupation and national wealth), while the attributes of temperature, degree of political freedom, and economic system are not represented in the image of China even though they are part of this person's image of the Soviet Union.

Of course, a characterization on any attribute may be forced by specific questions. The semantic differential technique of Osgood et al. (1957) may even require respondents to describe objects on nonsensical dimensions. This is presumably not a usual exercise for most people, so the semantic differential technique runs the risk of creating a set of transient beliefs instead of assessing a preexisting set.

We conceive of the multidimensional space of this model as having a Euclidean geometry, and thus consisting of points and lines with metricized dimensions. A Euclidean geometry greatly facilitates the development of measures. Even though many of the concepts lend themselves most obviously to non-Euclidean representation (that is, without precise distances and angles), they are not easily elaborated in this form. The algebraic elaborations and specifications provided by a Euclidean space are preferred because they are precise and easy to work with. It is unlikely that measures developed from a nonmetric geometry would be more valid, for limits on precision are set by the procedures for assessing cognitions rather than by the algebra involved. These procedures include rather imprecise questions which admit substantial response error; indeed, the actual state of cognitions for most people is probably quite imprecise. This means that it is virtually impossible to distinguish a linear relationship from any other form of monotonic relationship, so a Euclidean geometry is likely to provide as valid a representation as any other until the technology of assessment is greatly improved.

In our model there is a mutual relation between objects and attributes. Objects are defined by their projections onto attributes, and attributes are defined by the loci of object projections. If two objects are projected onto identical segments of all attributes to which they are assigned, they are indistinguishable. Correspondingly, if two attributes order or classify all

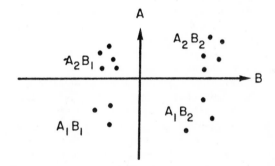

Object distributions proportional: Attributes orthogonal.

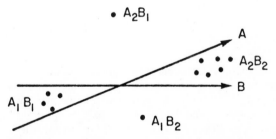

Object distributions disproportional: Attributes oblique.

Fig. 6. Relative location of dichotomous attributes A and B depends on relative frequencies of objects of types A_2B_1 and A_1B_2 compared to types A_1B_1 and A_2B_2.

objects in the same way, they are indistinguishable. Just because a person uses two different object names, or two different attribute names, this does not necessarily mean that they represent different cognitive elements. The names may be functionally synonymous, even if not explicitly recognized as such by the person.

The geometric structure of a cognitive space depends on how the concepts are used by the person. Object placement is given priority over attribute placement in defining the cognitive space; the arrangement of attributes is determined by the placement of objects. Considering just two attributes, A and B, with two characteristics (1 and 2) each, their relative placement would depend on the frequencies with which the four category combinations occur (see Figure 6). If all pairs $(A_1B_1, A_2B_2, A_1B_2,$ and $A_2B_1)$ occur with proportional frequencies, the attributes would be represented by orthogonal lines in the geometric space. If the first two combinations were much more numerous than the last two, or vice versa, the attributes would be represented as correlated (i.e., in acute-angle relationship), with the angle between the lines depending on the degree of disproportionality. Multicategory ordinal attributes may be represented in a similar way, as long as the implied relations among them are monotonic. Nominal attributes, and attributes related nonmonotonically to the rest, could not be conveniently represented in Euclidean space; it would be necessary first to subdivide them into two or more ordinal attributes yielding monotonic relations with the remaining set.

As the reader may have already surmised, the angle between a pair of lines reflects a relation of association between the attributes they represent. Because the model represents existing cognitions, relations between attributes across a set of objects are relations of association. Relations of implication are not distinctively represented in this model. Including them would increase the complexity of the model considerably because different directions of implication would have to be distinguished. Though relations of implication have received little attention in defining personality traits, it is quite plausible that they would be useful in this context (see Osgood, 1977).

INTER-DOMAIN COMPARISONS

With this geometric model it is possible to represent the degree of similarity or distinctness between two cognitive domains. Cognitive domains are similar, or overlapping, to the degree that their objects are appraised on the same attributes. Thus, a particular individual may conceive of technologically advanced and backward nations in quite different terms—the former in terms of political systems and military threat, the latter in terms of resources and natural beauty—in which case they constitute quite different cognitive domains. Another person may conceive of all nations in terms of attributes that typically apply to acquaintances—such as honesty, intelligence, and industriousness—in which case the domains of nations and acquaintances may be represented as merged or overlapping.

The centrality of a cognitive domain for a person may be represented by the density of points and lines within that region of a multidimensional space encompassing all domains he or she recognizes. Thus, for the casual student the domain of nations could be represented by enough points and lines to cover the countries and their characteristics called for in the textbook, while for the teacher the representation would be considerably more dense, displaying not only known objects and attributes but others imagined or inferred.

BELIEFS AS COMBINATIONS OF COGNITIVE ELEMENTS

The two elements of cognition, objects and attributes, are combined in various ways in beliefs about a domain. The *description* of an object on an attribute appears in the general form,

$$O_k \text{ is } A_{ji},$$

meaning that object k is assigned to the ith category of attribute j. Such a description is represented geometrically as the projection of a point onto a line segment.

Two objects may be combined by the cognitive process of *classification*, in which the basis of classification is left unspecified. The general form of a classification is,

$$O_i \text{ is similar to } O_j \text{ and different from } O_k,$$

where the subscripted Os refer to different objects. A classification may be more rudimentary than this, consisting perhaps of only a difference judgment. In terms of the geometric model, the judgment of similarity implies, at a minimum, that the two objects are located on the same segment of at least one attribute. Correspondingly, the judgment of difference implies that the two objects are placed on different segments for some attribute.

A third way of combining cognitive elements is by a *generalization* or *proposition* about relations among attributes; it takes the form,

$$X \text{ is related to } Y.$$

There is a more abstract belief than either description or classification, for it disembodies attributes from their particular manifestations in specific objects and generalizes about objects not yet explicitly contemplated. The description, "China is ethnically homogeneous," assigns an object to an attribute. The classification, "China and the Soviet Union are similar," assigns both objects to the same category of an unspecified attribute. The generalization, "ethnically heterogeneous nations are politically unstable," relates two attributes implicitly by associating one category from each (implying a corresponding association of their respective complementary characteristics, ethnically homogeneous and politically stable).

As relations between attributes, generalizations correspond to angles between lines in the geometric model. We have previously stated that these angles are determined, not by judgments about association, but by beliefs about particular objects. Generalizations are similar to trait-implication judgments in that they require abstraction by a respondent, and this abstraction may or may not correspond to the relations exemplified by the person's views about particular objects. Our concern will focus mainly on relations between attributes as inferred from measures of assocation (see p. 39).

The processes of description and classification would appear to be more primitive and more easily accomplished than the process of relating two abstract attributes with a proposition. One's conception of the relation between attributes such as friendliness and generosity is likely to arise, at first, out of experiences with people who can be classified on these attributes, and only secondarily will this conception of a generalized relationship affect the judgment of new objects. Hence, the location of attributes in the cognitive space depends more on the relative densities of objects than does the distribution of objects depend on the relative locations of attributes.

Relations of association, and beliefs respondents hold about these associations, provide ways in which objects and attributes may be combined in the model. The elements themselves and the relationships among them may be compared in a number of ways which constitute variable properties of the cognitive domain. Some of these properties have become well established in psychological theories; others are newly suggested by the present model. We shall consider in turn variable properties of objects, variable properties of attributes, and distinctively structural properties, those referring to relations among objects or attributes.

VARIABLE PROPERTIES OF OBJECTS

Complexity

Following Zajonc's (1960) usage of the term, we consider the *complexity* of an object to be the number of ideas the person has about it. Noble (1952) has called this meaningfulness. Geometrically, complexity is represented by the number of different attributes onto which an object is projected. A complex, richly conceived object is assigned many characteristics, while a simple object has an impoverished image containing few characteristics.

Valence

The valence of an object refers to its degree of likableness in the person's eyes. Valence has both an affective and a directional component, the former representing the strength of feeling and the latter representing like or dislike for the object. Identifying a direction of valence implies that objects can be clearly assigned to a single continuum, ranging from a high degree of liking to a high degree of dislike. This may be the case for some objects, in the view of some persons, but it need not be so for all. Some objects are seen as having both desirable and undesirable features making a univalent affective assignment unreasonable. Nevertheless, judgments of liking for objects capture a person's feelings toward objects in a summative (albeit simplistic) way, and are therefore quite useful in defining structural properties.

Ambivalence

The ambivalence of a phenomenal object refers to the degree to which it contains both desirable and undesirable features, resulting in no unique direction of valence. Geometrically, a univalent view may be displayed as a projection from the point representing an object to line segments which are either all of positive valence or all of negative valence for the person. An ambivalent view is displayed by projection from a point onto line segments that differ in the direction of their valence.

VARIABLE PROPERTIES OF ATTRIBUTES

Ordinality

The ordinality of an attribute refers to the nature of the scale represented in its categories. An ordinal attribute consists of ordered categories, while a nominal attribute consists of categories that are simply different, without representing more or less of the attribute. Examples of ordinal attributes applied to nations are size of population and amount of freedom permitted. Examples of nominal attributes are geographical location and ethnic composition. Ordinal attributes should provide more efficient bases for classifying objects than nominal attributes, for they admit intermediate categories and do not require detailed memory for category names. It is sometimes possible to convert a nominal attribute into one or more ordinal attributes by specifying particular bases of comparison as, for example, if geographical location is converted into the two ordinal attributes, latitude and longitude.

We do not distinguish a separate class of interval-scale attributes, but rather subsume them under ordinal. Although mechanical measurement typically yields an interval scale, judgmental assessment, with which we are concerned, rarely approaches that degree of refinement without mechanical aids.

Evaluation

The designation of an attribute as evaluative or neutral depends on the evaluation of characteristics comprising it. A neutral attribute consists of all neutral characteristics; hemispheric location of a nation (northern, southern, eastern, or western) is a likely example. Most evaluative attributes contain mixed sets of categories, ranging from positive to neutral and negative. While an attribute (represented geometrically by a line) may have mixed evaluation, a single characteristic (line segment) within it will not. A single characteristic is either positive, negative, or neutral from the standpoint of a particular observer. Of course, different observers may evaluate the same characteristic in different ways.

There may be instances—quite numerous for some people—in which the evaluation of a characteristic depends on the object to which it is applied. Shyness in men, for example, may be deplored, while shyness in women may be quite attractive. Here we shall ignore such complexities to keep the theory manageable.

Precision

The precision of an attribute is the degree to which it yields refined distinctions among objects. The more precise an attribute, the more categories are included in it and the greater is the dispersion of objects over all categories. Ordinal attributes of greatest precision are those dependent on mechanical measurement, such as distance and temperature. Nominal attributes of equal precision require enormous numbers of categories (e.g., the species of plants or the mineral compounds), which limits their use largely to specialists. Logically, minimal precision would be provided by a two-category attribute, for the recognition of one category implicitly requires at least its opposite or absence. It may be, however, that single-category attributes exist in the sense that objects are explicitly classified by the person into only one category, while the complementary category remains implicit but never used. Examples are particular historical, geographical, or personal associations with nations: The presence of pyramids may be associated with Egypt and Mexico, but their absence is never associated with any nation.

Centrality

The centrality of an attribute is the frequency with which it is used to describe objects in the domain. Centrality is similar to Kelly's (1955) notions of permeability and range of convenience for personal constructs, but is more precisely defined. Geometrically, centrality is represented by the proportion of objects that are projected onto an attribute. Some attributes may be used for describing almost any object the person recognizes; such an instance might be geographical location applied to nations. Other attributes are used only occasionally, either through the observer's ignorance or because they do not seem important for most objects. Single-category attributes (i.e., attributes of minimum precision) are likely to be of low centrality, as are attributes difficult for the person to infer from the information available, such as mineral resources of a nation. An attribute of high centrality is presumably very useful to the person in comprehending the domain, and he would want to classify new objects on it before determining how to act toward them.

VARIABLE PROPERTIES OF COGNITIVE STRUCTURE

Our model of cognitive structure specifies three relations among objects and attributes: description, classification, and generalization. These relations offer a basis for characterizing the structure of an entire domain, using variables which we term variable properties of cognitive structure. These structural variables apply, not to a particular object or attribute, but to a set of such elements as interconnected in a person's beliefs.

Within the proposed model, a number of different structural properties could be defined. In our work, we have concentrated only on seven variable properties, and a word regarding our choice of these variables is in order. The structural properties which we have investigated are those which have frequently been implicit in the work of others but which often have been treated only metaphorically. An additional consideration dictating our choice of properties was a realization that several properties of cognitive organization, treated by other theorists as constant over persons, might be more reasonably conceptualized as variable.

At any rate, the properties to be discussed below should not be considered as a definitive set of structural variables but rather as a selective and potentially useful set. In later chapters, we present evidence concerning the reliability, generality, and convergent and predictive validity of these properties. This strategy of exploring the utility of these and other properties, conceived as personality traits, might well be followed in future elaboration of the model, by ourselves or others.

Evaluative Centrality

Research with Osgood's "semantic differential" suggests that evaluation is an important aspect of connotative meaning. By implication, one concludes that cognitions are generally evaluative. Nevertheless, it seems reasonable to modify this generalization: The attributes employed by a person differ in valence and in centrality. Hence, the degree to which evaluative attributes are more central than attributes of neutral valuence may be treated as a variable property, one which we term evaluative centrality. In terms of our geometric model, a condition of high evaluative centrality is represented by a large proportion of objects' being projected mainly onto evaluative attributes, thereby implying psychologically that the person tends to think of objects primarily in evaluative terms. A condition of low evaluative centrality is represented geometrically by a small proportion of projections onto evaluative attributes and implies that the person tends to think of objects primarily in neutral terms.

Image Comparability

Kelly (1955) defined the range of a personal construct as the number of objects to which it is assigned. Our next property may be viewed as a generalization of this notion to the structural level. Image comparability is defined as the degree to which all objects are conceived with the same large set of attributes. In terms of the geometric model, high image comparability is represented by a large number of attributes with high centrality. If all attributes are of low centrality, and each is applied to a distinct set of objects, then the domain is characterized by a low degree of image comparability.

High image comparability implies that the attributes are abstract, in the sense that they can readily be applied to any object. By contrast, low image comparability implies concrete imagery, with each object conceived in its own unique terms, not comparable to any other object. This usage of the terms abstract and concrete is somewhat novel, and may be clarified by contrasting poetic and scientific descriptions. The former are typically object-specific, emphasizing unique characteristics salient in the particular object, while the latter typically display a high degree of image comparability, with all objects described in comparable terms. One need only contrast scientific descriptions of individual personalities, such as MMPI profiles, with literary descriptions to notice the limited, but general (and hence abstract), vocabulary of the former in comparison to the latter.

Centralization

A number of theories describe individuals whose cognitions are dominated by a given attribute, such as depression, alienation, patriotism, evaluation, and so on. In general terms, this condition may be termed centralization and defined as the degree to which all cognitive objects in a given domain are assigned to a single, dominant attribute. Geometrically, maximum centralization is represented by a single attribute with high centrality. Low levels of centralization may occur in two ways—namely, under conditions of either high or low image comparability, when all attributes have either high or low centrality.

The properties just discussed are all defined in terms of various types of attribute centrality. The next three properties are phrased in terms of degrees of consistency or inconsistency in attributed characteristics. Theories of cognitive consistency have been popular in social psychology (Abelson, Aronson, McGuire, Newcomb, Rosenberg, & Tannenbaum, 1968; Zajonc, 1968), but they have usually assumed that consistency is an invariant characteristic and that departures from it are quickly corrected, since inconsistency functions as an aversive drive. We make no such assumptions here. Rather, the degree to which a cognitive domain is inconsistent or consistent is conceived as variable. Inconsistency is defined only as a rare association, one which violates expectancy. The unexpected may be pleasant, as a long-awaited insight or the punch line to a joke, or unpleasant, as the death of one's child. Just what particular combinations of attributes are unexpected depends to some extent on individual experience and to some extent on collective experience.

Dissonance

Festinger's (1957) theory of cognitive dissonance is the best known consistency theory in social psychology, and his famous example of dissonance, "I'm standing in the rain, but I'm not getting wet" (p. 14), reports a combination of two attributes (proximity to rain and dryness) that is almost universally unexpected. The dissonance of a more complex set of cognitions would be quantitatively represented as the proportion of dissonant components, two components being dissonant if the opposite of one "follows from" the other. The term "follows from" may be defined as the degree to which a given combination of characteristics is usual in the person's experience and expected in his imagination. Geometrically, an expected association of categories is represented by the proximity of corresponding segments from two highly correlated vectors (see Figure 7). The higher the correlation—i.e., the smaller the angle between the lines—the stronger is the expectation about corresponding categories of the two attributes.

A dissonant state occurs when a new object (O_1) is assigned characteristics geometrically represented by segments at opposite ends of the two lines (see Figure 7). The stronger the expectation (i.e., the smaller the angle between the lines), and the more unusual the combination (i.e., the more remote the line segments), the greater should be the resulting dissonance.

Note that dissonance refers to the inconsistency of an event with an expectation, while ambivalence refers to the opposition of valences. Whether or not the latter is an instance of the former will depend on the observer. It is possible that, for a person accustomed to thinking of others in ambivalent terms, a univalent impression would be dissonant.

Without additional postulates, one cannot say that dissonance is uncomfortable or that there will be a strain to reduce it. But to the degree that the unexpected is accepted, there will be a change in the relative positions of the attributes in question (i.e., the angle between them becomes less acute). Hence, the unexpected quality of an event is soon diminished, and further events like it should arouse less dissonance.

Affective-Evaluative Consistency

Without knowing the distribution of events in the person's experience and imagination, it is difficult to predict which combinations of characteristics will be dissonant. Presumably, there are general as well as idiosyncratic contributions to expectations about the relations among attributes. One basis for expectations which has been regarded as universal is evaluative consistency. That is, it has been assumed that objects which are liked are assigned favorable characteristics and that objects which are disliked are assigned

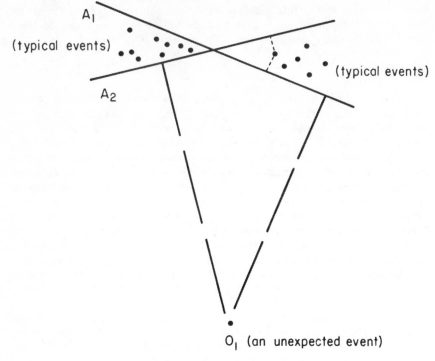

Fig. 7. A dissonant cognition, O_1.

unfavorable characteristics (cf. Abelson et al., 1968). Conceived as a variable property of cognitive structure, affective-evaluative consistency is the degree to which liked objects are assigned more favorable characteristics than disliked objects. A state of high consistency exemplifies the "universal" assumption, and is represented geometrically by acute angles between the affective attribute and various evaluative attributes. A state of low consistency occurs when liked objects are no more favorably evaluated than disliked objects. (A state of negative consistency is geometrically possible, but psychologically unlikely, as long as a representative set of objects is considered and the attribute designations are used by the person with their conventional meanings.)

Affective Balance

Heider (1946, 1958) described a state of balance as one in which a person's cognitions fit together "without stress." The meaning of stress is not indicated in general terms, but most of the illustrations of balance employed by Heider and subsequent investigators involve circumstances in which liked objects are seen as belonging together, disliked objects are seen as belonging together, and the two sets are viewed as mutually dissociated (e.g., Feather, 1971; Jordan, 1953; Morrissette, 1958). This idealized state gives rise to another structural variable which we call affective balance, defined as the degree to which similarly liked objects are classified together. The basis for classification is not specified (in contrast to the case of affective-evaluative consistency), so geometric representation in the present model is imprecise, implying only that similarly liked objects lie close together in the multidimensional space, hence are projected onto identical segments of various unspecified attributes.

Dimensionality

The final structural property to be defined here has been extensively considered by other researchers [see recent reviews by Goldstein & Blackman (1978) and by Streufert & Streufert (1978)]. Indeed, a number of psychologists have treated dimensionality as the only variable property of cognitive structure. An advantage of our approach, defining dimensionality within a general model of cognition, is that it makes possible a better understanding of the variable property, since the level of dimensionality can be expected to depend on, or affect, other properties of the cognitive domain.

As previously noted, the angles among lines in our geometric model are determined by the experienced or imagined characteristics of objects in the domain. Together, these lines constitute a multidimensional space in which all objects are accommodated and to which any new object may be assigned. The dimensionality of this space is, geometrically, the number of dimensions-worth of space required to accommodate the set of objects and attributes. Psychologically, dimensionality is the number of considerations independently brought to bear by a person in appraising a set of objects. To the degree that the angles between lines are orthogonal, dimensionality is high. As the angles become acute, attribute use becomes redundant (i.e., objects become similarly ordered), and dimensionality decreases. A set of k dichotomous attributes requires between 1 and k dimensions of geometric space. With 1 dimension only 2 types of objects can be distinguished; with k dimensions, 2^k different types of objects can be distinguished. Combinations of multicategory attributes permit correspondingly more distinctions among objects.

Refined discrimination among objects requires either high dimensionality or high attribute precision. When judgmental attributes are concerned (i.e., when no mechanical measures are available), it is likely that refined discrimination will be accomplished primarily by the proliferation of dimensions, rather than by the proliferation of categories along a single dimension. The capacity of most people to make refined discriminations along a single dimension of judgment appears quite limited (see Miller, 1956).

DERIVATIONS AND PREDICTIONS FROM THE STRUCTURAL MODEL

Next we shall consider a number of predictions about relationships among the variable properties defined here. Each of the predictions represents a presumably logical derivation from the model, but there is, of course, no

Table 5. Predicted Interrelations Among Variable Properties

Object properties	1	2	3	4	5	6	7	8	9	10	11	12	13
1. Complexity													
2. Valence (affect)													
3. Ambivalence	+												
Attribute properties													
4. Ordinality													
5. Evaluation		Def											
6. Centrality				+	+								
7. Precision				+	−	+							
Structural properties													
8. Evaluative centrality		Def			Def								
9. Image comparability				+		Def	+						
10. Centralization		+			+			+	±				
11. Dissonance	−	+	−		+		−	+					
12. Affective-evaluative consistency	−	+	−		+			+			+		
13. Affective balance	−	+	−		+			+			+	+	
14. Dimensionality	+		+			+	+		+	±	−	−	−
	1	2	3	4	5	6	7	8	9	10	11	12	13

Note. A positive correlation between two properties is designated by +, a negative correlation by −, and a tautological relation by Def (see text).

guarantee that the predictions will be corroborated by appropriate empirical research. To the degree that the predictions are supported, then confidence can be placed in the validity of the geometric model and in the appropriateness of our methodology. It is necessary to obtain evidence of such construct validity before the more interesting business of investigating external correlates of the properties can be fruitfully pursued.

Table 5 summarizes the predictions, which will be developed in detail below. The first three variables in the table are properties of objects, the next four are properties of attributes, and the last seven are properties of domain structure. Predictions are designated as "+" or "−", which refer respectively to positive and negative correlations between the properties of interest. Other predictions are designated as "Def," which means they will hold, by definition. In a sense, all the predictions which are made are based on definition, that of the geometric model, but the "Def" predictions are not derivations but simply tautologies. The reader may verify that these are tautologies by considering the operational meanings of the properties involved (see subsequent chapters).

All of the relationships are predicted for a particular cognitive domain. At this time, no assumption is made concerning the generality of the properties across domains. Even though some degree of individual consistency in these respects might be expected, this is a matter for empirical study rather than for postulation.

For the sake of convenience, the predicted relations are treated in the order presented in Table 5, from top to bottom.

Interrelations Among Properties of Objects

Let us first consider possible interrelationships among the three variable properties of a single object. These relationships might be computed for a single object over a sample of individuals, for a single individual over a sample of objects, or for a single individual and a single object over a sample of occasions. It is predicted that the ambivalence associated with cognitions about an object will increase as the complexity of the image increases. This prediction follows from the plausible argument that enrichment of an image is likely to add characteristics contravalent to those already present. This prediction must be qualified by the recognition that unknown objects will probably be neutral in valence; only initial information can establish a liking or disliking for them; hence, an initial increase above zero complexity should produce increased univalence. Beyond the minimal level, though, further increases in complexity of the image should increase ambivalence. In the studies reported later in this book, a linear, rather than a curvilinear, relationship is expected, since subjects were not questioned about unknown objects.

No other relationships among the variable properties of objects are predicted from our model. The effect of complexity on valence (affect or direction) will depend on the kind of information added to the image. Also, the relationship between affect and ambivalence is not clear from the model, as the highest degree of univalence, as well as the highest degree of ambivalence, can plausibly be associated with extreme affect. For the type of subjects used in most of our research (university students), it seems likely that greater ambivalence will be expressed toward objects of moderate to low degrees of affective involvement than toward objects of high affective involvement. The most affect-laden objects will tend to be seen in univalent terms, reflecting the widespread tendency toward affective-evaluative consistency in the general population.

Interrelations Among Properties of Attributes

Let us next consider predicted relationships among the variable properties of a single attribute. These relationships might be assessed over attributes within an individual, over individuals within an attribute, or over time for a single individual and a single attribute. The predictions summarized in Table 5 are generated from the substantive meanings of the properties and their implications. Presumably, a central attribute is one that the person cares about, and this is more likely to obtain for evaluative than for neutral attributes. High centrality implies that the attribute is widely applied to objects within the domain; hence, it is likely to consist of ordered categories (high ordinality) permitting fairly fine discriminations (high precision).

Because precise discrimination should be aided by an ordinal arrangement of categories, a positive association is predicted between attribute ordinality and attribute precision. On the other hand, it seems likely that precise discrimination will be impeded by high affective loading, and a negative relationship is predicted between attribute evaluation and attribute precision. The predicted effects of high attribute evaluation are a bit paradoxical; a larger number of objects can be described on an evaluative attribute, but with less precision, than for nonevaluative attributes.

Interrelations Among Structural Properties

Some of the predictions in Table 5 refer to relations between pairs of variables representing different units of analysis—objects, attributes, or entire domains. In order to make these predictions meaningful and allow empirical testing, it is necessary to make these units comparable. This can be done by computing the mean values of object properties over all objects, and the mean values of attribute properties over all attributes, within the structural unit of interest—typically, the cognitive domain. Although these summary properties of objects and attributes are not structural in the sense in which we use the term (they do not refer to relations among cognitive elements), it is possible to incorporate them in the structural model, and test predictions concerning their correlations with the strictly structural variables.

Correlates of evaluative centrality. The reader will remember that evaluative centrality is defined as the degree to which evaluative attributes dominate the person's cognitions. It is therefore redundant to state that evaluative centrality is positively associated with the mean affect expressed toward objects and with the mean attribute evaluation. Similarly, these correlates of evaluative centrality should be tautologically associated with each other. More interesting is the proposition that levels of affective balance and affective-evaluative consistency will depend on evaluative centrality. This proposition follows from the interpretation of a highly central attribute as a useful one. To the degree that a person employs a preponderance of evaluative attributes (displays high evaluative centrality), he or she should be likely to employ them as organizers of cognitions. Both affective balance and affective-evaluative consistency are principles of cognitive organization involving the affectively consistent description and grouping of objects; such principles seem most likely to obtain when evaluation is salient in the cognitive domain.

Correlates of image comparability. Image comparability, by definition, is high when the mean centrality of all attributes is high; it is low when the mean centrality of all attributes is low. Accordingly, the predicted relationship between mean attribute centrality and image comparability is a tautological one. The other predictions regarding image comparability are derived by considering factors which should make attributes "permeable," a term used by George Kelly (1955) to describe attributes which are, in principle, applicable to a wide range of objects, including those not yet encountered. Two characteristics of attributes which should affect their general applicability are precision and ordinality, which imply, respectively, many categories and inter-category locations into which an individual may place new objects not recognized at the time the categories were established. Thus, it is predicted that image comparability is positively associated with mean attribute ordinality and with mean attribute precision. Similarly, image comparability should also be enhanced by high dimensionality of a cognitive domain, since the more distinct attributes entertained by a person, the more likely they are to include some of high centrality.

Correlates of centralization. Centralization is the degree to which a single attribute dominates all object descriptions. As argued above, a central attribute is more likely to be evaluative than neutral and, thus, it follows that high centralization will be associated with high average affect expressed toward objects in the domain, and with a tendency to use evaluative attributes in describing them. This means that centralization as a principle of organization is most likely to be found in cognitive domains of high evaluative centrality.

It is predicted that centralization will correlate in curvilinear fashion with both image comparability and dimensionality. The lowest levels of dimensionality will be associated with both low image comparability and low centralization, since it is unlikely that a person will entertain only a single attribute of high centrality. As the number of independent attributes employed by a person increases, so too does image comparability, but the level of centralization should first increase, then decrease, as the number of permeable attributes expands.

Correlates of dissonance. In terms of our geometric model, dissonance results when hitherto unassociated characteristics are assigned to a single object. Dissonance theorists assume this to be a transient state, resolved in one way or another almost as soon as it arises. Although dissonance itself is not usually assessed, its presence is inferred, after the fact, from actions by the person that presumably serve to reduce the dissonance. The proposed model yields several predictions about the sorts of cognitive structures in which dissonance is most likely to arise. It thus provides a more explicit means for making predictions about the occurrence of dissonance than those used heretofore by dissonance researchers, whose dissonance-arousing manipulations were presumably guided by intuition.

In general, it is predicted that structures of limited complexity and high affect have the greatest potential for dissonance. A large number of orthogonal attributes implies that the person has experienced, or can imagine, a variety of combinations of characteristics, and is thus unlikely to find any two characteristics incompatible. If, on the other hand, a domain is characterized by high affect, the accompanying affective organization of concepts will tend to limit the number of combinations that can be accommodated without dissonance.

Finally, because a high level of mean attribute precision affords intermediate categories to which a strange event can be assigned, it is predicted that dissonance is negatively associated with mean attribute precision. The observation that "I am standing partly sheltered and partly in the rain, and I'm not getting particularly wet," presumably has less dissonance-arousing potential than the corresponding assertion on p. 67, which was phrased in terms of dichotomous attributes.

Correlates of balance and consistency. As already explained, affective balance and affective-evaluative consistency are theoretically related properties of cognitive structure. Balance implies that similarly liked objects are seen as similar, with the basis of similarity unspecified. Consistency implies that similarly liked objects are rated similarly on evaluative attributes. The predicted correlates of balance and consistency are the same (see Table 5). Clearly, the two properties should be correlated with each other. Both principles of organization imply that evaluative attributes predominate in descriptions and classifications of objects, so positive associations are expected with evaluative centrality, with mean object valence (affective intensity), and with the use of evaluative attributes.

A high degree of correspondence between evaluation of objects and other appraisals of them means that attributes are highly correlated. Thus, it is predicted that affective-evaluative consistency and affective balance will be found most frequently in structures of low dimensionality, where the various attributes entertained by the person order the objects in similar ways. The other predictions in Table 5, negative correlations between these properties and the variables of mean object complexity and mean object ambivalence, follow from the same line of reasoning.

Correlates of dimensionality. Most of the predictions regarding dimensionality have already been justified in the preceding pages. To summarize briefly these predictions, dimensionality is expected to correlate positively with image comparability (mean attribute centrality), curvilinearly with centralization, and negatively with dissonance, affective-evaluative consistency, and affective balance.

The other predictions involving dimensionality follow from consideration of the substantive meaning of the property in terms of the geometric model. High mean object complexity should be associated with high dimensionality, since a number of ideas about a variety of objects can occur to the extent that one brings a number of perspectives to bear on objects of a domain. This should also tend to increase ambivalence, for different perspectives imply differing appraisals of the same object. Finally, precision in the use of attributes implies attention to inter-object differences, which is also facilitated by high dimensionality.

SUMMARY

We have developed a multidimensional geometrical model that makes explicit many relationships hinted at or overlooked in previous studies of cognitive processes. Within this model one may define as variable properties certain structural properties that other investigators have treated as constant.

Predictions about interrelations among the variable properties have been made in light of the structural model. Most of the predictions have been tested. with data obtained from several samples of university students, who reported their cognitions about a variety of object-domains (see Chapter 11). For the most part, results support the predictions, although some levels of association are small, and other outcomes are inconsistent with the model.

Before these results are discussed, it will be necessary to describe in some detail the procedures by which the structural properties were assessed. This is the task of the next several chapters.

SECTION II

MEASURING COGNITIVE PROPERTIES

The next five chapters are concerned with procedures for measuring variable properties of cognition, both in our own studies and in the work of other investigators. Measurement consists of two aspects: (a) eliciting ideas that people hold about a particular cognitive domain, and (b) coding and scoring these responses in such a way as to reflect the intended properties. Chapter 6 discusses some considerations underlying our own choice of strategy and presents the questionnaires we have used for assessing respondents' ideas about their acquaintances. (Questionnaires pertaining to other cognitive domains appear in Appendix A.)

The coding and scoring of responses is described in Chapters 7 through 9, which are divided for convenience among measures of differentiation, measures of integration, and measures of other properties. Chapter 10 concerns the degree to which these properties are manifest similarly or distinctively in different domains of cognition.

Chapter 6

DEVELOPING MEASURES OF STRUCTURAL PROPERTIES

There is little consensus among psychologists concerning ways in which structural properties should be assessed. The conceptions in this area are fairly recent and have not often been expressed with sufficient clarity to encourage precise measurement. One is therefore faced with a range of procedures, from judgmental to quantitatively precise, which are not necessarily equivalent even when they bear similar names.

In the next four chapters, we shall emphasize measures which follow logically from the theoretical conception of structural properties developed in Chapter 5. In addition, we will discuss some procedures which have gained currency through the work of other investigators. First, it is appropriate to consider some general principles of psychological measurement which are especially pertinent to the assessment of cognitive structure.

SOME GENERAL CONSIDERATIONS IN MEASURING COGNITIVE STRUCTURE

Fundamental Measurement

Ideally, we would like to construct measures that have clearly interpretable meanings independent of the particular instrument used to obtain them. Physical properties such as length, volume, velocity, mass, and density, for example, can be measured in a variety of ways, any of which can be readily translated into any other because all refer to a single fundamental meaning of the concept. By contrast, the meanings of most psychological measures are so dependent on the particular procedures used to obtain them that translation among different measuring instruments is virtually impossible. For instance, the attitude toward China measured by the two questions "How do you feel about China?" and "Do you think the Chinese government is helpful to its people?" might be quite different, and no one could say which yields the more valid result. Even with "standard attitude scales," such as Middleton's (1963) and Dean's (1961) "alienation" scales, there is no necessary correspondence between measures having the same name, and one cannot say which is the more valid.

The problem lies partly in the way psychological concepts are defined and partly in the way they are operationalized by the measuring procedures. An attitude is conceptualized variously as "evaluation of a concept" (Fishbein, 1967) and as "a mental and neural state of readiness exerting a directive influence upon the individual's response to all objects and situations with which it is related" (Allport, 1935). It is not clear from these definitions just what should be done to "measure an attitude." The definitions certainly do not refer to any zero-point (a state of "no attitude") or to any upper limit of magnitude which should lie within the capacity of a measuring instrument. Psychologists have developed rather arbitrary measuring procedures, such as Likert scales and Thurstone scales, relying on particular sets of questions that may be appropriate to one group, not another, applicable today, but not tomorrow. The scores yielded by attitude scales typically depend on the number of items with which the subject agrees, and this in turn depends more than anything else on the number and type of items in the scale. There is no good way of translating a score from one sample of questions into that obtained from another sample, unless the two item samples are equated by randomization.

The best means that is currently available for coping with this unsatisfactory state is to employ a strategy of multimethod assessment in which a variety of different instruments are administered and some subset of mutually correlated measures is built into a composite. This method is not entirely satisfactory because it does not aid in defining a rational zero point or unit of measurement, and each different composite will give a different result. The typical way around this problem has been to convert all measures to standard scores in which the sample mean and standard deviation become the zero-point and measuring unit. This is a limited solution as well, because each different population studied will yield a different zero-point and unit of measurement.

Ad hoc measuring strategies will continue as long as psychologists use concepts that are not themselves expressed in fundamental terms—i.e., terms which imply a natural zero point and a reasonable unit of measurement. In order to develop measures that are applicable at different times and places, one needs to conceive of a fundamental measuring scale and aim one's instruments at yielding this scale. Fundamental measurement in turn implies fundamental concepts, which are not prevalent in psychology today.

The structural properties developed in Chapter 5 have a potential status as fundamental concepts; most of them have been, or can be, defined in ways that imply a natural zero point. There are logically minimal levels of dimensionality, precision, and evaluation, for example. For others, such as affective balance, affective-evaluative consistency, and ambivalence, meaningful upper and lower limits can be conceived theoretically. Some of the structural properties imply a meaningful unit of measurement, such as "dimensions-worth of information" or "categories-worth of discrimination." Thus, the model has the potential for fundamental measurement; it is largely a matter of ingenuity to develop instruments which tap this potential.

Convergent Validity

Unless there is consensus among investigators, based on clear empirical evidence, as to which measure of a variable is to be preferred, there is no alternative but to employ several measures. Any single one is subject to distortion by innumerable unwanted effects. Even if a measure proves useful in one setting, it may be inapplicable for another population. Without evidence that it corresponds to an alternative measure of the concept, one runs the risk of misinterpreting any findings that are obtained. Failure to support an expected relationship might be due to an invalid measure. Conversely, an outcome in the predicted direction could be due to some contamination in the measure.

Instruments depending on verbal reports are particularly vulnerable to contamination by the styles of writing, speaking, and self-presentation which literate people employ. Verbosity, use of unusual, complicated, or stereotyped words, the tendency to flatter or deprecate oneself, restraint or flamboyance in emotional expression—all such tendencies come to play when people are asked to express their own ideas. These or other response styles may appear even when subjects respond to "objective" or fixed-alternative questions, as in tendencies to check many or few alternatives, to use the extremes or midpoint of a rating scale, or to peruse a list diligently or carelessly.

The constructs we have identified as structural are intended to mean something other than such response styles. We are concerned with the ways in which ideas are related in an observer's typical thoughts rather than in the ways they might be expressed in a particular medium or circumstance. Yet it is virtually impossible to design a verbal instrument for assessing a property of cognitive structure that does not also call forth some irrelevant response style as a vehicle for expression. This means one must employ, not just one, but several methods of assessment and make sure that these do not call forth the same irrelevant response styles. It is not enough to use a single instrument that some other investigator has found valid for another purpose on a different population. Multiple measures are required for each new group and each new problem until the scientific field ultimately comes to accept one measure as preferred or adequate.

The investigator should seek several measures of a structural variable that yield correlated scores. If these correlations are clearly not due to similar contaminating features, then one may reasonably combine them into a composite score. If the sources of error are truly different, the composite will be more accurate and less biased than any of its components. One should stop and ponder before proceeding, however, when two measures are not correlated. This is very likely to mean that the instruments are not valid, at least for the particular subjects and circumstances, We have encountered at least one example of such apparent invalidity in our own research. When a set of questionnaires developed with university students to assess structural properties of the self-concept was applied to outpatients at a mental health center, some of the critical measures did not correspond (Scott, 1972). We could only surmise, after the fact, that the patients may have adopted quite a different response set than the students—perhaps to reveal themselves critically and exhaustively, rather than to perform a routine descriptive task. Why the measures were invalid for this population is not altogether clear, but at least we were alerted to problems which would not have been apparent if only one measure had been employed. In the present state of the art, there is no reasonable alternative to multiple measurement.

Content Validity

Content validity refers to the evident appropriateness of a measure as an indication of the intended concept. Though it is possible to have a valid measure for a concept to which it is not obviously related, it can only be proved valid by empirical association with a measure which does have content validity. Thus, in the initial development of measures, content validity is essential. To insure this, two considerations have been paramount in developing measures of our structural properties: to select tasks that fit the constructs and to require responses that made sense to the subjects.

Because most of our constructs refer to relations among objects and attributes within a particular cognitive domain, the questionnaires either specify objects and attributes or invite the respondent to specify them. In some cases the objects and attributes of a cognitive domain can be identified readily; in other cases considerable exploration and, eventually, some arbitrary restrictions may be required. The case of nations is simple, and this domain was studied partly for that reason: There is a limited number of objects, and most people are likely to conceive of them in a limited number of ways. Nevertheless, we always include at least one free-response instrument (*Listing and Comparing Nations*) in our test battery in order to check on the current appropriateness of fixed lists employed in other instruments (such as *Checklist Description of Nations*).

Definition of the self domain was more problematic. We started with a vague reference and asked subjects in a pilot study to fill in its elements, with the question, "When you think about yourself, what sorts of ideas come to mind? Just what does your self consist of, and what do you think about the various components of yourself?" A variety of answers emerged, ranging from physical characteristics (5'6") through roles (student) to evaluative appraisals ("I'm pretty satisfied with myself"). The evaluative appraisals could be readily accommodated within our conception of attributes, but the definition of objects posed a dilemma. We chose roles rather than physical parts, because they are more varied and give rise to a wider range of attributes. We did not attempt to incorporate both kinds of self-objects (roles and physical parts) in the same cognitive domain, because they tended to call forth rather different sets of attributes, and this violated our conception of a domain. Although the choice of objects obviously restricts the meaning of self somewhat, the resulting definition benefits from both sociological and psychological implications. Roles constitute a reasonable sociological definition of self, and the attributes of role performance constitute a reasonable psychological definition. One need not prejudge the question of whether any particular person will regard his or her self as fragmented into multiple roles or unified into a coherent, constant self. Appropriate analysis of responses to the questionnaires should reveal the answer.

Thus far we have developed questionnaires pertaining to 9 different cognitive domains (nations, acquaintances, self, family relationships, occupation, school, celebrities, societal groups, and psychological tests). These are not to be regarded as fixed instruments, but rather as tentative realizations of a strategy of assessment which can, in principle, be applied to cognitive domains not yet considered. The particular objects of a domain (for instance, celebrities) may become outmoded and require replacement in modified instruments; even the salient attributes of a domain (such as those for the self) could change through time and place, requiring modification in the questionnaires.

Since the structural properties refer to an entire domain of cognition, adequate sampling of objects and attributes is necessary for content validity. This requirement has been satisfied reasonably well across the complete set of instruments pertaining to a particular cognitive domain, but any single instrument may be grossly deficient in object or attribute sampling. The instrument called *Rating of Nations* (or other objects) contains only 20 objects and 10 attributes, too few to justify the dimensionality analyses applied to them. The *Checklist Description of Nations* (or other objects) contains just 10 objects, far too few for a dimensional analysis of the 36 bipolar attributes in the checklist. We score these instruments for dimensionality in spite of this limitation, hoping that their deficiencies would be offset by additional instruments aimed at the same property. It seemed that sufficient lengthening of the *Rating* and *Checklist Description* would have threatened the other main aim in questionnaire development, rapport with subjects. Rather than have one measure with an adequate sample of objects and attributes, we choose to have a series of individually less representative instruments that would permit multimethod convergence.

Acceptance by Subjects

We were fortunate in having access to university students recruited from general psychology courses; otherwise we would have encountered considerably more resistance to the tedious procedures often required. Some tedium is perhaps inevitable in early versions of instruments, but we were aiming at a final battery which at least made sense to subjects. We hoped they would feel they had benefitted from the 2 hours or more required to fill out the questionnaires. Comments received from many of them suggested that we had been at least partly successful in this attempt. Nevertheless, reaching this stage required certain intuitive decisions along the way which violated another consideration, namely continuity with the work of other investigators.

One such choice was to include in the fixed alternative instruments only attributes commonly used by observers to describe objects of the particular domain. We assumed that the structural properties in which we were interested would be more validly measured with domain-appropriate attributes than with a standard artificial set. This consideration precluded use of the standard attribute set employed by Charles Osgood and his colleagues in their well known "semantic differential." Our previous experience with that instrument suggested that even university students would not welcome the opportunity to rate nations and themselves on standard semantic differential attributes like "sweet-vs.-sour."

We also decided to aim at instruments that are "self-administering" or that at least can be administered to large groups of people without much individual attention. This decision, made on grounds of efficiency, eventually precluded the use of tests with rather complicated instructions, such as Kelly's *Role Constructs Repertory Test*. A self-administering version of this test was developed and its results compared with those from other instruments for the variable of dimensionality. The correlations between instruments were significantly larger than zero, though not high, leading us to believe that a common construct was tapped. There were, however, numerous faulty completions of the *Role Constructs Repertory Test* (requiring that results be discarded) and an excessive number of questions raised by students during the test period. These problems led us to abandon this group-administered form of the instrument in favor of our home-grown varieties, which are more readily understood by these respondents.

Although experience with university students in four cultures—U.S., New Zealand, Japan, and Australia—gives us confidence in the applicability of these procedures in such a literate population, there is still insufficient assurance that the measures are applicable to nonstudent populations. They have been used successfully with high school students (9th grade or higher) and their parents. Orally administered versions of a selected set of instruments appeared satisfactory for hospitalized psychiatric and surgical patients (see Scott, 1969). On the other hand, a pilot study of outpatients in a community mental health center showed poor convergence of structural measures within the domains of self and acquaintances (Scott, 1972), and a study of the domain of "occupation" for secretarial and clerical employees showed only fair convergent validities (Le Bach & Scott, 1969). It is likely that further attention must be given to subjects' motivation and to reducing the complexity of some instruments before they can be used successfully with nonstudent populations.

SAMPLE INSTRUMENTS

In this section appear the instruments currently used to assess structural properties of cognition defined in Chapter 5. Though developed over several years' pilot work on many samples of respondents (all university students), these instruments should still be regarded as prototypes rather than as final versions to be copied uncritically. Before administering them to any group, one should consider changing some of the objects—and perhaps some of the attributes—to make these more appropriate to the particular population of respondents.

The instruments shown here all pertain to the four cognitive domains investigated most thoroughly so far. They are listed in the order of administration, which should be used when a single domain is being assessed. In this case, 1½ to 3 hours is required for completion, depending mainly on subjects' diligence in the free-response instruments. When two or more cognitive domains are assessed from the same respondents, it is desirable to alternate instrument format, as well as domain. In general, free responses should be obtained first, so that they are not contaminated by the particular objects and attributes appearing in the fixed-response instruments.

The "average time" indicated for each instrument should be interpreted as the time within which 80% of university students can finish. Testing time is markedly skewed, particularly for the free-response instruments. If one plans a 2½-hour session based on the average times given, a large majority of respondents will have completed by that time, some in 90 minutes or less. An additional 30 minutes will accommodate nearly all students, but a few slow or hyperconscientious persons will want to take the booklets home and finish them. We have usually permitted this, with admittedly unknown effects on validity. As thoughtfulness and thoroughness are required for manifesting the traits being studied, it seems unreasonable to truncate individual differences by imposing arbitrary time limits. We would prefer to develop other fixed-response instruments, which would still be affected by thoughtfulness, but not so much by writing time and sheer perseverence.

We have attempted to avoid more than 50% overlap between the objects or attributes of any two instruments in order to make the scores they yield as independent as possible. This goal proved rather difficult in such domains as self, where the number of common roles, and perspectives for appraising them, are limited. Ideally, one would want these instruments to sample representatively from every respondent's own cognitive domain. This ideal can only be approximated, of course, but the culturally defined domain will presumably match individuals' domains best if it includes those objects and attributes that appear most commonly in the free-response instruments.

For simplicity, the instruments will be described in reference to the domain of acquaintances; their application to other domains is quite similar. The specific instructions used for the domains of family activities, nations and self-roles appear in Appendix A.

Listing and Comparing Objects

Average time: less than 20 minutes

The *Listing and Comparing* instrument was among the first developed to assess dimensionality. It was originally called *Listing and Grouping*, as the earliest format required only that groups of similar objects be constructed. Subsequently, the format was expanded to elicit groups of "different" objects as well, so that responses could be scored for image comparability. Also, liking for objects was added so that the instrument could be scored for affective balance. It is the only instrument which elicits the respondent's own conception of both objects and attributes. Hence, it is routinely included early in the test batteries. One suspects, however, that its validity may be lower than that of other instruments because scores are unduly affected by the particular sample of objects which the respondent lists and by the total number of groups formed.

LISTING AND COMPARING ACQUAINTANCES (first page)

In the spaces below please write the initials of 20 people with whom you have been acquainted. Include both people you have liked and those you have disliked. Following each person's initials, please identify him by a short phrase indicating his role (e.g., doctor, grocer) or relationship to you (e.g., younger sister). Try to make these identifications unique, so that no two people on the list will be identified alike. For example, instead of "friend" beside several different initials, write such things as "best girl friend in secondary school" or "ex-shopkeeper."

———— 1. ————————————————————
———— 2. ————————————————————
———— 3. ————————————————————

(20 lines)

LISTING AND COMPARING ACQUAINTANCES (second page)

Tear off the previous sheet and place it beside this one. Consider the entire list of acquaintances and pick out some people who are alike in an important way. Write their *line numbers* in the left-hand box and, at the bottom of the box, write whatever it is that the acquaintances in that group have in common—that is, why you put them together.

Then, in the right-hand box, write the *line numbers* of any acquaintances remaining on the list that are *clearly different* from the first group in this respect. That is, include in the right-hand box acquaintances who *do not* possess the characteristic written at the bottom of the left-hand box.

It is not necessary to include all acquaintances on your list in either box. If a particular acquaintance's standing on this characteristic is not relevant, or if you do not know how a particular acquaintance stands on the characteristic, omit him from both boxes.

Line numbers of similar acquaintances (from *your* list):	*Line numbers* of acquaintances who differ in this respect from group at left:
Way in which above acquaintances are alike.	

On the following pages are more pairs of boxes. Consider your entire list of acquaintances again, and pick out another group who are alike in an important way. Write their line numbers in the left-hand box of a pair, and, at the bottom, write their common characteristic. Then, in the right-hand box, write the line numbers of acquaintances who clearly differ in this respect from the left-hand group.

And so on, using as many pairs of boxes as you need in order make groups of acquaintances who are alike in an important way. Any particular acquaintance may be included in more than one group if you wish. Just be sure that, for every group of similar acquaintances, you write their common characteristics after the numbers in the left-hand box, and also write in the right-hand box the numbers of acquaintances who clearly do not possess this characteristic.

(There followed 9 more pairs of boxes, 3 pairs per page.)

LISTING AND COMPARING ACQUAINTANCES (last page)

Now would you please go back to the first page, on which you listed the 20 acquaintances, and *beside each one* write a number from the following scale, indicating how much you like that person.

SCALE

7 Like very much
6 Like considerably
5 Like for the most part, with some degree of dislike
4 Neither like nor dislike
3 Dislike for the most part, with some degree of liking
2 Dislike considerably
1 Dislike very much

You may tear this sheet out, if you wish, to make the rating easier. (*Listing and Comparing* instruments for the other 3 cognitive domains have pages 2–6 like the above except that the appropriate object class is substituted for acquaintances throughout the instructions.)

Free Description of Objects

Average time: 20 minutes

These instruments were once called *Open Description and Rating*, but the colloquial adjective "open" did not make much sense to students in New

Zealand, so a more appropriate adjective was found. Although respondents provide their own attributes, the sample of objects is chosen by the investigator, thus permitting some control over the range of desirability represented in them. This control is advantageous because the instrument is intended mainly for assessing evaluative centrality, ambivalence, and affective-evaluative consistency; for the last of these, at least, it is necessary that every respondent find a range of attractiveness in the objects.

Only the respondent's own evaluative ratings are required to assess these three properties. If, in addition, one wants to assess object complexity, centralization, and image comparability from this instrument, it is necessary either to assume that each different description represents a distinct attribute or else to develop a reasonably exhaustive set of categories for coding and descriptions. Codes developed for studies of university students in the U.S., Japan, and New Zealand are available from the authors.

Identification of some of the people designated as the subject's acquaintances (e.g., a neighbor) may be ambiguous. As it is necessary to keep these objects constant within a given instrument, each respondent filled out a list of initials identifying the several persons designated; they were asked to refer to this list whenever a particular acquaintance was called for.

FREE DESCRIPTION OF ACQUAINTANCES (first page)

On the following pages specific people are described at the top of a set of lines. In the designated space, copy the initials of the person from your *List of Acquaintances*. Please think about each of the people, then on the blank lines below, write down some of the characteristics which describe him (or her). State each characteristic by a word, phrase, or sentence and start each different characteristic on a new line. You may use as many or as few lines as your wish for each person, but try to list all those characteristics which you feel are *important* in describing him.

(second page)

A clergyman (priest, minister, or rabbi) (initials _____)

———— 1. _____
———— 2. _____
———— 3. _____
(12 lines)

A person who excels in sports (initials _____)
(3rd, 4th, 5th and 6th pages, 2 acquaintances per page, each followed by 12 lines)
An old person, e.g., your grandmother or grandfather (initials _____)
A person you have played games with (initials _____)
A teacher you disliked (initials _____)
A very popular person (initials _____)
A person you have studied with (initials _____)
A former classmate (initials _____)
Someone who frightens you (initials _____)
Someone you don't trust (initials _____)

FREE DESCRIPTION OF ACQUAINTANCES (next to last page)

Now, would you please go back to the beginning of this booklet, and rate *every characteristic* that you have written down for each person, by writing a number from the following scale in front of the description. Make sure you write a number on *every line* you have used, not just one number per person.

SCALE

7 Very pleasant characteristic
6 Quite pleasant
5 Sometimes pleasant, but depends on the circumstances
4 Neither pleasant nor unpleasant
3 Sometimes unpleasant, but depends on the circumstances
2 Quite unpleasant
1 Very unpleasant characteristic

You may tear this sheet out, if you wish, to make the rating easier.

LIKING OF ACQUAINTANCES FROM FREE DESCRIPTION (last page)

Please write a number from the following scale beside each person listed below to indicate how much you like him (or her).

SCALE

7 Like very much
6 Like considerably
5 Like for the most part, with some degree of dislike
4 Neither like nor dislike
3 Dislike for the most part with some degree of liking
2 Dislike considerably
1 Dislike very much

———— 1. A clergyman (priest, minister, or rabbi) (initials———) (etc.)

Free Comparison of Objects

Average time: less than 20 minutes

These instruments were developed mainly for assessing image comparability and centralization. These properties require that responses be coded into the same dimensional categories that were developed for coding the free descriptions (see preceding). In addition, overall object complexity for the domain may be scored, crudely, as the total number of different attributes employed.

It was initially anticipated that image comparability would be measured by the similarity between attributes used for describing objects and attributes used for comparing them. This would require a constant sample of objects, so the pairs used for *Free Comparison* were selected from the *Free Description*. Subsequent analyses indicated that this method of combined scoring was no more valid than scoring each instrument separately, which is preferable because it yields two measures of image comparability instead of just one. Future versions of this instrument should probably use a set of objects quite different from those appearing in the *Free Description.*

FREE COMPARISON OF ACQUAINTANCES (first page)

On the following pages, pairs of acquaintances are designated. Please refer to your *List of Acquaintances* and copy the initials you assigned to these designations into the spaces provided. Think about the two acquaintances in each pair and try to decide on the *major ways* in which they are alike. Write these principal similarities on the lines provided. Then, think about the *major ways* in which the two acquaintances are different and write these *principal differences* on the lines provided for them. You do not need to use all the lines provided. Just make sure you cover the major similarities and differences you are aware of between the two acquaintances described.

(second page)

A clergyman (priest, minister, or rabbi) (initials _____)
Someone you don't trust (initials _____)

Major similarities:

1. _____
2. _____

(12 lines)

Major differences:

1. _____
2. _____

(12 lines)

(Subsequent pages presented pairs of acquaintances from FREE DESCRIPTION OF ACQUAINTANCES, composed of acquaintance numbers 2 and 9, 3 and 8, 4 and 7, 5 and 6. This basis for selecting pairs is no longer recommended – see above).

Free Comparison instruments for the domains of family, nations, and self were identical in format to the above, except that instructions were modified to designate the appropriate object class.

Checklist Description of Objects

Average time: less than 15 minutes

These instruments were developed as fixed-response counterparts to the *Free Description* instruments (page 88). They were intended to circumvent individual differences in the tendency to give extreme or neutral ratings to the various descriptions of objects by using a checklist of adjectives with evaluative characteristics that could be assumed similar for all respondents. The assumption is justified to the extent that adjectives in the list had received clearly positive, negative, or neutral ratings from previous samples of judges in the same population. The adjectives were selected from Anderson's (1968) lists, supplemented by similar pilot work at the University of Colorado, in which students rated the desirability of trait names on a 7-point scale, ranging from +3 (very desirable) through 0 (neither desirable nor undesirable) to −3 (very undesirable). The only adjectives used were those for which the mean rating was +2 or higher, −2 or lower, or between +1 and −1, with standard deviations less than 1.00. Other adjectives were omitted from the lists because there was not adequate agreement among subjects about their affective value. Subsequent comparisons indicated that mean ratings are very stable among our samples in the U.S. and New Zealand, and Anderson's samples, with all interlist correlations above .95, and averaging .97.

The present lists obviously contain restricted samples of attributes. Though this limitation was reasonable given the initial purposes of the *Checklist* instruments, their subsequent adaptation for assessing dimensionality made the decision questionable. In future modifications we propose to include a more representative sample of adjectives in order to measure dimensionality, but to use only those with standard affective values for measuring evaluative centrality, ambivalence, and affective-evaluative consistency. The present instruments typically include 18 evaluative pairs of adjectives and 18 neutral pairs.

CHECKLIST DESCRIPTION OF ACQUAINTANCES (first page)

At the top of each of the following pages is designated a person whom you know. Please refer to your *List of Acquaintances* and copy the initials of the specified person alongside the heading. Below each person is a list of adjectives that might be used to describe him or her. Please circle the words which come to mind when you think about that person. Do not circle all the words that might be used, but only those which you consider essential. For instance, if you do not usually think of the person who has given you advice in terms of how reliable he (or she) is, you would not circle the word "reliable" or "unreliable."

Each adjective is paired with another adjective which is roughly its opposite. It is *not* necessary to circle either member of any pair. Circle it only if you think it is an important characteristic of that person. Occasionally, both words of a pair could apply to the same person. If you feel that they do in an important way, you may circle both.

(second page)

A person who has given you advice (initials ⎯⎯⎯⎯)

1. reliable (+)	25. conformist	49. quiet
2. unreliable (−)	26. nonconformist	50. excitable
3. religious	27. changeable	51. trustworthy (+)
4. nonreligious	28. unchanging	52. untrustworthy (−)
5. selfish (−)	29. unassuming	53. dependable (+)
6. generous (+)	30. demanding	54. undependable (−)
7. tactful (+)	31. emotional	55. wise (+)

8. rude (−)	32. unemotional	56. foolish (−)
9. intelligent (+)	33. forgiving (+)	57. open minded (+)
10. unintelligent (−)	34. spiteful (−)	58. narrow minded (−)
11. conventional	35. honest (+)	59. sincere (+)
12. eccentric	36. dishonest (−)	60. deceitful (−)
13. friendly (+)	37. kind (+)	61. cool
14. hostile (−)	38. cruel (−)	62. tense
15. aggressive	39. sophisticated	63. indifferent
16. unaggressive	40. naive	64. persistent
17. argumentative	41. neurotic (−)	65. appreciative (+)
18. compliant	42. well adjusted (+)	66. ungrateful (−)
19. considerate (+)	43. loyal (+)	67. strict
20. conceited (−)	44. disloyal (−)	68. lenient
21. cooperative (+)	45. ordinary	69. large
22. uncooperative (−)	46. unusual	70. small
23. complex	47. shy	71. rich
24. simple	48. bold	72. poor

(Evaluative coding of the attributes, + and −, did not appear in the instrument. Subsequent pages presented the same adjective checklist, with different acquaintances designated at the top, as in the following rating form, which appeared on the last page.)

Please write a number from the following scale beside each person described below to indicate how much you like that person.

SCALE

7 Like very much
6 Like considerably
5 Like for the most part, with some degree of dislike
4 Neither like nor dislike
3 Dislike for the most part, with some degree of liking
2 Dislike considerably
1 Dislike very much

_____ 1. A person who has given you advice (initials _____)
_____ 2. A good friend of the same sex (initials _____)
_____ 3. Your father (or the man who raised you) (initials _____)
_____ 4. Someone you have lived with (initials _____)
_____ 5. Someone who has failed at something (initials _____)
_____ 6. A person who excels academically (initials _____)
_____ 7. A person who you have studied with (initials _____)
_____ 8. A doctor (initials _____)
_____ 9. A person you regard as worthless (initials _____)
_____10. Someone who does peculiar things (initials _____)

Checklist Comparison of Objects

Average time: less than 15 minutes

The *Checklist Comparison* instruments were developed for assessing image comparability as fixed-response counterparts to the *Free Comparison* instruments (see page 89). They were constructed with adjectives identical to those in the *Checklist Descriptions* and the objects to be compared were also selected from that instrument. This choice was made to permit a combined scoring of the two instruments. However, subsequent analyses indicated that separate scoring was preferable, so there is now no reason why the objects and attributes should be identical; in fact, different sets would assure wider sampling within each domain and therefore seem preferable.

CHECKLIST COMPARISON OF ACQUAINTANCES (first page)

On the following pages are designated pairs of acquaintances. Please consult your *List of Acquaintances* and copy their initials into the spaces provided. Underneath each pair of acquaintances is a list of adjectives or pairs of contrasting characteristics. Please think about the two acquaintances in each pair and try to decide what are their principal similarities and differences. On the pages labeled "similarities," circle all the *major* ways in which the two acquaintances are alike. Do not circle all the words which might apply to both, but only those which represent what, to you, are important similarities.

On the pages labelled "differences," consider each adjective-pair. If the two acquaintances described *do not* differ on the characteristic represented by a particular pair of adjectives, or if you think the difference between them is unimportant, leave it blank. If the two acquaintances differ on a characteristic to a degree which you regard as important, circle the two words. Then write beside each adjective in that pair the initials of the acquaintance to whom it applies. For instance, if you think "a person who has given you advice" is reliable, while "someone who does peculiar things" is unreliable, and that this is an important difference between the acquaintances, you would circle the word-pair "reliable-unreliable," then write the initials of "a person who has given you advice" above "reliable" and the initials of "someone who does peculiar things" above "unreliable."

Two pages of adjectives will appear for each pair of acquaintances. The first one will ask for important ways in which the two acquaintances are alike; the second will ask for important ways in which they are different. If you see no important similarities, you may leave the first page blank; if you see no important differences, you may leave the second page blank.

SIMILARITIES (second page)

Important ways in which A person who has given you advice (initials _____) and Someone who does peculiar things (initials _____) are alike; both are:

1. reliable	25. conformist	49. quiet
2. unreliable	26. nonconformist	50. excitable

(ect., as in *Checklist Description of Acquaintances*, page 91).

DIFFERENCES (third page)

Important ways in which A person who has given you advice (initials _____) and Someone who does peculiar things (initials _____) *differ*:

(Circle major differences, then write the initials of the acquaintances over the appropriate words.)

1. reliable—unreliable
2. religious—nonreligious
(etc., for all adjective pairs on the *Checklist*.).

19. kind—cruel
20. sophisticated—naive

Succeeding pages alternated the "similarities" checklist and the "differences" checklist, for comparing the following pairs chosen from the *Checklist Description of Acquaintances* (p. 92) 2 and 9, 3 and 8, 4 and 7, 5 and 6.

Grouping Objects

Average time: 20 minutes

This instrument format was initially developed for assessing attribute precision. The objects and attributes were specified, and the respondent was encouraged to make as many or as few groups as he or she wished on each attribute. Subsequently a procedure was developed for scoring dimensionality from this instrument. An attribute representing "liking for the objects" was then added to permit scoring for affective balance and affective-evaluative consistency. Finally, instructions were modified to encourage respondents to omit objects whose classification on a particular attribute was not clear; this permitted scoring the instrument for image comparability. Altogether, this has proven to be one of the more versatile instruments—along with *Free Description, Checklist Description*, and *Rating*—from which to score structural properties of cognition. Nevertheless, it is surprisingly difficult for respondents to understand the required task, and one must be prepared to answer questions during the testing session. It is necessary to make sure that all groups are labeled; otherwise their appropriateness for the attribute cannot be ascertained.

Some editing and coding of the groups is necessary, to make certain that all refer to the designated attribute and that they are ordered monotonically to represent decreasing amounts. The most common response error is forming groups irrelevant to the specified attribute—for instance, designating different *kinds* rather than different *degrees* of maturity in acquaintances. Editing in this case consists in pooling all groups labeled at a given *level* of the attribute—for instance, "intellectually mature" and "interpersonally mature" would be combined into a single category, "mature."

GROUPING ACQUAINTANCES (first page)

Here is a list of people who are known to you. Please refer to your *List of Acquaintances* and write their initials alongside the designations. On the following pages are 10 attributes on which these acquaintances could be described. In the space underneath each attribute, please write down all the different ways by which you could describe your acquaintances on that attribute. Then, for each description, write the *numbers* of the acquaintances that belong in it. For instance, under "How happy they are," you might decide that there will be two descriptions, "very happy" and "very unhappy." Then you would write numbers beside these labels to indicate which people belong in each. If you do not think of a particular acquaintance in terms of how happy he is, you would not write his number anywhere in this space.

You may divide each attribute in as many ways as you wish and you may assign as many acquaintances as you wish to any description.

You may tear off this page and put it at the side to keep track of the acquaintances' numbers.

ACQUAINTANCES

1. A friend of your parents (_____)
2. A person who excels in sports (_____)
3. An old person, e.g., your grandmother or grandfather (_____)
4. A neighbor (past or present) (_____)
5. A person to whom you have taught something (_____)
6. A person who appears to dislike you (_____)
7. Someone who disappointed you (_____)
8. A person you admire (_____)
9. A person you dislike (_____)
10. A person you have played games with (_____)
11. A teacher you disliked (_____)
12. A very popular person (_____)
13. A person who has given you advice (_____)
14. An aunt or uncle (or close friend of your parents' age) (_____)
15. A good friend of the same sex (_____)
16. Your cousin (or child of your parents' friends) (_____)
17. Your mother (or the woman who raised you) (_____)
18. A person you like to avoid (_____)
19. A person who has failed at something (_____)
20. A former classmate (_____)
21. An ex-friend of the opposite sex
22. A salesman or shopkeeper (_____)
23. A person you would like to know better (_____)
24. A person who excels academically (_____)
25. A person you have worked with (_____)
26. A doctor (_____)
27. Someone who helped you (_____)
28. Someone who got you into trouble (_____)
29. Someone who does peculiar things (_____)
30. Someone who frightens you (_____)

(Subsequent pages presented these attributes, two per page, each followed by one-half page of blank space: How happy they are, How mature they are, How much respect (or disrespect) they command, How flexible (or rigid) they are, How healthy they are, How intelligent they are, How introverted (or extroverted) they are, How conventional (or unconventional) they are, How energetic (or sluggish) they are, How friendly you feel toward them.)

Most Similar Pairs of Objects

Average time: 5 minutes

This instrument was developed to assess affective balance only. Although respondents are required to indicate "principal similarities" and "principal differences" for the pairs selected, this is mainly to encourage their serious attention to the task, and the information is not presently utilized in scoring. It is possible that, with appropriate lengthening and elaboration of instructions, the instrument could be scored for other structural properties, such as dimensionality or evaluative centrality.

MOST SIMILAR PAIRS OF ACQUAINTANCES (first page)

1. A friend of your parents
2. Someone who excels in sports
3. A casual acquaintance
4. A person who bores you
5. Someone who disappointed you
6. A person who has supervised your work
7. A person you admire
8. A person you dislike
9. A favorite teacher
10. A very talented person
11. A good friend of the same sex
12. Your brother or sister (or close childhood friend)
13. Your cousin (or child of your parents' friends)
14. Your mother (or the woman who raised you)
15. A person you like to avoid
16. Someone who has failed at something
17. A salesman or shopkeeper
18. A doctor
19. Someone you regard as worthless
20. Someone who got you in trouble

The 20 designations above have been selected from the *List of Acquaintances*. Please refer to that sheet as you complete this instrument so that you can be sure you are thinking of the same people you designated on the *List of Acquaintances*. Pick out 2 people who you feel are *very similar* to each other (on whatever basis you choose). Write their *numbers* in the spaces beside A. To the right of the pair, please write the main way in which they are similar. Then pick out 2 other people who are very similar to each other; write their numbers and their principal similarity in the spaces beside B. Do the same with C. You may use a person more than once but do not repeat the same pair.

Most Similar Pairs of Acquaintances	*Principal Similarity*
A. No. _____ & No. _____	_____
B. No. _____ & No. _____	_____
C. No. _____ & No. _____	_____

From the list at the top of the page, please pick out 2 people you regard as *very different* from each other. Write their *numbers* beside D. To the right indicate their principal difference. Do the same for E and F.

Most Different Pairs of Acquaintances	*Principal Difference*
D. No. _____ & No. _____	_____
E. No. _____ & No. _____	_____
F. No. _____ & No. _____	_____

(second page)

Beside each person listed below, write a number from the following scale, indicating how much you like that person.

SCALE

7 Like very much
6 Like considerably
5 Like for the most part, with some degree of dislike
4 Neither like nor dislike
3 Dislike for the most part, with some degree of liking
2 Dislike considerably
1 Dislike very much

——————1. A friend of your parents
——————2. Someone who excels in sports
      (etc.)

Similarity of Paired Objects

Average time: 5 minutes

This brief instrument is presently used only to assess affective balance.

SIMILARITY OF PAIRED ACQUAINTANCES

Below are descriptions of people from your *List of Acquaintances*. Please think about the persons you assigned to each of the descriptions in the pair. Then rate them according to how similar you feel they are. Mark the column which best expresses your opinion.

Acquaintances	Degree of Similarity: High	Medium	Low
1. A person who has given you advice & A brother or sister	—	—	—
2. An old person & A casual acquaintance	—	—	—
3. A neighbor & A person who appears to dislike you	—	—	—
4. A person who bores you & A person who has supervised your work	—	—	—
5. A person you have played games with & A favorite teacher	—	—	—
6. Your father & Your mother	—	—	—
7. Your spouse or good friend of the opposite sex & Someone you have lived with	—	—	—
8. A person you like to avoid & Someone who has failed at something	—	—	—
9. A former classmate & An ex-friend of the opposite sex	—	—	—
10. A doctor & Someone who got you in trouble	—	—	—
11. An old person & Your father	—	—	—
12. A casual acquaintance & Your mother	—	—	—
13. A neighbor & Your spouse or good friend of the opposite sex	—	—	—
14. A person who appears to dislike you & Someone you have lived with	—	—	—

15. A person who bores you & A person
    you like to avoid   — —— —
16. A person who has supervised your work
    & Someone who has failed at something   — —— —
17. A person you have played games with
    & A former classmate   — —— —
18. A favorite teacher & An ex-friend of
    the opposite sex   — —— —
19. A person who has given you advice &
    A doctor   — —— —
20. A brother or sister & Someone who
    got you in trouble   — —— —

(last page)

Please write a number from the following scale beside each acquaintance
described below to indicate how much you like him (or her).

SCALE

7 Like very much
6 Like considerably
5 Like for the most part, with some degree of dislike
4 Neither like nor dislike
3 Dislike for the most part, with some degree of liking
2 Dislike considerably
1 Dislike very much

———— 1. An old person
———— 2. A casual acquaintance
(etc. for 20 acquaintances)

Constructing Sets of Objects

Average time: 5 minutes

This brief instrument is used only for assessing affective balance. It was
initially called *Homogenizing Sets*, but the first term was changed to be more
intelligible to respondents in New Zealand. The common basis for the
designated set (indicated at the right of each group) is not presently used in
scoring the instrument, but it is intended chiefly to encourage serious
attention to the task.

CONSTRUCTING SETS OF ACQUAINTANCES (first page)

Listed below are descriptions of people who are known to you. Please
refer to your *List of Acquaintances* for the specific person you assigned to
each description and use that *same person* in this instrument. Think about
all persons in the group and what they are like. On this basis, please cross
out the number of any person who you feel *doesn't belong* with the rest of
the group. You may cross out as many numbers in each group as you wish,
including all of them or none of them. To the right of each group, please
give the main reason why you feel the remaining acquaintances belong
together.

*Main reason why persons remaining
in group belong together*
(excluding persons crossed out)

1.   02 A casual acquaintance
     03 A neighbor
     05 A person who bores you
     06 Someone who disappointed you
     07 A person who has supervised your work
     14 Your spouse or a good friend of the opposite sex
     16 An ex-friend of the opposite sex

(Acquaintances in the other 9 groups were identified by both number and designation in the rating list, which appeared on the last page. The numbers were used to facilitate keypunching. The groups consisted of the following acquaintances:)

Group	List numbers						
2.	08	09	10	11	12	13	14
3.	01	04	15	17	18	19	20
4.	01	03	05	11	13	15	20
5.	04	06	08	10	12	16	18
6.	02	03	08	09	10	17	20
7.	04	05	07	08	10	14	15
8.	02	04	06	12	13	17	18
9.	02	06	12	14	16	19	20
10.	01	07	09	11	16	18	19

(last page)

Beside each person listed below, write a number from the following scale, indicating how much you like that person. Please think of the same person you used on the previous pages.

SCALE

7 Like very much
6 Like considerably
5 Like for the most part, with some degree of dislike
4 Neither like nor dislike
3 Dislike for the most part with some degree of liking
2 Dislike considerably
1 Dislike very much

———— 1. A friend of your parents
———— 2. A casual acquaintance
———— 3. A neighbor
———— 4. A person who appears to dislike you
———— 5. A person who bores you
———— 6. Someone who disappointed you
———— 7. A person who has supervised your work
———— 8. A person you dislike

_____ 9. A teacher you disliked
_____ 10. A favorite teacher
_____ 11. Your cousin (or child of your parents' friends)
_____ 12. Your father (or the man who raised you)
_____ 13. A person you have studied with
_____ 14. Your spouse or a good friend of the opposite sex
_____ 15. Someone you have lived with
_____ 16. An ex-friend of the opposite sex
_____ 17. A salesman or shopkeeper
_____ 18. A person who excels academically
_____ 19. Someone you regard as worthless
_____ 20. Someone who helped you.

Rating of Objects

Average time: 15 minutes for original test, 10 minutes for retest

The _Rating_ instruments are generally quite versatile, yielding measures for five different structural properties. Evaluative centrality, ambivalence, and affective-evaluative consistency can be scored from a single administration. Scoring for attribute precision requires a retest later in the test battery, and measurement of dimensionality is generally improved by use of a retest, so that inter-attribute correlations can be corrected for unreliability of ratings.

The format is rather inefficient, requiring one page for each of the 20 objects; this was deemed most appropriate, however, as it focused respondents' attention on a single object at a time, thereby discouraging inter-object comparisons, which were presumably elicited by other instruments.

It would be desirable to increase both the number of objects (now 20) and the number of attributes (now 10) to provide for better representation of the cognitive domains and more reliable scoring of the structural properties. Indeed, a similar point could be made for many of the other instruments. Since respondents' tolerance for tedious activity ultimately sets a limit on the length of instruments intended for general use, we felt it preferable to fill the approximately 2 hours required to assess a single domain with many instruments of diverse format, rather than with just two or three long instruments in a single format. This choice was in line with our multimethod strategy, aimed to reduce the degree to which structural measures are contaminated by particular stylistic tendencies that are instrument-specific.

RATING OF ACQUAINTANCES (first page)

Each of the following pages refers to an acquaintance of yours. Please refer to your _List of Acquaintances_ and copy the initials of the person designated into the space at the top of the page. Below the initials are 10 characteristics on which the person can be rated. Each characteristic has been polarized (so that it has opposite meanings on either end of the line). Please put _one_ mark on each line to indicate where you think the person stands on the characteristic.

For instance, if you think that the clergyman is very attractive, put a mark on the first line, under the word "very." If you think he is quite unattractive, put a mark on the first line, second box from the right, under the word "quite." If you think he is of moderate or average attractiveness, put a mark in the middle of the first line, under the words "equally or neither," meaning in this case neither attractive nor unattractive.

Then continue to rate this clergyman on the other nine characteristics, making *one* mark on each line.

Then do the same for the other acquaintances designated at the tops of subsequent pages. There are 20 pages in all. If you do not know how to rate a particular acquaintance on one of the characteristics, please make the best guess you can, using a question mark (?).

(20 subsequent pages were each headed by one of the following designations: A clergyman (priest, minister, or rabbi), A person to whom you have taught something, A person who appears to dislike you, Someone who disappointed you, A person who has supervised your work, A person you admire, A person you dislike, A person you have played games with, A teacher you dislike, A favorite teacher, A very popular person, A very talented person, Your aunt or uncle (or close adult of your parents' age), A good friend of the same sex, Your brother or sister (or close childhood friend), Your father (or the man who raised you), Your mother (or the woman who raised you), Your spouse or a good friend of the opposite sex, Someone who does peculiar things, Someone you don't trust.)

(Below the designation appeared 10 bipolar attributes identified by the following words at opposite ends of the rating space: attractive-unattractive, competent-incompetent, humble-arrogant, interesting-dull, likable-not likable, reliable-unreliable, religious-nonreligious, selfish-altruistic, strong-weak, tactful-tactless.)

(Between the antonyms were 7 spaces, numbered (to facilitate keypunching), with the following designations at the top: Very, Quite, Slightly, Equally or Neither, Slightly, Quite, Very.)

(Later in the test battery appeared the same rating instrument with the following instructions:)

RATING OF ACQUAINTANCES—II (first page)

Earlier in this series of questionnaires, you rated each of 20 acquaintances on 10 different characteristics. You were probably more certain of some of the ratings than you were of others. This is because some people cannot be clearly categorized on some characteristics.

In order to find out how clear or ambiguous each person's standing is on the various traits, we would like you to rate them again. This time, just rate each person as he (or she) seems to you *now*. *Do not* try to remember your previous rating. We are not interested in checking your consistency, but rather in seeing which persons clearly fall into one category or another and which persons do not clearly fit the rating scales provided.

Chapter 7

MEASURES OF
DIFFERENTIATION

The concept of cognitive complexity, or differentiation, has given rise to a great many measures, intended to represent, in various ways, the number of cognitive elements and the extent to which they are distinguished from one another. Following the model proposed in Chapter 5, we will consider three major types of differentiation: object complexity, dimensionality, and attribute precision. Each of these has been measured in several ways, using the instruments described in Chapter 6.

DIFFERENTIATION AMONG CHARACTERISTICS:
OBJECT COMPLEXITY

Object complexity has been defined conceptually as the number of attributes on which an object is projected. A prototype measure was proposed by Zajonc (1960). His respondents, after receiving information about a person, were asked to describe that person's characteristics. Zajonc's measure of differentiation was simply the number of characteristics mentioned; it is heavily confounded by individual differences in verbosity, which may not be desirable. We have attempted to reduce this confounding to some extent by coding each characteristic listed in *Free Description* of objects according to an empirically developed set of categories. Object complexity if scored as the number of categories used which are distinct within the coding system, ignoring characteristics which duplicate the meaning of others already counted. No such control for redundancy is provided for *Checklist Description*, which is simply scored as the number of adjectives checked. A mean score for each cognitive domain is computed by averaging over all objects in a particular instrument.

Free Comparison of objects provides an overall domain complexity score, which is the total number of different categories in the code utilized for all comparisons. *Checklist Comparison* is scored by counting the number of different attributes (adjective pairs) used to describe similarities and differences between the pairs of objects presented. (An adjective pair is counted if either antonym is used.) Finally, *Listing and Comparing* objects is scored for mean object complexity as the mean number of groups to which the listed objects are assigned.

DIFFERENTIATION AMONG ATTRIBUTES: DIMENSIONALITY

Dimensionality is defined in the structural model as the number of dimensions required to represent objects for the person. Measures of this variable reflect the number and distinctness of attributes which the person uses to describe objects. To the extent that attributes overlap in their meaning for the individual, dimensionality will be less than the number of attributes used. Intercorrelations among attributes depend on the manner in which they distinguish objects.

Bieri's (1955) measure of cognitive complexity, based on Kelly's (1955) *Role Constructs Repertory Test*, reflects differentiation among attributes, even though it was not defined to represent dimensions of cognitive space. Bieri's original index was formed by counting the number of attribute pairs which the subject used in a nearly identical fashion. The higher this score, the lower the complexity. A wide variety of measures bearing the name cognitive complexity have followed from Bieri's (see Bonarius, 1965; Fransella & Bannister, 1977; Goldstein & Blackman, 1978), while others with the same name have little to do with differentiation among attributes. Because there are many ways in which cognitive structure may be complex, and because the term has been used so loosely, we prefer the more specific term, dimensionality.

Listing and Comparing of Objects

Among the objections that have been raised to Kelly's procedure are the tedium of generating the object-by-attribute matrix and the requirement for dichotomous judgments, which many respondents find too restrictive (see p. 39). A somewhat more efficient approach is embodied in our *Listing and Comparing* measure (p. 86). The respondent first generates a set of objects, then picks successive subsets that are alike for some characteristic. Objects that clearly differ on that attribute are also noted, but a classification of every object is not required.

Table 6. Computation of H (Index of Dimensionality) from *Listing and Comparing Nations*

Groups formed

A	B	C	D
1. $\boxed{1, 2, 4}$	$\boxed{1, 5, 17, 20}$	$\boxed{2, 4}$	$\boxed{8, 9, 10, 11, 12}$

2. Object: 1 2 3 4 5 6 7 8 9 10 11 12 13 14 15 16 17 18 19 20

    Groups: A A   A B   D D D D D   B   B
                 B C   C

3. Group
    combinations: –   A B C D AB AC AD BC BC BD CD ABC ABD ACD BCD ABCD
             n_i: 9 – 3 – 5 1   2 –   –   –   –   –   –   –   –   –   –

4. $H = \Sigma p_i \log_2 \dfrac{1}{p_i} = \log_2 n - \dfrac{1}{n} \Sigma n_i \log_2 n_i$

   $= \log_2 20 - \dfrac{1}{20} (9 \log_2 9 + 3 \log 3 + 5 \log 5 + 1 \log 1 + 2 \log 2)$

   $= 4.32193 - \dfrac{1}{20} (28.52932 + 4.75489 + 11.60964 + 0 + 2.00000)$

   $= 4.32193 - 2.34469 = 1.97724$

The measure of dimensionality computed from this instrument is based on H, the index of disperson derived from information theory (Attneave, 1959). It represents the number of dimensions of information implicit in the respondent's grouping system. Its calculation is illustrated for data presented in the first section of Table 6, showing groups of nations constructed by one respondent. Only the positive groups—those possessing the designated characteristics—are considered. Each group is designated by a letter, and the letters underneath an object number indicate the groups to which it belongs (Table 6, Section 2). For instance, object 1 appears in Groups A and B; object 2 in Groups A and C; object 3 in no groups, and so on.

Each different *combination* of group memberships (including no group memberships) is considered as a distinct way of combining the dichotomous attributes (Table 6, Section 3). The more different combinations appear, the greater is the independence of the several attributes and the higher the resulting index of dimensionality. The largest number of combinations possible is the smaller of two numbers: n, the number of objects (in this case 20), or 2^k, where k is the number of groups formed by the respondent (in this case $2^4 = 16$). Whenever a particular group combination is missing, it implies that the attributes involved are not independent; for instance, in the present data, characteristic C appears only with characteristic A; characteristic D always appears alone; etc. Calculation of H requires the use of logarithms to the base

Table 7. Computation of D from *Grouping of Nations*

A. Attribute   Groups of objects (ordered in magnitude)

Attribute	Groups of objects (ordered in magnitude)
1	`4, 7, 8, 9, 13, 14` `1, 2, 3` `19, 22, 27, 28` `11`
2	`3, 4, 6, 7, 8` `11, 23` `21, 25, 28, 30`
3	`7` `4, 6, 8, 13, 14` `1, 2, 3, 5, 9, 10, 11, 12, 15, 16, 17, 18` `22, 25, 27` `19, 20, 21, 23, 24, 26, 28, 29, 30`
4	`3, 6, 7, 18, 19` `8, 21, 24` `1, 4, 11` `20, 23, 25, 30` `27, 28` `13, 14`
5	`6, 7,` `8`
6	`3, 4, 6, 7, 8, 13, 14` `1, 11, 12` `20, 22, 24, 27, 28, 30` `18, 23, 24`
7	—
8	`3, 7,` `6, 24,` `4, 16, 17,` `2, 5, 8, 9, 15` `1, 13, 14,` `30` `28` `21, 25` `18, 23, 27` `19, 20, 22`
9	`6, 7, 8,` `3, 4, 13, 14,` `1, 2, 5, 9, 11, 12, 15, 18,` `24, 30` `21, 28, 29` `20, 22, 23, 25, 26, 27`
10	`3, 7,` `1, 2, 5, 6, 8, 9, 11, 12, 13, 14, 15, 16,` `18, 30` `19, 20, 21, 22, 23, 24, 25, 26, 27, 28`

B. Object   Attribute

Object	1	2	3	4	5	6	7	8	9	10
1	2		3	3		2		5	3	2
2	2		3					4	3	2
3	2	1	3	1		1		1	2	1
4	1	1	2	3		1		3	2	
5			3					4	3	2
6		1	2	1	1	1		2	1	2
7	1	1	1	1	1	1		1	1	1
8	1	1	2	2	1	1		4	1	2
9	1		3					4	3	2
10			3							
11	2	2	3	3		2			3	2
12			3			2			3	2
13	1		2	3		1		5	2	2
14	1		2	3		1		5	2	2
15			3					4	3	2
16			3					3		2
17			3					3		
18			3	1		2		4	3	1

Table 7. (cont'd)

B. Object — Attribute

	1	2	3	4	5	6	7	8	9	10
19	1		3	1				5		2
20			3	1		1		5	3	2
21		1	3	2				3	2	2
22	1		2			1		5	3	2
23		2	3	1		2		4	3	2
24			3	2		X		2	1	2
25		1	2	1				3	3	2
26			3						3	2
27	1		2	2		1		4	3	2
28	1	1	3	2		1		2	2	2
29			3						2	
30		1	3	1		1		1	1	1

C. Attribute — Inter-attribute correlations

	1	2	3	4	5	6	7	8	9
2	.63								
3	.58	.39							
4	.11	.22	-.10						
5	–	–	–	–					
6	.77	1.00	.56	.09	–				
7	–	–	–	–	–	–			
8	-.14	.48	.08	.40	–	.30	–		
9	.41	.65	.39	.11	–	.64	–	.65	
10	-.18	.33	.12	.48	–	.08	–	.59	.35

$$D = \frac{k^2}{k + 2\Sigma r^2} = \frac{(8)^2}{8 + 2\,(5.8269)} = 3.26$$

2. [Tables may be found in Attneave (1959) and in Scott and Wertheimer (1962).] The maximum value of H is k, the number of groups formed, or $\log_2 n$, whichever is smaller. This means that dimensionality is limited by the number of objects and attributes included in the instrument. Thus, we do not have a measure of dimensionality for the entire domain, but for the sample of objects and attributes generated by the subject. A comparable limitation is inherent in all our measures; their validity therefore rests on the assumption that objects and attributes are representative of the entire domain for each subject.

Grouping, Checklist Description, and Rating Instruments

In these three instruments, respondents apply a standard set of attributes to a standard set of objects. This provides a common basis for calculating redundancy among attributes. Redundancy between a pair of attributes is inferred from the magnitude of their squared correlation (r^2) over the set of objects. This means that two attributes which order objects identically (or inversely) are treated as identical, and therefore comprise only a single dimension. The index of dimensionality currently used is:

$$D = \frac{k^2}{k + 2\Sigma r^2}$$

where k is the number of attributes employed by the respondent and Σr^2 is the sum of all squared intercorrelations among the k attributes.

An illustrative computation from the *Grouping* instrument (see p. 94) is shown in Table 7. The formula requires that the groups of objects constructed by the respondent from each attribute be ordered from maximum to minimum value on that attribute before keypunching (see section A of Table 7). The number of groups may vary from one attribute to another, so scores assigned to the 30 objects (section B of Table 7) will have different upper limits. If fewer than two groups are formed, correlations involving that attribute cannot be computed, and it is omitted from the index, D. Also, the subject is permitted to omit from any attribute those objects for which classification is uncertain. Because these omitted objects will differ from one attribute to another, the several inter-attribute correlations may be based on quite different sets of scores. Whenever the number of objects shared by two attributes is less than 3, that correlation is also omitted from the table, and the value of k is reduced accordingly.

The inter-attribute correlations (Table 7, section C) form the basis for the index of dimensionality, D, which varies between 1.00 and k, the number of attributes with at least two categories of objects. The denominator of the index will be equal to k when all inter-attribute correlations are 0, implying maximum independence. When all inter-attribute correlations are +1 or −1, the denominator of the index will be k^2. In the present example, k has been reduced from 10 to 8, because no groups were formed on the seventh attribute, and only one group was formed on the fifth. If, in addition, some of the remaining pairs of attributes had fewer than 3 objects in common, the correlations between them would be ignored and a new value of k would have to be provided to take account of the reduced limit of Σr^2. This (noninteger) value is computed as:

$$k = \frac{1 + \sqrt{1 + 8n}}{2}$$

where n is the number of inter-attribute correlations actually used, out of the $k(k-1)/2$ possible.

Calculation of D from the *Checklist Description* (p. 90) is straightforward.

One member of each antonymic pair is scored 1 and the other -1. The scoring for that bipolar attribute is taken as 0 if both are circled or if neither member of the adjective-pair is circled. The 36 bipolar attributes (scored +1, 0, or -1) are then intercorrelated over the 10 objects. Although 36 is used as the value of k in calculating the index of dimensionality, there are not enough objects in the instrument to show complete independence among these attributes even if they were, in fact, quite distinct. This sets a spuriously low upper limit on D.

D is calculated from the *Rating* instrument by the same formula. Some gain in validity is typically achieved if the inter-attribute correlations are first corrected for unreliability, utilizing the test-retest correlations of the several attributes. The corrected inter-attribute correlations are computed as:

$$r_{ij_{\text{cor}}} = \frac{r_{ij}}{\sqrt{r_{ii}r_{jj}}} \, ,$$

where r_{ii} and r_{jj} are the respective test-retest correlations of attributes i and j, and r_{ij} is the correlation between attributes i and j computed on the first test. If any of the test-retest correlations equals 0 or less, all corrected correlations involving that attribute are ignored in the computation of D, and k is reduced accordingly. Thus k is taken to mean the number of attributes with positive reliability. If any corrected r_{ij} exceeds 1 in absolute value, it is taken to be +1 or -1.

Other, more complicated measures of dimensionality have been employed, yielding results very close to D (see Scott, 1966b). When *Ratings of Nations* provided by 35 university students were subjected to a principal components analysis, the proportion of variance accounted for by the first component correlated $-.94$ with D. The dispersion of variance over all components, as measured by the information statistic, H, correlated $.92$ with D. It thus seems that D provides a measure of dimensionality very close to the more complicated measures available through factor analysis. Given the savings in computer time afforded by the simpler index, D is preferable.

Multidimensional Scaling

Although we have not done so, dimensionality could also be calculated by the statistical technique of multidimensional scaling (Carroll & Chang, 1970; Kruskal, 1964). Like our geometric model, this technique assumes that phenomenal objects may be depicted in a multidimensional space. Multidimensional scaling estimates the number of independent dimensions defining this space and attempts to offer substantive interpretations of these dimensions. The technique of multidimensional scaling has often been used to describe results for groups of subjects, but it is in principle applicable to the calculation of individual dimensionality scores. The individual-differences models of multidimensional scaling surveyed by Rosenberg and Sedlak (1972) were mainly concerned with substantive interpretation of the dimensions employed by individual subjects, but again, there is no reason in principle why attention could not be paid to the number of dimensions per se.

Multidimensional scaling starts with consideration of the psychological *distance* between pairs of objects in the space. The technique requires a data matrix in which distances between all pairs of objects in the space are represented. A variety of techniques for obtaining this matrix have been specified (Guilford, 1954, pp. 248–250), but in general, one of two approaches is followed. First, subjects may be asked directly to provide distances between every possible pair of objects in the space, as by rating each pair on a similarity (or dissimilarity) scale. This may prove to be a tedious task, since the number of judgments required for n objects is $n(n-1)/2$. Second, subjects may be asked to rate objects on a variety of attributes, allowing an inference about the distance between each pair to be calculated from the similarity (or dissimilarity) of their ratings. This procedure seems less tedious than the first, but care must be taken that the attributes employed constitute a representative sample of those actually used in direct distance judgments.

In Chapter 6, we argued that researchers should require of their subjects responses which make sense. Far too little is known about the relative reasonableness of judgments about global similarity and judgments about similarity on specified attributes.

After a distance matrix is obtained, multidimensional scaling proceeds by calculating a one-dimensional solution for the space. The procedure creates a straight line which best fits the provided distances; i.e., the hypothetical distances of a linear solution are made as close as possible to the actual distances between pairs of objects. The discrepancy is termed stress. Zero stress means that the solution corresponds perfectly to the provided distance matrix. Because of measurement error, zero stress is never achieved, and the goodness of the linear solution can only be assessed by calculating further solutions. Thus, a two-dimensional solution is next calculated; the plane is found which minimizes stress. Next, a three-dimensional solution is found, stress is calculated, and so on. Since stress necessarily decreases (or stays the same) as the dimensionality of the solution increases, the dimensionality of a space is defined as the level after which subsequent solutions do not appreciably decrease stress. This is a matter of judgment by the researcher, of course, although certain heuristics have been specified (Kruskal, 1964).

A number of our questionnaires could be used to create a distance matrix for multidimensional scaling. The degree of solution for an individual subject's responses is conceptually similar to our construct of dimensionality. There is, however, an important distinction between the approach of multidimensional scaling and the approach inherent in our object-attribute model. Multidimensional scaling defines its space in terms of distances between objects and *then* attempts to find attributes corresponding to the space. Our geometric model defines its space in terms of the attributes assigned to objects and *then* attempts to estimate the dimensionality (and other properties) of the assignment. Whether or not this difference is critical in practice can only be ascertained with appropriate empirical data.

DIFFERENTIATION AMONG CATEGORIES: ATTRIBUTE PRECISION

A crude measure of attribute precision is constructed from the *Grouping* instrument simply by counting the number of groups formed on each attribute and averaging this over all 10 attributes (including those for which no groups are formed). Though highly reliable, in the sense that respondents show very great consistency in number of categories formed for the 10 different attributes, this score appears too instrument-specific to be adequate by itself. There is a strong tendency among subjects to perseverate on a particular number of groups (usually two or three) even though they could probably distinguish more for many of the attributes.

The *Rating* instrument was initially scored for precision by simply counting the number of different categories on the 7-point rating scale actually used by a respondent to describe the 20 objects, or computing the dispersion of ratings over the 7 categories, using the index of disperson, H (see p. 105). These procedures proved unsatisfactory, however, as many subjects checked the rating scale rather sloppily, sometimes marking 6, sometimes 5, thereby spuriously increasing their indices of precision when, in fact, the two categories were indistinguishable for them. This artifact was counteracted by administering a second *Rating* instrument, and treating two categories as indistinguishable if they were spanned by the first and second rating of an object. In practice, some objects are rated consistently on both occasions, while other objects show two or more categories difference in ratings from one time to the next. An index, P, was constructed which combines results for all 20 objects in the following way:

Each time an object is rated identically on first and second test, that category of the rating scale is given one unit of distinctiveness. Each time an object is rated differently on the two occasions, the two categories, and all categories between them, are assigned a single category-value. If all objects were rated with perfect consistency, the final P would equal the number of different categories used. If all objects were rated with maximum inconsistency—that is, at opposite extremes of that portion of the scale used by this particular respondent—the final P would equal 1, implying that only one category could be distinguished. Figure 8 shows a sample response pattern for six objects rated on a single attribute. Four of the objects (numbered 1, 3, 4, and 6) are consistently rated on both tests, but they fall in only three categories (7, 4, and 2). Object 2 confuses categories 7 and 6, but distinguishes these from all other categories, while object 5 confuses categories

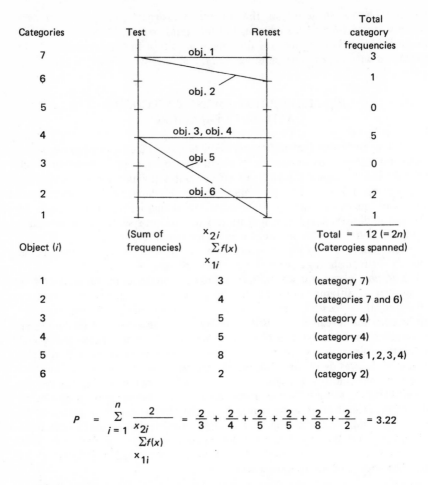

Object (*i*)	(Sum of frequencies)	$\frac{x_{2i}}{\Sigma f(x)}$ x_{1i}	Total = 12 (= 2n) (Caterogies spanned)
1		3	(category 7)
2		4	(categories 7 and 6)
3		5	(category 4)
4		5	(category 4)
5		8	(categories 1, 2, 3, 4)
6		2	(category 2)

$$P = \sum_{i=1}^{n} \frac{2}{\dfrac{x_{2i}}{\Sigma f(x)}} = \frac{2}{3} + \frac{2}{4} + \frac{2}{5} + \frac{2}{5} + \frac{2}{8} + \frac{2}{2} = 3.22$$
$$\phantom{P = \sum_{i=1}^{n}}x_{1i}$$

Fig. 8. Test and retest rating of six objects, showing computation of *P* (index of attribute precision).

1 through 4, but distinguishes these from categories 6 and 7. Categories 3 and 5 are not used at all. The resulting index of attribute precision, *P*, is 3.22, implying that slightly more than 3 categories-worth of discriminations have been made by this respondent.

The formula for *P* is:

$$P = \sum_{i=1}^{n} \frac{2}{\dfrac{x_{2i}}{\Sigma f(x)}}$$
$$x_{1i}$$

where x_{1i} and x_{2i} are the first and second ratings of object i, and $f(x)$ is the frequency with which category x was used for this attribute (both first and second ratings for all objects). Thus, the denominator for object 1 is 3 because it was rated only in category 7 and there were 3 ratings in that category (2 for object 1 and 1 for object 2). The denominator for object 5 is 8 because its first rating was in category 4 and its second was in category 1; in between, and including, those categories, were 5 ratings in category 4, none in category 3, 2 in category 2, and 1 in category 1.

P reflects ratings for a single attribute. A mean P is calculated over all 10 attributes to represent average attribute precision within the domain.

This index, though logically and empirically superior to its predecessors, is still defective, in that its magnitude depends substantially on the number of categories in the rating scale. Crabbe (1969) found a steady increase in mean P scores as the rating scale was lengthened from 5 to 15 categories, with no indication of an asymptotic limit, as one might expect. Clearly, further work is required in the measurement of attribute precision.

CORRELATIONS AMONG MEASURES OF DIFFERENTIATION

The various measures of differentiation presented above have been administered to several groups of respondents, though not all measures have been included in any single study. Table 8 presents correlations among the currently preferred measures, combining results for seven cognitive domains. They are based on the following samples of subjects:

(a) 88 students, University of Colorado, domains of acquaintances, family, nations, school, self, and societal groups.

(b) 80 psychology students, 40 from each of Doshisha and Shiga University (Kyoto and Otsu, Japan), domains of acquaintances, family, nations, and self.

(c) 136 first-year psychology students, Victoria University of Wellington (New Zealand), domains of nations, and self.

(d) 129 first-year psychology students, Victoria University of Wellington (New Zealand), domain of acquaintances.

(e) 122 first-year psychology students, Victoria University of Wellington (New Zealand), domain of family.

(f) 104 students, University of Colorado, domains of acquaintances, celebrities, nations, and self.

(g) 121 students and their parents from Boulder High School, domains of nations and self.

Subjects in samples a, f, and g, were paid for their time (about 2 hours per domain); other subjects were tested as part of their practical work in psychology courses. All samples contained about equal numbers of males and females.

In addition to these samples, numerous earlier groups of students at the University of Colorado took various pilot forms of these instruments. Two of

Table 8. Mean Intercorrelations Among Selected Measures of Cognitive Differentiation

	1	2	3	4	5	6	7	8	9	10
Object complexity										
1. Free Description										
2. Free Comparison	.49									
3. Checklist Description	.21	.15								
4. Checklist Comparison	.26	.28	.60							
5. List and Compare	.41	.30	.11	.18						
Dimensionality										
6. List and Compare	.30	.31	.05	.14	(.72)					
7. Grouping	.18	.20	.20	.24	.17	.11				
8. Checklist Description	.12	.14	(−.20)	−.02	.08	.11	.03			
9. Rating	.10	.08	−.02	−.01	.10	.08	.20	.02		
Attribute precision										
10. Grouping	.09	.14	.08	.08	.11	.12	(.26)	.08	.18	
11. Rating	.12	.16	.05	.11	.11	.10	.02	−.03	(.22)	.21

Note. Mean Intercorrelations for variables 6, 7, 9 and 10 are each based on 20 correlation coefficients from 7 separate subject samples (*a* through *g*), covering 7 different cognitive domains. Mean correlations involving variables 1, 2, 3, 4, 5, and 8, are each based on 14 correlation coefficients from 5 separate subject samples (*a* through *e*) covering 6 different cognitive domains. See accompanying text for particulars. Parentheses indicate correlations between measures derived from a common instrument.

these samples (n = 53 and 54) filled out a modified form of Kelly's *Role Constructs Repertory Test* (see Campbell, 1960), as well as the *Listing and Comparing* instrument, both applied to nations. The correlations between these two measures of dimensionality were .28 and .43 (see Scott, 1964, 1965a).

Mean correlations among measures of object complexity average .29; mean correlations for dimensionality and attribute precision are .09 and .21, respectively. Though the mean *r*s for dimensionality are lowest, even these values attained statistical significance, considering the number of samples on which they are based, and represent some improvement over previous efforts to measure this property reliably. Studies reviewed by Goldstein and Blackman (1978, pp. 106-117) generally found no relationship among measures of dimensionality unless they were derived from a common instrument format—the *Role Constructs Repertory Test* of Kelly (1955) and Bieri (1955). Still, intercorrelations among our dimensionality measures are no larger than the mean correlation between dimensionality and object complexity. It thus appears that mean object complexity and dimensionality of a cognitive domain are not well distinguished by the measures used here, even though for subsequent analysis we treat them as separate scales.

Table 9. Homogeneities and Reliabilities of Composite Measures of Cognitive Differentiation

Sample and domain	Object complexity		Dimensionality		Precision	
	H.R.	r_{tt}	H.R.	r_{tt}	H.R.	r_{tt}
U.S.−Acquaintances	.26	.63	.20	.49	.00	.00
(a) Family	.26	.64	.13	.34	.23	.35
Nations	.33	.71	.19	.47	.14	.25
Self	.23	.59	.13	.38	.13	.22
Japan−Acquaintances	.34	.72	.04	.13	.35	.51
(b) Family	.26	.63	.03	.09	.27	.43
Nations	.44	.79	.08	.23	.28	.44
Self	.24	.61	.05	.17	.15	.25
New Zealand −						
Acquaintances (d)	.28	.64	.08	.26	.18	.31
Family (e)	.23	.58	.09	.26	.26	.41
Nations (c)	.43	.79	.08	.25	.21	.35
Self (c)	.38	.75	.10	.30	.19	.31
Mean	.31	.67	.10	.28	.20	.32

Note. Letters in parentheses refer to samples described on page 113. H.R. is Scott's (1960) Homogeneity Ratio; r_{tt} is Cronbach's (1951) coefficient alpha.

Statistics on composite scores for four cognitive domains studied in three countries appear in Table 9. The homogeneity ratio (Scott, 1960) indicates the average correlation among different components of the score, and Cronbach's (1951) coefficient alpha estimates the reliability of the composite score. In general, reliabilities for the composite scores on object complexity approach acceptable standards, while those for dimensionality and mean attribute precision do not. Clearly, it will be necessary to construct additional measures of the latter properties to obtain composite scores that have sufficient reliability to permit a good understanding of their correlates. Meanwhile, we tentatively accept the present composite measures as offering at least some improvement on single-instrument scores previously employed.

Chapter 8

MEASURES
OF INTEGRATION

While there is some agreement among investigators about the meanings—if not the measures—associated with cognitive differentiation, there is no such consensus for cognitive integration at either the conceptual or operational level. The term is typically used as an evaluative one and is diversely applied to ways in which respondents process or emit information. Typically, integrated structures have been implicitly regarded as desirable while unintegrated structures have not. In this chapter, we shall not seek a single meaning of integration, but will classify under this rubric a variety of measures that pertain to ways in which people's ideas are interrelated. Although we describe measures developed by other investigators besides ourselves, only a few of these were explicitly conceived by their originators as representing an integrative style (e.g., Zajonc's unity, and Schroder et al.'s integrative complexity).

ABSTRACTNESS vs. CONCRETENESS:
HARVEY'S "THIS I BELIEVE" TEST

The first two measures to be considered, Harvey's and Schroder's, are the most global. They pertain to the entire set of ideas entertained by a person. Both depend on a content analysis of verbal productions. In Harvey's (1966) "This I Believe" Test, the objective is to classify respondents into one of four "conceptual systems" or "stages" of cognitive development based on written responses to statements starting with "This I believe about . . . . (a variety of objects)." Each system is described for coders in terms of the content of ideas and manner of expression. Coders read through the test's 12 statements (beliefs about friendship, sin, compromise, etc.) and classify the respondent from the following manifestations (Harvey, 1966, p. 42):

> *System 1.* High absolutism and closedness of beliefs; high evaluativeness; high positive dependence on representatives of institutional authority; high identification with social roles and status positions; high conventionality; high ethnocentrism or strong beliefs that American values should be instituted as a model for the rest of the world.
>
> *System 2.* Uncertainty, distrust of authority, rejection of socially approved guidelines to action, while at the same time other stable referents are lacking. Guided more by rebellion against social prescriptions than by positive adherence to personally derived standards. Manifests a high drive toward autonomy and avoidance of dependency on God, tradition, and most of the referents that serve as positive guides for System 1 individuals.
>
> *System 3.* Concern with interpersonal relationships. Oriented toward establishing dependencies on others, but displays more autonomous internal standards, especially in the social sphere, than does the System 1 individual, and more positive ties to the prevailing social norms than does the System 2 person.
>
> *System 4.* A highly differentiated and integrated cognitive structure; more flexible, more creative, and more relative in thought and action than the other three systems. Displays a set of internal standards that are most truly independent of external criteria, in some cases coinciding with social definitions and in others not.

As only one score is obtained per respondent, it is not possible to calculate the test homogeneity or to estimate parallel forms reliability. With sufficient training of coders, 90% agreement in classification of respondents has been achieved (Harvey, 1966). However, it is typically found that only about two-thirds of respondents can be classified clearly into one or another of the types. Ambiguous and mixed cases are usually ignored, thus limiting the generality of results in an unknown way. At the time of this writing, no completely specified system for coding protocols has been published, and users of this test are advised to have their coding performed under Harvey's supervision. A serious limitation of the measure is that the coder's judgment is made to depend on so many considerations that it is difficult to attribute any single basis to the classification system.

INTEGRATIVE COMPLEXITY:
SCHRODER'S PARAGRAPH COMPLETION TEST

Schroder et al. (1967) developed a procedure for coding the level of integrative complexity without reference to content. They score this variable from paragraphs subjects write on such topics as "doubt," "confusion," and "parents." Integrative complexity is conceived by these authors as the degree to which people base their judgments on combinations of conditional rules, rather than on a single, absolute rule. After reading an entire paragraph or essay, ·the coder is required to rate it on a 7-point scale of integrative complexity, with 4 critical points defined as follows:

1. (lowest index) "... the response could be generated by a single fixed rule, no alternative interpretations were considered, and subtle changes would produce no changes in the response. Responses that fit the event into a category (inclusion vs. exclusion) with a high degree of certainty, that unambiguously reduce conflict and avoid the use of gradations (shades of gray and continua), are typically generated by simple structure .... More specific indications of a low integration index include (a) viewing conflict, uncertainty, or ambiguity as unpleasant or as a flaw or weakness in people or functions; (b) seeking fast and unambiguous closure or resolution, and reacting in such a way as to engage internally consistent processes that reduce incongruity or dissonance; (c) offering a specific guide or rule for reducing conflict; (d) implying that an absolute solution can be found; (e) stating that effects are compartmentalized, are all one way or all another way; and (f) presenting only one side of a problem while ignoring differences and similarities with other views" (Schroder et al., 1967, p. 187).

3. (medium low) Displays "alternative rule structures for perceiving the event .... It may also include a conditional rule for specifying when each interpretation is used. Compared to the first level, conditionality, probability, and alternatives indicate a slight increase in the degrees of freedom involved. A score of 2 is given when the response signifies a qualification of an absolute rule (scored 1) but the qualification is not clearly identified as an alternative interpretation... Specific operations include (a) the listing of similarities and differences between views without considering relationships; (b) the specification of at least two different interpretations of the event in the sentence stem; (c) the presence of "either-or" type of responses expressing a possible conditional rule about two ways of categorizing; (d) probability statements about the occurence of different views or outcomes; (e) reactions against absolutism in general; (f) the avoidance of dependency on external imposition .... " (p. 188).

5. (medium high) Utilizes "comparison rules for considering the joint as opposed to the conditional outcome of these different perceptions .... The response implies alternate interpretations and also implies that both can interact, but the interaction is expressed as qualification rather than as the emergence of comparison rules. Specific indications include (a) the integration of two conflicting or different interpretations so as to preserve and not "ward off" the conflict; (b) the generation of various meanings of the perception of conflicting views about a person; (c) evidence that the completion implies the ability to take another person's intentions (or perspectives) into account and to relate different perceptions of different people; (d) the implication that one's behavior is affected by the way another behaves, as in a give-and-take strategy game; (e) a view of social relationships as anchored in mutual responsibility (as opposed to fixed beliefs or rules), in which each person can place himself in the other person's shoes (relate alternate schema); and (f) the consideration of alternate reasons for similarities and differences between views" (p. 189).

7. (highest index) Responses "not only state or imply that alternative perceptions occurred and were simultaneously held in focus and compared, but also indicate that the outcomes of various comparisons can be considered in producing causal statements about the functional relations between ways of viewing the world. Such statements are relativistic rather

than absolutistic ... Responses that indicate the simultaneous operation of alternatives and give some evidence of the consideration of functional relations between them are given a score of 6. Specific references ... include (a) conflicting alternatives that are viewed as leading to new organizations and information; (b) utilization of alternatives through exploratory action in order to obtain new information; (c) generation of functional relations between alternatives; (d) consideration of relationships among similarities and differences between sides of a problem or question, and development of relationships between alternate reasons as to why these differences and similarities exist; and (e) production of more connectedness between alternatives by theorizing as to why these reasons exist" (p. 189).

Obviously, these coding instructions are abstract and require considerable training for coders to reach substantial levels of agreement. Such levels have been obtained by Schroder and his colleagues, who also report fairly high consistency in integration level displayed in different paragraphs written by the same respondent (see Gardiner & Schroder, 1972; Goldstein & Blackman, 1978). Other investigators, using less rigorous training procedures and less literate respondents (high school students), have not obtained such reliable results (see Burgoyne, 1975; Cox, 1970). Although the conception concerning the multiplicity-vs.-simplicity of perspectives underlying this body of work is provocative, we do not favor the measure any more than Harvey's "This I Believe" Test. Because the measure is judgmental rather than analytical, it is prone to distortion by coders' preconceptions. Also, the multiple bases for coding integrative complexity may very well confuse a number of different structural variables which cannot be disentangled when only a single composite index is employed.

UNITY AND ORGANIZATION: ZAJONC'S MEASURES OF OBJECT INTEGRATION

Zajonc (1960) was perhaps the first investigator to derive systematic indices for various types of cognitive integration.[1] His unit of analysis is a single cognitive object (such as a particular person), rather than a cognitive domain in our sense (such as all persons known to the respondent). The respondent first describes the object by listing its characteristics, and is then asked to consider each pair of characteristics included in the description, according to the instruction: "If trait A changed, would trait B change also?" This is a rather tedious task, if the number of characteristics is large, and requires judgments which are probably unreal for most respondents (much like the trait-implication method). Hence, we have not pursued this strategy of assessment in developing our own measures. Nevertheless, the quantitative indices of integration are ingenious and merit further consideration in

[1]Though published in 1960, Zajonc's research was originally presented in his doctoral dissertation in 1954.

connection with more realistic tasks. They are based on the indices of trait dependency and determinance, which are obtained simply by counting for each trait the number of changes that it would induce and the number of changes that would be induced in it by other traits. Specifically, the dependency of trait i is defined as:

$$\text{dep}_i = \sum_{j \neq i}^{n} X_{ij},$$ where X equals 1 if trait i depends on trait j, and 0 if it does not. Values of X are summed over all traits j, resulting in a dependency score for trait i.

The determinance of trait i is defined as:

$$\text{det}_i = \sum_{j \neq i}^{n} Y_{ij},$$ where Y equals 1 if trait j depends on trait i, and 0 if it does not. Values of Y are summed over all traits j, resulting in a determinance score for trait i.

The *unity* of a cognitive object is defined as the sum of dependencies among all traits in ratio to the maximum sum possible—that is, to $n(n - 1)$—given the number (n) of traits listed.

$$\text{uni} = \frac{\sum_{i=1}^{n} \text{dep}_i}{n(n - 1)}$$

The index of unity thus varies between 0 and 1, and represents the degree to which all characteristics of an object depend on every other characteristic.

Zajonc's index of organization is defined as the highest determinance divided by the unity of the structure:

$$\text{org} = \frac{\text{det}_{max}}{\text{uni}}$$

It represents the degree to which the unity of the structure depends on a single determining characteristic.

IMAGE COMPARABILITY

The first type of integration defined in terms of our model and measured by the instruments presented in Chapter 6 is image comparability, the tendency to conceive of all objects of a domain in terms of the same large set of attributes. In our model an attribute is conceived as a bipolar, dimensional construct. The attribute is "used" whenever either pole or any intermediate category is ascribed to an object. *Free Description* and *Free Comparison* are initially coded into bipolar attributes (or multicategory nominal scales, which are treated the same way). The *Checklist Description* and *Checklist Comparison* present only the 2 poles for each of 36 attributes. The *Rating* instrument presents the poles and intermediate categories (2 to 6) of 10 attributes. Nevertheless, this instrument is of little help in measuring differential use of attributes because most respondents tend to rate every object on all of the scales presented.

The following formula provides a rational index of image comparability for the first four of these instruments.

$$COMP' = \frac{\sum\limits_{j=1}^{k} p_j^*}{k}$$

where k is the total number of attributes used at least once by the respondent to describe any one of the n objects, and p_j^* is the proportion of the remaining $(n - 1)$ objects that are also described on the jth attribute. The unit of measure for this index is the proportion of objects described on any attribute that is used at least once. If all attributes used were applied to every object, $COMP'$ would equal 1.00. If each attribute described only one object, $COMP'$ would equal 0.00.

It is desirable to correct this index, so that respondents who use more attributes are given higher scores. A correction affecting small attribute sets, by adjusting their scores downward, is provided by the multiplier, $k/(k + 1)$. Computation is made easier by converting p_j^* algebraically into p_j, which is the proportion of all n objects described on attribute j. These modifications yield the following formula for the index of image comparability:

$$COMP = \frac{n \sum\limits_{j=1}^{k} p_j - k}{(n - 1)(k + 1)},$$

where n is the number of objects, k is the number of attributes used at least once by the respondent, and p_j is the proportion of the n objects described on the jth attribute. *COMP* has a lower limit of 0 and approaches an upper limit of 1 as the number of used attributes becomes large. In *Free Comparison* instruments, n is set equal to the number of pairs (5) in the formula for *COMP*, and an attribute is considered used if it is employed to designate either a similarity or a difference between members of a particular pair. A sample calculation of *COMP* from *Free Description of Nations* is presented in Table 10.

Table 10. Computation of COMP and CENT from *Free Description of Nations*

Nation	Description (and code number)
1. Australia	large (02), new country (60), in Southern hemisphere (01)
2. France	old country (60), refined culture (63)
3. Greece	old country (60), now poor (54), ruled by a dictator (40)
4. India	large (02), poor (54), densely populated (03)
5. Israel	small (02), new country (60), surrounded by hostile neighbors (25)
6. Japan	island nation (10), technologically advanced (52), enemy of U.S. in World War II (80)
7. Mexico	neighbor of U.S. (01), arid (12), poor (54)
8. Soviet Union	large (02), Communist (43), U.S. ally in World War II (80), now an antagonist (20)
9. U.A.R.	developing country (51), dependent on the Nile River (48), ancient civilization (60)
10. U.K.	declining world power (18), once ruler of an empire (16), source of English language and culture (81)

Attribute code[a]	Object										p_j
	1	2	3	4	5	6	7	8	9	10	
01	x						x				.20
02	x			x	x			x			.40
03				x							.10
10						x					.10
12							x				.10
16										x	.10
18										x	.10
20								x			.10
25						x					.10
40			x								.10
43								x			.10
48									x		.10
51									x		.10
52						x					.10
54				x	x		x				.30
60	x	x	x		x				x		.50
63		x									.10
80						x		x			.20
81										x	.10
										Σp_j	3.00

$$\text{COMP} = \frac{n\sum\limits_{j=1}^{k} p_j - k}{(n-1)(k+1)} = \frac{10(3.00) - 19}{9(20)} = .06$$

$$\text{CENT} = p_h - M_{p*} = .50 - \frac{3.00 - .50}{18} = .36$$

[a]Code available from authors.

The notion of image comparability can be similarly applied to *Listing and Comparing Objects* (p. 86) and to *Grouping Objects* (p. 94). In the former instrument, an attribute is considered "used" if an object is assigned either to a group which possesses the characteristic or to a group of objects which clearly do not possess the characteristic (and is thus placed in the "nil" category of the attribute). The attribute is regarded as not used in any case that an object is omitted from both groups. The index, *COMP*, is then defined as the average proportion of the 20 listed objects that are assigned to one group or the other for each of the attributes (bases of grouping) provided by the respondent.[2] Similarly, objects omitted from any attribute designated in the *Grouping* instrument are considered evidence that the respondent does not consider the attribute generally applicable to the domain. Hence, the mean proportion of objects included in some group is interpreted as an index of image comparability.[3]

Although *COMP* indices computed from all these instruments have the same upper and lower limits and the same logical basis, their means and standard deviations are quite different. This indicates that though the unit of measurement is conceptually the same, it does not result in a standardized measure from various tasks. In particular, free descriptions and comparisons typically generate quite a diverse and idiosyncratically applied set of attributes, while attributes specified in the *Grouping* instruments are typically applied to most of the objects listed, resulting in high image comparability scores.

CENTRALIZATION

Centralization is defined as the centrality of the most central attribute minus the mean centrality of all remaining attributes, i.e.,:

$$\text{CENT} = p_h - M_{p*}$$

where p_h (highest proportion) is the largest number of objects assigned to any attribute, divided by the total number of objects, and M_{p*} is the mean proportion of objects assigned to all other attributes. If two or more attributes are tied for highest p, it does not matter which one is chosen for p_h; the other is included with the remaining attributes.

---

[2]Again, it is desirable to multiply this mean p by $k/(k + 1)$, where k is the number of attributes (here groups of similar objects) formed by the respondent. This has the effect of reducing the index for respondents who consider a small number of attributes as bases for grouping. This recommendation comes from hindsight; the correction was not made for the analyses to be reported here.

[3]No correction for differing numbers of attributes is necessary, as this number is constant over all respondents.

This index applies to *Free Description* and *Checklist Description*. In the *Free Comparison* and *Checklist Comparison* instruments, the number of pairs (5) is treated as the basis for calculating ps, and a pair is considered "assigned to an attribute" if that attribute is used to describe either a similarity or a difference between pair members. See Table 10 for an illustrative calculation.

AFFECTIVE-EVALUATIVE CONSISTENCY

The principle of affective-evaluative consistency in attitudes was formulated systematically by Rosenberg (1956) and Carlson (1956); the measures of individual differences utilized here are derived from their work. Our basic measure is the correlation of liking for objects with the mean evaluation (favorableness) of characteristics ascribed to them, computed over the sample of objects included in a particular instrument. In *Free Description of Objects* (p. 88), mean evaluation is calculated from the respondent's desirability ratings of the several descriptions given to each object. In *Checklist Description* (p. 91), a priori ratings (+1, 0, or −1) of those adjectives circled by the respondent are averaged for each object. In *Rating of Objects* (p. 100), the mean rating on attributes deemed (a priori) desirable or undesirable provides an index of evaluation. An index of affective-evaluative consistency is then:

$$AEC = r_{LE},$$

where L is the respondent's expressed liking for each object, E is the mean evaluation of that object, and r_{LE} is the correlation between these two scores over all 10 or 20 objects.

Grouping of Objects (p. 94) does not yield a constant rating scale, because respondents may form different numbers of groups on each attribute. It is therefore necessary, with this instrument, to correlate each evaluative attribute separately with liking for the 30 objects, and then average these correlations over all evaluative attributes. For all instruments, the index of affective-evaluative consistency varies, maximally, between +1 and −1, with the highest scores indicating that the best liked objects are assigned more favorable characteristics than the least liked objects.

AFFECTIVE BALANCE

The last group of instruments to be discussed here provide means of assessing affective balance. Early studies of Heider's (1946) construct by Jordan (1953), Morrissette (1958), and others were aimed mainly at demonstrating cognitive balance as a structural principle, rather than at assessing individual differences in this tendency. Hence, indices of balance were typically not quantified beyond what was required to compute a level of statistical significance. Also, balance was studied only within two- and three-object systems. ("If A likes B and B likes C, how will A feel about C?").

Cartwright and Harary (1956) developed a continuous index of the degree of balance. Based on the proportion of cycles in a graph that are positive, it applies, in principle, to any number of objects. In graph theory (Flament, 1963), a cycle is a path connecting points. Applied to cognition, the points represent objects (such as people), and a path connecting two points represents a perceived connection between the two objects (such as a respondent's judgment that person A likes person B). A positive path (+1) between points A and B indicates that A likes B or B likes A; a negative path (−1) indicates that one dislikes the other. A cycle is a series of paths that leads back to the original point. Thus, A's judged liking for B, B's judged liking for C, and C's judged liking for A could be represented as a cycle. A positive cycle is one in which the product of connected paths is positive. Therefore, A likes B (+1), B likes C (+1), and C likes A (+1) is a positive cycle. Also, A dislikes B (−1), B dislikes C (−1), and C likes A (+1) is a positive cycle. A dislikes B (−1), B likes C (−1), and C likes A (+1) is a positive cycle. A dislikes B (−1), B likes C (−1), and C dislikes A (−1). If many objects are considered, the number of possible cycles becomes enormous, and they are best counted by computers rather than people, using matrices rather than graphs.

Cartwright and Harary's index of balance (see Harary, Norman, & Cartwright, 1965) is

$$BAL = \frac{Cy+}{Cy}, \text{ where}$$

Cy is the total number of cycles in the graph and Cy+ is the number of cycles that are positive. Figure 9 represents the relations among five persons as seen by a particular respondent: A and B like each other; C and E like each other, and both of them dislike B, who reciprocates the sentiment; A likes D, but D dislikes A. Although several of the points are left unconnected in this graph, the total number of cycles is rather large—49. Figure 9 lists only those cycles beginning (and ending) at point A. All of them are positive, except the cycle ADA. If one ignored point D, and considered only the other four points, the graph would be balanced. The effect of the A-D relationship is to unbalance an otherwise balanced graph, yielding 18 negative cycles out of the total 49. By Cartwright and Harary's index, the total balance is thus:

$$BAL = 31/49 = .63$$

One can readily appreciate the complexity introduced by connecting a few more points in this graph; the total number of cycles in a graph consisting of just 10 points, completely connected, is enormous. This index of balance was intended primarily for application to groups, in which each member's liking for all others could be conveniently assessed by a sociometric questionnaire. Application to a single person's cognitions about a group requires that all the

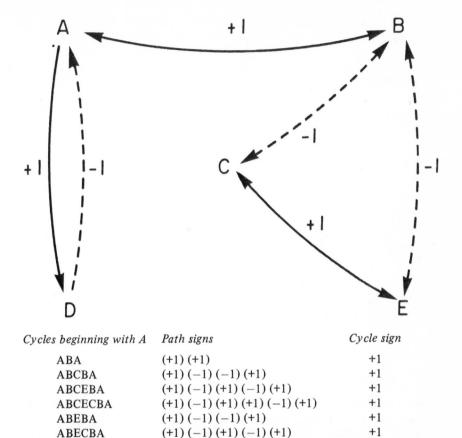

Cycles beginning with A	Path signs	Cycle sign
ABA	(+1) (+1)	+1
ABCBA	(+1) (−1) (−1) (+1)	+1
ABCEBA	(+1) (−1) (+1) (−1) (+1)	+1
ABCECBA	(+1) (−1) (+1) (+1) (−1) (+1)	+1
ABEBA	(+1) (−1) (−1) (+1)	+1
ABECBA	(+1) (−1) (+1) (−1) (+1)	+1
ABECEBA	(+1) (−1) (+1) (+1) (−1) (+1)	+1
ADA	(+1) (−1)	−1

Fig. 9. A graph representing relations among 5 cognized objects.

Note. A solid line indicates liking (scored +1), a dotted line dislike (scored −1), in the direction of the arrow.

judged interconnections be elicited from that one person, which could be an overwhelming task. We have followed a different course in constructing measures of individual differences in balance. They are based on the same idea of Heider, but permit much more efficient assessment.

Affective Balance from Listing and Comparing Objects

We designate our variable *affective balance*, rather than simply balance, in recognition that "harmonious relations among cognitions" (Heider, 1958) on

Table 11. Computation of BAL (Index of Affective Balance) from *Listing and Comparing Nations*

Object (list number):	1	2	3	4	5	6	7	8	9	10
Liking:	7	4	1	5	6	7	5	4	3	2
Object number (cont.)	11	12	13	14	15	16	17	18	19	20
Liking:	3	6	2	4	5	1	6	4	6	5

Liking for objects in group:	A	B	C	D
	7	7	4	4
	4	6	5	3
	5	6		2
		5		3
				6
Mean liking:	5.33	6.00	4.50	3.60
σ^2	1.56	0.50	0.25	1.84
$M_{\sigma_w^2}$ =	0.87			
σ_b^2 =	0.81			

$$BAL = \frac{\sigma_b^2 - M_{\sigma_w^2}}{\sigma_b^2 + M_{\sigma_w^2}} = \frac{0.81 - 0.87}{0.81 + 0.87} = .04$$

Note. Based on data of Table 6 (p. 105).

bases other than affect might be conceived. Previous operational definitions of balance have also been restricted to liking.

In the *Listing and Comparing* instrument (see p. 86) each object is rated by the respondent on a 7-point scale, indicating degree of liking. This liking score is considered for all objects within each group labeled as "similar" (ignoring the groups identified as "different" or "not possessing the characteristic"). To the extent that objects within a single group are more alike than objects in different groups, the entire set will appear as balanced by the following formula:

$$BAL = \frac{\sigma_b^2 - M_{\sigma_w^2}}{\sigma_b^2 + M_{\sigma_w^2}}$$

where σ_b^2 is the variance among group mean liking scores and $M_{\sigma_w^2}$ is the mean within-group variance in liking scores. Thus, BAL indicates the degree to which objects seen as similar are liked to the same degree.

BAL has theoretical limits between +1.00 and −1.00, but the unit of measurement is not readily defined. Hence we regard the index as preliminary, and would urge the exploration of alternate indices, including those which take into account group size. The computation of BAL is illustrated in Table 11, based on the data of Table 6 (p. 105).

Affective Balance from Grouping Objects

One of the attributes specified in the instrument for grouping objects is the affective attribute—that is, the degree to which the respondent likes each object. The number of categories in the liking scale depends on the number of groups formed by the respondent; it ranges from 2 upwards. Protocols with fewer than two categories are not scored. Liking scores are considered in relation to the groups formed on all the other 9 attributes specified in the instrument. Considering one attribute at a time, the index BAL is computed in the same way as for the *Listing and Comparing* instrument (see Table 11). The mean BAL score is computed over all 9 attributes to yield an index of affective balance for the domain. Attributes for which fewer than two groups are formed and those for which the grouped objects show no variance in liking scores are ignored.

Table 12. Computation of BAL (Index of Affective Balance) from *Most Similar Pairs of Nations*

Nation number:	1	2	3	4	5	6	7	8	9	10
Liking:	4	5	6	5	3	2	4	5	3	1
Nation number (cont.):	11	12	13	14	15	16	17	18	19	20
Liking:	2	3	3	4	4	7	4	2	2	5

		d^2
Most similar pairs:	6 and 15	4
	7 and 9	1
	4 and 16	4
Most different pairs:	10 and 16	36
	1 and 20	1
	8 and 12	4

$$M_{d^2_{diff}} = \frac{36 + 1 + 4}{3} = 13.67$$

$$M_{d^2_{sim}} = \frac{4 + 1 + 4}{3} = 3.00$$

$$M_{d^2_{max}} = \frac{(7-1)^2 + (6-2)^2 + (5-2)^2}{3} = 20.33$$

$$BAL = \frac{M_{d^2_{diff}} - M_{d^2_{sim}}}{M_{d^2_{max}}} = \frac{13.67 - 3.00}{20.33} = .52$$

Most Similar Pairs of Objects

In scoring balance from *Most Similar Pairs* (p. 95), the respondent's expressed liking for objects judged similar is compared with liking for objects judged different, by means of the following index:

$$\text{BAL} = \frac{M_{d^2_{diff}} - M_{d^2_{sim}}}{M_{d^2_{max}}},$$

where $M_{d^2_{diff}}$ is the mean squared difference in liking between objects in the "most different" pairs, $M_{d^2_{sim}}$ is the mean squared difference in liking between objects in the "most similar" pairs, and $M_{d^2_{max}}$ is the maximum squared difference possible, considering the three highest and three lowest ratings of liking given by this respondent. A sample calculation is presented in Table 12. This index has theoretical limits of +1 and −1; a score of 0 indicates that similar objects are about as similarly liked as are different objects. However, the unit of measurement has no clear interpretation.

Similarity of Paired Objects

The index of balance for *Similarity of Paired Objects* (p. 97) is the product-moment correlation, over all 20 pairs of objects, between the judged similarity of the pair and the similarity in the respondent's liking for the two objects in the pair. The maximum score (+1) indicates that greatest liking similarity is found in the most similar pairs, and least liking similarity in the least similar pairs. The minimum score (−1) indicates the reverse, and a score of 0 indicates that judged similarity and similarity in liking for the objects are unrelated responses for this subject.

Constructing Sets of Objects

In *Constructing Sets of Objects* the respondent is presented with a group of objects and asked to eliminate those that do not belong together. The result is a set of groups of objects seen as similar, just like *Listing and Comparing Objects*. The index of balance for *Listing and Comparing Objects* can therefore be applied to *Constructing Sets of Objects* as well.

CORRELATIONS AMONG MEASURES OF INTEGRATION

No single study has investigated more than a few of these integrative styles at once, so we can report only partial information concerning their interrelations. Harvey's "This I Believe" Test and Schroder's *Paragraph*

Table 13. Mean Intercorrelations Among Selected Measures of Cognitive Integration

	1	2	3	4	5	6	7	8	9	10	11	12	13	14	15	16	17	18
Image comparability																		
1. List and Compare																		
2. Free Description	.05																	
3. Checklist Description	.09	.11																
4. Free Comparison	.09	.28	.11															
5. Checklist Comparison	.11	.12	.66	.18														
6. Grouping	.29	.17	.26	.14	.29													
Centralization																		
7. Free Description	.06	(.54)	.11	.23	.14	.16												
8. Checklist Description	−.04	.02	(.00)	.06	.06	−.02	.03											
9. Free Comparison	.06	.19	.10	(.50)	.15	.12	.18	.03										
10. Checklist Comparison	−.02	.08	.02	.04	(.02)	.00	.08	.24	.09									
Affective-evaluative consistency																		
11. Free Description	.00	(.08)	−.01	.08	.02	−.02	(.06)	.00	.12	.01								
12. Checklist Description	.06	.10	(.12)	.04	.08	.08	(.07)	.08	.05	.18								
13. Grouping	−.09	−.02	−.12	−.01	−.11	(−.33)	−.02	.00	−.02	−.01	.10	.11						
14. Rating	−.01	.03	.05	.02	.03	.04	.01	.04	−.01	.00	.20	.19	.15					
Affective balance																		
15. List and Compare	(−.22)	.00	−.05	−.04	−.05	−.12	.00	.06	−.02	−.01	.06	.05	.05	.04				
16. Grouping	−.15	−.05	−.15	−.02	−.12	(−.44)	−.06	.04	−.03	.06	.12	.14	(.59)	.17	.07			
17. Most Similar Pairs	−.01	.03	.01	.02	.03	−.01	.02	.01	.05	.01	.08	.13	.13	.10	.03	.09		
18. Similarity of Pairs	.02	.05	.03	.03	.02	.06	.05	.03	.06	−.02	.03	.09	.10	.12	.00	.11	.13	
19. Constructing Sets	−.04	.06	−.05	.00	−.04	−.02	.00	−.05	.04	−.05	.09	.10	.12	.14	.13	.12	.11	.10

Note. Mean intercorrelations for variables 11, 12, 14, 15, and 16 are each based on 20 correlation coefficients from 7 separate subject samples covering 7 different cognitive domains (p. 113). Mean correlations involving the other variables are each based on 14 correlation coefficients from 5 separate subject samples covering 6 different cognitive domains (p. 113, samples *a* through *e*). Parentheses indicate correlations between measures derived from a common instrument.

Completion Test were administered in three studies reviewed by Goldstein and Blackman (1978); only one of the three correlations was significantly greater than zero. Thus, evidence concerning the relationship between level of abstractness and level of integrative complexity as defined by these two investigators is ambiguous.

Zajonc's two measures of integration (unity and organization) are derived from a single task, so it is not possible to assess the relationship between them uncontaminated by instrument-specific factors. By definition, the two properties must be negatively correlated, and it is not yet clear that they can be empirically distinguished when measured from different instruments.

The several measures developed in our own research program have been administered to some of the university student samples identified on p. 113. Mean correlations among the measures, computed over five samples (groups *a* through *e*) for six cognitive domains, are reported in Table 13. The mean of all correlations among measures of image comparability is .20; comparable means for centralization, affective-evaluative consistency, and affective balance are .11, .16, and .09, respectively.

In general, coefficients pertaining to a single integrative style tend to be larger than those across styles (ignoring measures derived from a single instrument). The main exception to this general pattern of discriminant measurement is found in the apparent confusion between affective balance and affective-evaluative consistency. In spite of the fact that these properties are assessed from different instruments (with one exception, *Grouping of Objects*), their cross-property correlations average about as high (.10) as the

Table 14. Homogeneities and Reliabilities of Composite Measures of Cognitive Integration

Sample and domain	Comparability		Centralization		Consistency		Balance	
	H.R.	r_{tt}	H.R.	r_{tt}	H.R.	r_{tt}	H.R.	r_{tt}
U.S.—Acquaintances	.22	.63	.05	.17	.13	.36	.10	.36
(a) Family	.18	.55	.10	.31	.22	.49	.22	.58
Nations	.12	.43	.15	.41	.16	.40	.02	.10
Self	.20	.60	.10	.30	.10	.29	.07	.27
Japan—Acquaintances	.16	.54	.22	.54	.16	.42	.17	.51
(b) Family	.16	.53	.03	.09	.27	.59	.18	.52
Nations	.22	.61	.05	.18	.24	.56	.14	.44
Self	.24	.64	.11	.34	.22	.53	.14	.44
New Zealand—								
Acquaintances (d)	.27	.69	.15	.41	.25	.56	.11	.38
Family (e)	.13	.45	.12	.35	.10	.30	.18	.49
Nations (c)	.23	.65	.07	.22	.27	.59	.08	.26
Self (c)	.18	.56	.08	.25	.12	.35	.09	.33
Mean	.19	.57	.10	.30	.19	.45	.13	.39

Note. Letters in parentheses refer to samples described on p. 113. H.R. is Scott's (1960) Homogeneity Ratio; r_{tt} is Cronbach's (1951) coefficient alpha.

mean intra-property correlation for affective balance (.09). This finding suggests that the two integrative styles amount to the same thing, that when objects of similar valence are seen as belonging together, they also tend to be evaluated similarly.

When the several measures for each integrative style are pooled into their respective equally weighted composites, reliabilities and homogeneities approach acceptable levels for image comparability, but are far from satisfactory for the other three integrative styles (see Table 14). It is clear that centralization has not yet been well measured, and that the two constructs, affective balance and affective-evaluative consistency, may as well be combined into a single construct when referring to individual differences in use of this integrative style. Such a combination would also raise the composite reliability to a more acceptable level.

Chapter 9

MEASURES OF OTHER PROPERTIES

In the studies to be described in subsequent chapters, we have employed measures of other cognitive properties besides differentiation and integration. Some of these are standard in attitude measurement, but others were developed for the present purposes. The organization of this chapter will follow that introduced in Chapter 5—properties of objects, attributes, and cognitive structure.

PROPERTIES OF OBJECTS

The three variable properties of cognitive objects identified in Chapter 5 are complexity, valence, and ambivalence. Measures of object complexity have been presented in Chapter 7. Here we shall briefly describe measures of object valence and ambivalence.

Object Valence

Object valence includes both the direction and the intensity of affect expressed toward an object; directional valence can be measured with almost any of the standard self-report procedures for assessing attitudes (see Cook & Selltiz, 1964; Dawes, 1972; Scott, 1968; Triandis, 1970). Two simple methods of assessing directional valence were employed in our studies: a rating of the object itself ("object liking") and the evaluative description of an object ("object evaluation").

To assess "object liking", the respondent was asked to rate objects on a 7-point scale, in which 7 represents "like very much" (or some equivalent expression), 1 represents "dislike very much," and 4 represents "neither like nor dislike." Such rating scales were included on many of the instruments (see Chapter 6). "Object evaluation" was assessed as the average evaluation of characteristics the respondent assigned to it. In the case of the *Checklist Description*, evaluation of the adjectives could be ascertained from ratings provided by Anderson (1968) or from judgments made by other samples of students at the University of Colorado and Victoria University of Wellington, New Zealand. This scoring assumes similar evaluation of a characteristic by all respondents—an assumption which was strengthened (though not assured) by including in the checklist only adjectives for which there was high consensus (σ less than 1 on a 7-point evaluative rating scale). In several comparisons between Anderson's mean evaluative ratings and our own, correlations across samples of identical adjectives always exceeded .95 and averaged .97. When object descriptions were obtained from *Free Description*, the respondent rated the desirability of each assigned characteristic on a 7-point scale, and the mean of all these ratings was taken as the directional valence for the object described.

Scores for object valence measured by those two procedures showed considerable agreement; within-subjects correlations over various sets of 10 cognitive objects averaged .70 in the Colorado sample, .56 in Japan, and .64 in New Zealand. This still left substantial room for individual differences in correlation, and these provided the basis for our measures of affective-evaluative consistency (see p. 125).

Affective intensity is the strength of affect independent of its direction. Our sole measure of intensity was the absolute deviation of object liking from the scale midpoint (i.e., the absolute distance from 4 on a 7-point scale).

Object Ambivalence

Although ambivalence has been of interest to several researchers (e.g., Kaplan, 1972; Katz, 1971), assessment techniques have lagged far behind those developed for measuring directional valence and affective intensity. Our definition of ambivalence (Chapter 5) suggests a number of straightforward operational definitions, all based on the balance of favorable and unfavorable characteristics assigned to an object. To assess ambivalence from a *Checklist Description*, each circled adjective was assigned a value of +1, 0, or −1, representing its average desirability in the larger population of students. In scoring *Free Description*, the respondent's own ratings of the characteristics were used, but the rating scale was converted to a range from +3 to −3, so that sums of favorable and unfavorable evaluations could be distinguished. Several of the attributes included in *Rating of Objects* were defined, a priori, as evaluative. In scoring ambivalence, deviations from the scale midpoint were added separately over favorable and unfavorable ratings.

We required an index of ambivalence that approached a maximum when an object was assigned a large number of favorable and a large number of unfavorable characteristics, and approached a minimum when an object was assigned a large number of characteristics all of which had the same extreme desirability. A preliminary index, with boundaries of 0 and 1, was defined as follows:

$$Am' = 1 - \frac{L - S}{L + S}$$

$$= \frac{2S}{L + S}$$

where L is the sum of desirable *or* undesirable characteristics, whichever is the larger, and S is the smaller sum of desirable or undesirable characteristics. (Neutral characteristics are ignored.)

It may easily be seen that the maximum value (1) of Am' occurs when $S = L$, and its minimum value (0) occurs when $S = 0$. However, the total number of characteristics does not affect Am' as it should; the maximum value of 1, for instance, is achieved when both S and L are 1 and also when they are both 100. To make the index sensitive to the total number of characteristics assigned, two constants were added to the formula:

$$Am = \frac{2S + 1}{S + L + 2}$$

Am scores for some representative values of S and L are shown in Table 15. In practice, *Am* will approach its limits only in a *Free Description* where the rating scale allows a large range for S and L. In the present studies, the maximum value of L was 36 when calculated from *Free Description*, and 18 when calculated from *Checklist Description*. The corresponding limits on S were 18 and 9. Thus, the range of *Am* scores was bounded by .03 and .97 in *Free Description*, and by .05 and .95 in *Checklist Description*.

Consistency Among Domain Ambivalence Scores

We have only indirect evidence for convergence among the three measures. Because ambivalence is defined as a property of a single cognitive object, it would be most appropriate to assess convergence by comparing scores for a single object measured from different instruments. This assessment was not possible with the data we have collected. In order to reduce redundancy among the instruments (and thus increase their combined generality), we chose sets of objects that were almost completely nonoverlapping.

The consistency among measures of ambivalence could, however, be ascertained at a different level. By averaging a respondent's ambivalence scores from each instrument, we calculated indices of the tendency to hold

Table 15. *Am* Scores for Selected Values of *S* and *L*

S:	0	1	2	3	4	5	6	7	8	9	10	15	20	30	40
L: 0	.50*														
1	.33*	.75													
2	.25	.60	.83												
3	.20	.50	.71	.88											
4	.17	.43	.63	.78	.90										
5	.14	.38	.56	.70	.82	.92									
6	.13	.33	.50	.64	.75	.85	.93								
7	.11	.30	.45	.58	.69	.79	.87	.94							
8	.10	.27	.42	.54	.64	.73	.81	.88	.94						
9	.09	.25	.38	.50	.60	.69	.76	.83	.89	.95					
10	.08	.23	.36	.47	.56	.65	.72	.79	.85	.90	.95				
15	.06	.17	.26	.35	.43	.50	.57	.63	.68	.73	.78	.97			
20	.05	.13	.21	.28	.35	.41	.46	.52	.57	.61	.66	.84	.98		
30	.03	.09	.15	.20	.25	.30	.34	.38	.43	.46	.50	.66	.79	.98	
40	.02	.07	.11	.16	.20	.23	.27	.31	.34	.37	.40	.54	.66	.85	.99

*Note. Ambivalence has no clear meaning when fewer than 2 characteristics are assigned to an object, so these values of *Am* are excluded under current scoring practice.

ambivalent images within a specific domain. Correlations among the three instruments are shown in Table 16; they range from small to moderate, and average about .24. The uniformly positive results indicate two types of consistency: Consistency in the degrees of ambivalence held toward different sets of objects and consistency among different methods of assessment.

Table 16. Intercorrelations Among Mean Ambivalence Scores

Measure	Free Description			Checklist Description		
Sample	U.S.	Japan	N.Z.	U.S.	Japan	N.Z.
Checklist Description						
Acquaintances	.30	.14	.12			
Family	.15	.04	.08			
Nations	.11	.06	.30			
Self	.23	.09	.24			
Rating						
Acquaintances	.37	.14	.35	.48	.17	.40
Family	.23	.06	.19	.29	.28	.23
Nations	.29	.17	.19	.19	.24	.13
Self	.53	.05	.30	.37	.51	.47

PROPERTIES OF ATTRIBUTES

The four variable properties of attributes defined in Chapter 5 are ordinality, valence, precision, and centrality. Precision has been considered in Chapter 7 along with other measures of differentiation. It is likely that individuals differ in the ordinality and valence with which they use any particular attribute, but we have not considered individual differences in our investigations. Instead, we have assumed standard values of these properties for any particular attribute, that is, every attribute coded from *Free Description* was designated either ordinal or nominal for all subjects who used it, and either neutral or evaluative for all subjects. The proportion of a particular respondent's descriptions that were coded into ordinal (as opposed to nominal) attributes, and the proportion of descriptions that were coded into evaluative (as opposed to neutral) attributes, were used as measures of individual differences in tendencies to use these a priori types. Thus, the measures referred to an entire cognitive domain, rather than to a single attribute.

Centrality

Measures of attribute centrality were derived from four instruments: *Free Description, Checklist Description, Free Comparison*, and *Checklist Comparison*. This property represents the degree to which an attribute is used in describing or comparing objects named on the instrument. The attributes coded from *Free Description* are available from the authors. The measure of attribute centrality extracted from these two instruments is simply the proportion of objects (or object-pairs) coded on the particular attribute.

Correspondingly, pairs of antonymic adjectives in the checklists were taken to represent single bipolar attributes. The justification for this pairing was both conceptual and empirical. Conceptually, the model of cognitive structure defines attributes in dimensional terms, and thus as including more than one category. Empirically, it was found that respondents who used one adjective to describe any given object were more likely than average to use the opposite adjective in describing some other object in that instrument. In other words, when the antonymic pairs were treated as single attributes, they yielded more reliable measures of attribute centrality than when each adjective was considered separately (see Scott, Kline, Faguy-Coté, & Peterson, 1979).

These measures of centrality may be evaluated from two perspectives, within-subjects and between-subjects. A within-subjects perspective concerns the degree to which the several measures yield similar rankings of attribute centrality for a particular person. A between-subjects perspective focuses on the degree to which the several instruments similarly appraise differences among individuals in centrality of a particular attribute.

Within-subjects consistency in relative centralities of attributes has been considered by Scott et al. (1979). In a series of earlier studies of students at the University of Colorado, these authors analyzed measures of centrality based on *Free Description* and *Checklist Description*. The mean correlations between relative centrality scores (computed within subjects, then averaged over subjects) were .49, .24, and .35 for the cognitive domains of acquaintances, nations, and self, respectively. A comparable study in 1978 among introductory psychology students at the Australian National University yielded an average intra-subject correlation of .19 for the domain of self. In the Boulder, Kyoto, and Wellington samples described on p. 113, the mean within-subjects correlation was .42 for *Free Description* and *Free Comparison*, and the mean within-subjects correlation from *Checklist Description* and *Checklist Comparison* was .51. These results come from highly similar instrument formats, however, so their degree of correspondence is exaggerated.

Determining the degree of between-subjects consistency is somewhat more complicated. A simple correlation between the centrality scores produced by two instruments, calculated across subjects for a single attribute, is seriously contaminated by individual differences in verbosity. To the extent that some individuals generally include more attributes in their descriptions, their centrality scores will tend to be higher for all attributes. This factor spuriously inflates between-subjects correlations. In order to eliminate the effects of individual differences in the tendency to name or check many attributes, centrality scores were standardized within each respondent. The result of this standardization was that correlations among centrality scores of *different* attributes (calculated across subjects) became predominantly negative and that correlations between centrality scores of the same attribute calculated from *different* instruments were greatly reduced.

In general, we found that there is between-subject consistency in centrality scores, but it is considerably less than within-subject consistency. For example, introductory psychology students at the Australian National University in 1978 completed the *Checklist* and *Free Description* instruments for the domain of self. Correlations between the two measures of centrality for particular attributes ranged from −.11 to .22 with a mean correlation of .08. This is a very low level of correspondence, but it will be recalled that these correlations were reduced by the correction for verbosity. As another indication of the consistency between these two measures of centrality, we compared the between-instrument correlations of centrality scores for identical or similar attributes with those for different attributes. On the average, correlations between identical or similar attributes exceeded 78% of the correlations between different attributes.

When attribute centrality scores came from similar instrument formats, the degree of correspondence was somewhat higher. The correlation between standardized centrality scores for particular attributes in *Checklist Description* and *Checklist Comparison* averaged .32 over all 36 attributes in each of 4 domains for all 3 samples. The mean cross-subjects correlation between centrality scores for single attributes used at least 10 times in both *Free Description* and *Free Comparison* was .27, when averaged over all 453 relevant correlations.

It may be concluded from the analyses of within- and between-subjects

Table 17. Mean Intercorrelations Among Measures of Evaluative Centrality

Measure	Free Description			Checklist Description		
Sample	U.S.	Japan	N.Z.	U.S.	Japan	N.Z.
Checklist Description						
Acquaintances	.31	−.02	.32			
Family	.08	.36	.22			
Nations	.00	.30	.08			
Self	.23	−.07	.31			
Rating						
Acquaintances	.42	.46	.48	.08	.00	.27
Family	.30	.56	.48	.29	.25	.22
Nations	.37	.37	.35	.11	.25	−.05
Self	.54	.19	.34	.12	.30	.45

consistency that the relative centralities of several attributes within a single respondent can be assessed with some reliability by the present instruments, but intersubject differences in centrality on any particular attribute are markedly affected by the instrument from which centrality scores are obtained—whether from free descriptions or from checklists. We do not yet have a reliable method of measuring individual differences in the centrality of particular attributes.

EVALUATIVE CENTRALITY

Measures for most of the designated structural properties were discussed in the two preceding chapters under the headings of differentiation and integration. There remains one other property that is structural, in that it refers neither to objects nor to attributes, but to the relations among them. This is evaluative centrality, the degree to which most objects are described in evaluative terms rather than with purely descriptive or neutral attributes.

Our measure of evaluative centrality was the average evaluation (nondirectional valence) of the attributes assigned to the set of objects included in an instrument. Evaluation of attributes in the *Checklist Description* and *Rating* instruments was assumed constant for all respondents (on the basis of preliminary studies described earlier in this chapter). Adjectives in the checklist were scored as 1 (evaluative) or 0 (neutral). In the *Rating* instrument, evaluation was scored as the degree of deviation from the scale midpoint on evaluative attributes. Neutral attributes did not enter into the calculation of evaluative centrality for this instrument. The respondents' own ratings of evaluation (absolute deviations from the scale midpoint) were used to calculate evaluative centrality from *Free Description*.

Within each instrument, an evaluation score was computed for every object, as the mean evaluation of all attributes assigned to it by the subject, divided by the maximum mean score possible (1 for *Checklist*, 3 for *Free Description* and for *Rating* instruments). This evaluation score was then averaged over all objects to yield an evaluative centrality score for the instrument, which varied between 0 and 1. It represents the degree to which any particular respondent's object-conceptions are evaluative in tone.

The degree to which the three instruments yielded similar evaluative centrality scores for each domain may be ascertained from Table 17. The correspondence ranged from small to moderate, with an average between-instruments correlation of .26. Though the previous analysis of between-subjects consistency for centrality scores showed that our instruments do not yield very reliable measures of centrality for particular attributes, the instruments appear adequate for measuring the mean centrality of evaluative attributes as a class.

Chapter 10

GENERALITY OF COGNITIVE PROPERTIES

It has commonly been assumed in theories of cognitive structure and process that a person has a characteristic mode of organizing or utilizing information that pervades all mental activity. Thus, Gardner (1953) defined equivalence range as a consistent individual difference in what is accepted as "similar or identical in a variety of adaptive tasks" (p. 229). Pettigrew (1958) conceived of category width as an individual consistency in estimating "the extremes of a number of diverse categories—from length of whales to rainfall in Washington, D.C." (p. 543). Harvey et al. (1961) described varying degrees of abstractness and concreteness as pervasive individual tendencies. The most securely established psychological construct about individual differences in cognitive processes is that of intelligence, which is usually conceived as a general capacity to learn or to profit from experience or to anticipate consequences in almost any situation.

The adoption of such monolithic concepts is congruent with major historical trends within psychology, resulting in substantial methodological simplification. For example, in the study of animal learning, an assumption of equipotentiality—that all learning occurs in the same manner—reigned unchallenged for 50 years. [For an example of recent criticism, see Rozin and Kalat (1971).] This assumption legitimized the use of the so-called arbitrary operant in the study of learning. If all behavior is acquired in the same manner, one might as well study something as convenient as a pigeon pecking a key. Similarly, the use of simple tasks by experimental psychologists studying cognition is based on the assumption that problem solving strategies are similar regardless of the specific problem. The use of projective tests such as the Rorschach and the TAT to assess personality characteristics presumes that people cognize ambiguous pictures and ink blots in a manner equivalent to that employed for interpersonal relations, for example.

The utility of monolithic constructs depends in large part on the behavior to be predicted, on the range of scores available for the independent variable, and on the degree of theoretical precision desired at the time. In a number of cases, there are good reasons to assume that a particular theoretical construct is pervasive. It is possible, however, to define personality and cognitive constructs in a more differentiated way. Several aspects of intelligence may be identified either theoretically or through factor analysis of test scores. Theoretically, one can also conceive of cognitive structure and process as pertaining, not to the total mental sphere, but to more limited classes of mental activity. This is what we have done in defining a structural model in terms of a given cognitive domain. Our strategy is a cautious one, allowing empirical corroboration or disconfirmation of the hypothesis that the properties are pervasive.

The question remains whether this is a useful perspective to have taken—whether it leads to understandings more accurate or more refined than those which follow from global constructs about individual differences in cognitive structure. In our research, we have approached the question of generality with two different strategies. The first strategy is to compare inter- and intra-domain correlations among measures of structural properties. This approach resulted in the work to be reported in this chapter. The second strategy is to correlate external variables with cognitive properties of two or more domains that are differentially relevant. This analysis will be postponed to Chapter 15, where we consider correlates of interpersonal adjustment.

INTER- AND INTRA-DOMAIN CORRELATIONS

If the several measures of dimensionality, for example, correlate more highly within a particular domain than between domains, then it is fair to infer that there is some degree of domain-specificity, that the level of dimensionality depends to some extent on the category of objects the person is considering. If, on the other hand, measures of dimensionality correlate as highly between as within domains, then the most reasonable conclusion is that people tend to show a characteristic level of cognitive dimensionality regardless of the objects considered.

Three limitations of our data must be recognized. The first limitation results from the number and type of cognitive domains considered. To avoid imposing unduly on subjects' time and patience, we assessed, at most, six domains from a single person. (Only the four treated in all three main samples are reported here.) These domains were hardly representative of all the types of objects that people typically consider. The second limitation is on the respondents—university students in three cultures. Hardly any of these people can be considered either expert or ignorant concerning the four cognitive domains; the range of cognitive organization is restricted to an intermediate level of sophistication. It is not known whether the results obtained here will generalize to circumstances in which the subjects are expert or ignorant in the domains considered.

The third limitation is due to our use of parallel instrument formats in assessing properties of the four cognitive domains. Responses to any attitude or personality test reflect not only the variable characteristic that the test is designed to measure but also the manner in which the information is elicited, i.e., the format of the test itself. There are characteristic modes of response to a checklist (e.g., to check many or few adjectives), to a free description (e.g., to write much or little), and to a rating scale (e.g., to use the extremes or the middle of the range provided). Therefore, a substantial degree of cross-domain similarity in scores can be expected simply from the similarity of response formats underlying the measures.

A Multimethod Correlation Coefficient

The first two limitations cannot be overcome after the data are collected, but the third one can. The correlation between two scores can be corrected by subtracting the part that is due to common instrument formats. This is done by subdividing the total score from each domain into its components, and considering only the cross-domain correlations between those parts which do not depend on identical instrument formats. For instance, dimensionality scores from *Rating of Nations* may be correlated with dimensionality scores in the domain of acquaintances obtained from every instrument except *Rating of Acquaintances*. And so on, for every instrument within each pair of cognitive domains. From the average of these correlations based on instruments of different format, one can predict how composite scores from two domains would correlate if they had no instrument formats in common.

This derivation may be briefly sketched. Consider the following computational formula for the product-moment correlation between variables A and B:

$$r_{AB} = \frac{\sum_{k=1}^{N} AB - NM_A M_B}{N\sigma_A \sigma_B}$$

Suppose A and B are composite measures with, respectively, means and standard deviations of M_A and σ_A, M_B and σ_B. A is calculated from m instruments of different format (completed by N participants), scores from which are standardized over participants. B is calculated from n standardized instruments. Let c equal the number of pairs of instruments with the same format. The effect of standardization is to make $M_A = M_B = 0$. We may rewrite the correlation between A and B in terms of the component standard scores, a_i and b_j:

$$r_{AB} = \frac{\sum\limits_{k=1}^{N} \sum\limits_{i=1}^{m} \sum\limits_{j=1}^{n} a_{ik}b_{jk}}{N\sigma_A\sigma_B} = \frac{\sum\limits_{i=1}^{m} \sum\limits_{j=1}^{n} \sum\limits_{k=1}^{N} a_{ik}b_{jk}}{N\sigma_A\sigma_B}$$

In terms of the correlations among the component scores, a_i and b_j, this becomes:

$$r_{AB} = \frac{\sum\limits_{i=1}^{m} \sum\limits_{j=1}^{n} r_{a_ib_j}}{\sigma_A\sigma_B}$$

There are mn component correlations, $r_{a_ib_j}$. Of these, c are calculated from similar instruments, and the remaining $mn - c$ are calculated from instruments of different format. The term $M_{r_{sim}}$ may be used to represent the mean correlation between scores from similar instruments, calculated across participants, while $M_{r_{diff}}$ is used to represent the mean correlation between scores from different instrument formats. The correlation between composite instruments may then be written as:

$$r_{AB} = \frac{cM_{r_{sim}} + (mn - c)M_{r_{diff}}}{\sigma_A\sigma_B}$$

The correlation between A and B is assumed to be artificially inflated by common instrument factors to the extent that $M_{r_{sim}}$ exceeds $M_{r_{diff}}$. One way of correcting for the inflation is to set $M_{r_{sim}}$ equal to $M_{r_{diff}}$. This results in:

$$r_{AB} = \frac{mnM_{r_{diff}}}{\sigma_A\sigma_B}$$

or, alternatively:

$$r_{AB} = \frac{mn}{mn - c} \cdot \frac{\sum\limits_{i=1}^{m} \sum\limits_{j=1}^{n} r_{a_ib_j}}{\sigma_A\sigma_B}$$

where a_i and b_j are paired only for instruments of different format.

It is these corrected inter-domain correlations that are presented here in our first investigation of the degree of domain specificity or generality of structural properties. The reported correlations were usually reduced from their uncorrected levels, confirming our suspicion that parallel instrument formats introduced a contamination.

Subjects

The data come from students at three universities (see p. 113)—88 at the University of Colorado and 40 each at Doshisha and Shiga Universities. The two Japanese samples are combined into one. Though students at the University of Colorado completed questionnaires pertaining to six domains of cognition, only four are utilized here—those which were also described by the Japanese sample. (Students in New Zealand were tested on just one or two cognitive domains, so their results are not considered here.) Questionnaires were administered so as to proceed from maximally open instruments (*Free Description*) to maximally closed instruments (*Rating*), alternating among cognitive domains. This order avoided confounding intra-domain similarity of scores with temporal adjacency of testing.

Index of Domain-Specificity

Table 18 presents mean squared correlations between domains, compared with mean squared reliability coefficients within domains. (The mean reliabilities are averaged over the four cognitive domains, and the mean corrected between-domains correlations are averaged over six pairs of domains, within each sample.) The mean squared correlation (column b) represents the proportion of variance shared between measures from different domains (after subtracting that part due to common instrument formats). The mean squared reliability (column a) represents the proportion of variance shared by instruments within a single domain. The difference between the latter and the former index represents the degree of domain specificity.

These are not the only possible indices of domain-specificity and inter-domain generality, and the sample of cognitive domains is quite restricted, so one should not take the exact figures too seriously. Nevertheless, we may note those instances in which similar results occur in the two samples for which inter-domain analyses were possible:

Mean object complexity scores show substantial degrees of consistency both within and across domains. This is perhaps attributable in part to a general verbosity factor—the tendency to list many or few traits in describing an object (or to circle many or few traits in a checklist). At present, we are unable to separate this response style from the measurement of object complexity (if, indeed, it should be separated). In any case, the degree of domain-specificity is small compared to the degree of inter-domain generality.

Object valence is much more domain-specific. The general level of inter-object consistency is higher by the direct measure of object liking than

Table 18. Common Variance Among Structural Measures Within and Between Cognitive Domains

Property	Within-domains (a)		Between-domains (b)		Domain-specificity (a)–(b)	
	U.S.	Japan	U.S.	Japan	U.S.	Japan
Mean object complexity	.414	.477	.391	.302	.023	.175
Mean affect	.578	.624	.269	.274	.309	.350
Mean object liking	.644	.637	.219	.220	.425	.417
Mean object evaluation	.312	.257	.098	.041	.214	.216
Mean object ambivalence	.315	.175	.083	.058	.232	.117
Use of ordinal attributes	.166	.211	.057	.039	.109	.172
Mean attribute precision	.057	.174	.022	.082	.035	.092
Evaluative centrality	.230	.265	.142	.108	.088	.157
Image comparability	.311	.358	.269	.163	.042	.195
Centralization	.097	.122	.076	.061	.021	.061
Affective-evaluative consistency	.156	.287	.084	.020	.072	.267
Affective balance	.134	.232	.038	.006	.096	.226
Dimensionality	.179	.026	.157	.013	.022	.013
Mean for object properties	.453	.434	.212	.179	.241	.255
Mean for attribute properties	.112	.193	.040	.061	.072	.132
Mean for structural properties	.185	.230	.128	.062	.057	.153
Total mean	.276	.296	.147	.107	.130	.189

Note. Column (a) contains mean squared reliability coefficients, estimated from Cronbach's (1951) coefficient alpha. Column (b) contains mean squared correlation coefficients that have been corrected to eliminate the effect of common instrument formats (see accompanying text).

by the indirect measure based on the desirability of traits assigned to the objects, but the relative proportions of domain-specific and cross-domains covariance are consistent between the two measures. Similarly, the degree of object ambivalence shows a higher domain-specific than between-domains component in both samples.

The tendency to use ordinal (as opposed to nominal) attributes in describing objects is not nearly so consistent as are the several variable properties of objects, either within or between domains. Nevertheless, the level of domain-specificity is high in comparison with the level of inter-domain generality. The degree of consistency displayed in either crude or refined categorization of attributes is relatively low, and about equally divided into between-domains and domain-specific components.

For the structural properties pertaining to entire cognitive domains, the results are not altogether consistent in the two samples, but it may be noted that, where differences occur, dimensionality, centralization, and image comparability tend to show a higher between-domains than domain-specific component (this is entirely within the U.S. sample), while affective balance and affective-evaluative consistency show a reverse tendency (mostly within the Japanese sample).[4] The overall level of covariance for the structural properties tends to be lower than that for object properties, but higher than that for attribute properties. This is in part due to the relative numbers of components included within each measure. The object properties were assessed from 50 or more objects appearing in at least half a dozen different instruments. Properties of attributes were assessed from just 10 attributes in the *Grouping* instruments and 20 attributes in the *Rating* instruments. Structural properties pertaining to the entire cognitive domain were assessed from only four to seven measures each. On the other hand, each of these measures is based on the description of many objects with many attributes.

A tentative conclusion from these analyses is that those cognitive properties reflecting complexity (dimensionality, image comparability, and object complexity) are likely to show a relatively high degree of generality across domains, whereas those properties reflecting affective processes (object valence, affective balance, and affective-evaluative consistency) are likely to show relatively high levels of domain-specificity. This conclusion is compatible with that emerging from reviews of the personality assessment literature (see Mischel, 1968), which report the greatest degree of cross-situational generality for measures of intellectual ability.

A far safer conclusion is that the properties of cognition investigated here are to some extent similarly manifest in all cognitive domains and to some extent dependent on the particular domain the person is thinking about. Such a conclusion could not have been reached if we had built the assumption of cross-domain generality into a single composite index.

Inter-Domain Similarity

Although results are not reported separately for the several domains, our impression from more detailed analyses is that properties assessed from similar domains (acquaintances and family relations) show more correspondence than properties assessed from quite different domains (nations and self). This interpretation is not pursued here because of the small number of domains,

---

[4]Results in Table 18 are essentially equivalent to those previously reported by Peterson and Scott (1975), allowing for the use of different indices and for some minor corrections in the data since those analyses. The major exception is for the structural property of dimensionality, which has been redefined operationally since previous reports (Scott, 1969, 1974b) to correspond more appropriately with the conceptual definition. Some of its former components have been reassigned to the measure of mean object complexity.

but it would be a reasonable task to operationalize inter-domain similarity in terms of the degree to which their central attributes are similar. This could be done either for an entire sample, using measures of mean centrality over subjects, or for each respondent separately, thereby permitting one to investigate the consequences of individual differences in domain similarity—for example: Does the tendency to structure similarly thoughts about groups and thoughts about people bear any relationship to leader behavior or follower behavior? Does the tendency to structure similarly thoughts about nations and thoughts about acquaintances bear any relationship to nationalism or to experience in international negotiations? Does the tendency to structure similarly the domains of self and acquaintances relate to the level of interpersonal adjustment? Unfortunately, we shall have to leave most of these intriguing questions to a future study.

RELIABILITY OF MEASURES

The reliability of a measure depends on two things—the number of items contained in it and the average intercorrelation among those items. Most of the structural properties are measured by a very small number of instruments within each cognitive domain, the main exception being image comparability, which is based on six instruments. Their reliabilities are thus not high by usual test standards. Though it would be theoretically possible to increase reliabilities by adding more instruments, practical limits on time are imposed in most research circumstances. It is best to think of these structural measures as tentative, subject to improvement with more testing time and better control over the testing situation.

Table 19 reports the mean reliabilities of composite scores within the four cognitive domains considered separately, and combined over four domains (acquaintances, family, nations, and self) for the American and Japanese samples. As implied by the preceding analyses (Table 18), the within-domains reliabilities are highest for object properties, lowest for attribute properties, and intermediate for structural properties pertaining to the entire domain. Where the degree of cross-domain generality is substantial (i.e., for dimensionality, image comparability, centralization, and object complexity), the reliabilities of cross-domains composites substantially exceed those of single-domain scores. By contrast, the cross-domain composite measure of the tendency to describe objects with ordinal attributes shows substantially less reliability than the within-domains measures, in spite of the larger number of scores on which it is based.

Although mean object complexity and mean object liking are measured with relatively high reliability, it is difficult to be satisfied with most of the other scores, in comparison with what we have come to expect from traditional measures of psychological variables, such as intelligence and attitudes. On the other hand, highly reliable intelligence tests are typically administered individually, and require about as long to measure a single

Table 19. Reliability of Measures

Property	Mean reliability			Composite reliability	
	Within domains			Across 4 domains	
	U.S.	*Japan*	*N.Z.*	*U.S.*	*Japan*
Mean object complexity	.64	.69	.69	.86	.83
Mean affect	.76	.79	.72	.77	.79
Mean object liking	.80	.80	.73	.76	.76
Mean object evaluation	.56	.51	.58	.46	.36
Mean object ambivalence	.56	.42	.50	.44	.47
Use of ordinal attributes	.41	.46	.37	.12	.21
Mean attribute precision	.24	.42	.34	.48	.61
Evaluative centrality	.48	.51	.53	.60	.58
Image comparability	.56	.60	.60	.83	.77
Centralization	.30	.29	.31	.51	.52
Affective-evaluative consistency	.39	.54	.44	.49	.39
Affective balance	.37	.48	.35	.49	.29
Dimensionality	.42	.16	.27	.69	.40
Mean for object properties	.66	.60	.64	.66	.64
Mean for attribute properties	.33	.44	.36	.30	.41
Mean for structural properties	.42	.44	.42	.60	.49
Total mean	.50	.50	.49	.58	.54

Note. Reliabilities are estimated from Cronbach's (1951) coefficient alpha within each cognitive domain and averaged for results reported in the first three columns. Composite reliabilities (last two columns) are estimated from the generalized Spearman-Brown formula (Nunnally, 1967, p. 193), based on average intercorrelations among scores from all instruments measuring each property.

variable on one subject as was required in the present battery to assess 12 variables on 80 or more subjects. Highly reliable measures of attitudes (Thurstone scales and Likert scales, for example) typically have a large instrument-specific component built into them, as all questions are answered in a common format (agree-vs.-disagree or magnitude of agreement). If scores from different formats were pooled for attitude measures, as we have done for these cognitive properties, lower reliabilities would most certainly result. When different measures of the same attitude are compared, correlations are high when they share a response format, such as 7-point rating scales (e.g., Brigham & Cook, 1970; Selltiz & Cook, 1966), but essentially nil when they have dissimilar formats (e.g., Brigham & Cook, 1969; Waly & Cook, 1966). Our modest but positive correlations among measures with different formats should be viewed with this in mind.

Although there is substantial room for improvement in reliabilities of measuring these cognitive properties, the present results represent quite an advance over most previous studies. Typically, these have included only one measure of a property, so there was no way of estimating reliability. When multiple measures were utilized, average intercorrelations were usually near zero. For instance, the average intercorrelation among 19 measures of equivalence range obtained by Sloane, Gorlow, and Jackson (1963) was .056, which yields a composite reliability estimate of .53. The average intercorrelation among 20 measures of cognitive differentiation reported by Vannoy (1965) was −.005, yielding a negative composite reliability estimate. Kenny and Ginsberg's (1958) 13 instruments for measuring tolerance of ambiguity correlated .022, on the average, yielding an estimated composite reliability of .23.

It is hard to account for the difference between our results and the results of these previous studies solely on the basis of our attention to particular domains of cognition, for the levels of domain-specificity obtained in our research are not that great. It is possible that the measures used by these previous investigators were less appropriate for their constructs and invited too many diverse task-specific response sets. For instance, Sloane et al. utilized tasks including size-constancy judgments, brightness judgments, syllogistic reasoning, and tolerance for grammatical ambiguities. A number of these tasks possess little face validity for measuring equivalence range, e.g., the number of different interpretations of inkblots checked from a list of 10 possibilities.

Our results suggest that when attention is given to developing convergent measures of a particular cognitive property, they can usually be achieved— though often only after many attempts and discards of promising leads. Having selected mutually intercorrelated measures separately for each of several domains of cognition, we find that they share some degree of variance across domains, and we conclude that the structural properties we have been investigating have both general and domain-specific components.

QUESTIONNAIRE MEASURES AND OTHER MEASURES

A direction we would like to have followed in assessing the generality of structural properties is toward less reactive measures—measures that do not depend on questionnaires administered in a restricted testing situation. While it is hard to imagine completely nonverbal measures of the cognitive properties of concern here, at least we would like to find measures based on spontaneous verbal productions not restricted by our particular lines of questioning and instrument formats. Some appropriate directions of development are suggested by the work of Du Preez (1975), who scored political debates for dimensionality, and of Rosenberg and Jones (1972), who scored Theodore Dreiser's *A Gallery of Women* for association of personal traits in the characters depicted. Coding newspaper editorials, letters-to-the-editor, sermons, national constitutions, and other documents intended for public display might reveal as much about assumed characteristics of the audience as about the cognitive structure of their authors, but it is conceivable that more private communications, such as letters and conversations, would be amenable to such scoring and more readily interpretable as reflecting cognitive structure of their producers.

Our research on the generality of cognitive structure is a mere beginning. This preliminary state requires no apology, for it is duplicated in almost every other aspect of personality study. Nevertheless, it is well to bear such limitations in mind when interpreting the correlates to be discussed in subsequent chapters.

SECTION III

SOME CORRELATES OF STRUCTURAL PROPERTIES

Chapters 11 through 15 are concerned with the ways in which properties of cognitive structure relate to each other and to external variables. Our analyses will focus on three types of relations. First, in Chapter 11, we summarize the relations of the several structural variables to each other and to the variable properties of objects and attributes. Next, in a preliminary effort to understand how people think about different classes of events, Chapter 12 reports mean differences among four domains of cognition and among the three major samples. The remaining three chapters of this section (13, 14, and 15) focus on relations between cognitive structure and variables outside the theoretical system developed in Chaper 5. Analyses such as these are essential for establishing the utility of concepts and measures presented in the previous section. Only a few such external connections have been established so far, but their results have been informative and, in some cases, surprising.

Chapter 11

RELATIONS AMONG
VARIABLE PROPERTIES
OF COGNITION

Predictions regarding a number of relations among variable properties of cognition were derived from the geometric model in Chapter 5. The present chapter tests those predictions. Confidence both in the model and in our operationalizations of its properties is warranted to the degree that the predictions are confirmed. Disconfirmation would suggest that changes in the model or its associated methods are necessary. The present chapter also includes analyses of relations for which no predictions were made. Such relations have less immediate theoretical significance, but they are of interest for increasing our understanding of the cognitive properties.

Our model specifies two types of variable properties: structural properties, which characterize relations among objects and attributes, and formal properties of the cognitive elements (objects and attributes) themselves. The structural properties of cognition constitute individual difference variables that apply to a person's views of an entire domain of objects. Though the formal properties of cognitive elements were defined for particular objects and attributes, they may also be averaged over these elements to define individual differences for an entire domain. Just as one speaks of a person's ambivalence regarding the Soviet Union, so one may also speak of a more general tendency to hold ambivalent images of all nations.

Thus, all of the variable properties may be assessed at the domain level, but some of them may also be assessed at the level of individual attributes or objects. For that reason, tests of all predicted relations were performed at the domain level; i.e., relations were studied as the covariation across subjects of cognitive variables that referred to an entire domain. In addition, analyses at the attribute level were performed for the attribute properties and analyses at the object level were performed for the object properties. These entailed correlating variables over attributes (or objects) within a single person.

We consider the structural properties to be the most important. Therefore, relations among those properties will be considered first. Attribute- and object-level analyses follow. The remainder of the chapter is devoted to a domain-level analysis of relations among the formal properties of cognitive elements and of their relations to the structural properties.

RELATIONS AMONG PROPERTIES OF COGNITIVE STRUCTURE

Table 5 (p. 70) depicts the predictions regarding relations among structural properties derived from the model of cognitive structure, and that scheme is followed in discussing our results. The reader may wish to review that table now. Because many of the predicted relationships refer to variables assessed from common instruments, it is necessary first to exclude common instrument factors from the reported correlations. This was done by means of the multimethod correlation developed in Chapter 10.

Results for the four cognitive domains assessed in the three international samples are summarized in Table 20, which reports means computed from 12 multimethod correlations for each pair of variables. In parentheses underneath each mean correlation appears the standard deviation of these 12 correlations. This standard deviation may be used to estimate the standard error of the

Table 20. Mean Intercorrelations Among Structural Properties (Standard Deviations of rs in parentheses; reliabilities in diagonal brackets)

Property	Evaluative centrality	Image comparability	Centralization	Affective-evaluative consistency	Affective balance	Dimensionality
Evaluative centrality	.51 (.11)					
Image comparability	.15* (.15)	.59 (.07)				
Centralization	.08 (.11)	.23* (.10)	.30 (.12)			
Affective-evaluative consistency	.15* (.10)	.01 (.09)	.05 (.10)	.46 (.11)		
Affective balance	.13* (.13)	−.07 (.07)	.04 (.08)	.29* (.17)	.40 (.14)	
Dimensionality	.00 (.11)	.19* (.10)	.11 (.13)	−.16* (.12)	−.16* (.11)	.28 (.12)

Note. Means and standard deviations of correlation coefficients were computed over 12 values (3 samples of 4 cognitive domains each). These are based on multimethod correlations (see p. 143), from which the spurious component due to identical instruments has been removed. Means indicated by asterisks are at least three times their standard errors (estimated from the standard deviation of the correlation coefficients). Reliabilities are estimated from Cronbach's (1951) coefficient alpha.

mean correlation coefficient. Our convention will be to regard a mean multimethod correlation as "significantly" different from zero, when it is at least three times as large as its standard error. Such a conservative level of significance, ($p < .003$) is appropriate because the 12 correlations, which come from only 3 samples of subjects, are not independent. The assumption behind such a significance test is, of course, that the subjects and cognitive domains employed in our research constitute representative samples of some larger populations to which results can be generalized.

As predicted in the theoretical model, both affective-evaluative consistency and affective balance are significantly correlated with the degree of evaluative centrality. This result indicates that these two simplistic modes of organizing cognitive structures—grouping similarly liked objects together and appraising objects consistently with one's feelings about them—are most commonly found in cognitive systems that are affect-laden. When objects are viewed primarily in evaluative terms, there is a tendency to use liking and evaluation as principles of cognitive organization.

In addition to these two predicted correlates of evaluative centrality, this property is significantly correlated with image comparability. Thus, for the domains studied, consistent application of a standard set of attributes is associated with an evaluative orientation toward the domain. In other words, the attributes used as systematic bases for appraising all objects within a domain are more likely to be evaluative than purely descriptive. It appears that image comparability—an abstract basis for describing objects—is not necessarily an emotionally detached perspective.

The relation between dimensionality and image comparability predicted in the model is affirmed by a mean correlation of .19. When people conceive of objects in terms of many distinct attributes, they are also more likely to apply systematically a common set of attributes. When the number of distinct attributes is small, the person is likely to describe each object in its own specific terms.

Curvilinear relations of centralization to dimensionality and image comparability were predicted, so the product-moment correlation coefficient is not the appropriate index. Analyses of these data, however, showed only 4 significant tendencies toward curvilinearity out of 12 relationships between dimensionality and centralization and only 2 significant tendencies toward curvilinearity out of 12 relationships between centralization and image comparability; these were not generally in the inverted-U-shape anticipated by the hypotheses. Therefore, the linear relationships reported in Table 20 may be taken as adequately representing the results. They show a significant mean correlation (.23) of centralization with image comparability, but no notable correlations of centralization with other structural properties. Image comparability, on the other hand, correlates as expected with dimensionality (mean $r = .19$).

Considering the three structural variables of dimensionality, centralization, and image comparability together, the following relationships may be inferred: Increasing dimensionality is accompanied by an increasing tendency to utilize all available cognitive attributes in appraising objects within the domain, but (as will be seen in Chapter 12) for most subjects, the proportion of available attributes which are used frequently is not large. As a consequence, increasing image comparability is often tantamount to increasing centralization. That is, most people tend to appraise objects either in concrete, object-specific terms or in terms of a small number of central attributes. It is rare for a person to take a truly abstract, multidimensional view of all objects within the domain, appraising them according to a standard, large set of independent attributes. Perhaps this result reflects the kinds of subjects and domains chosen for these studies: If philatelists had been asked about postage stamps, or professors of international relations about nations of the world, higher scores for image comparability might have emerged. The present samples of respondents evidently think about these four classes of objects in a fairly concrete, object-specific way, with little systematic comparison.

As predicted in the model, affective-evaluative consistency and affective balance are significantly correlated with each other, and both are negatively correlated with dimensionality. The tendency to display a balanced cognitive organization (seeing as similar objects that are similarly liked or similarly disliked) is associated with a tendency to judge all objects in accordance with one's affective reaction to them. Both tendencies are found most commonly within cognitive domains of low dimensional complexity.

RELATIONS AMONG PROPERTIES OF OBJECTS
(OBJECT-LEVEL ANALYSIS)

There are numerous ways to study relationships among the specified properties of cognitive objects. The possibilities can be traced in the schematic data matrix of Figure 10. The entries in this matrix (X_{ijk}) represent an object property score at time i, for subject j, on object k. The analyses to be presented here reflect association between different object properties (e.g., complexity and valence) across a row of the matrix, i.e., association within a subject, across objects, at one point in time. Such a correlation was computed for each subject, and the correlations were then averaged over the entire sample.

Another mode of analysis would be to consider each object separately—e.g., correlating the entries in the first column over the n subjects with entries in the first column of another data matrix, representing a different property (e.g., valence) of object 1 for the same n subjects. This mode of analysis was neglected here because it confounds intersubject differences in the intended attribute with other differences unintentionally measured by the instrument. A within-subjects correlation presumably avoids such a confounding—although it is substantially affected by the particular sample of objects chosen and might vary considerably from one object set to another.

Yet a third mode of analysis would result from correlating complexity and valence scores in the same object over time. Thus entries X_{111}, X_{211}, X_{311},

Time 1

	Object						
Subject	1	2	3	.	.	.	m
1	X_{111}	X_{112}	X_{113}				X_{11m}
2	X_{121}	X_{122}	X_{123}				X_{12m}
3	X_{131}	X_{132}	X_{133}				X_{13m}
4	X_{141}	X_{142}	X_{143}				X_{14m}
.							
.							
.							
n	X_{1n1}	X_{1n2}	X_{1n3}				X_{1nm}

Time 2

1	X_{211}	X_{212}	X_{213}				X_{21m}
2	X_{221}	X_{222}	X_{223}				X_{22m}
3	X_{231}	X_{232}	X_{233}				X_{23m}
4	X_{241}	X_{242}	X_{243}				X_{24m}
.							
.							
.							
n	X_{2n1}	X_{2n2}	X_{2n3}				X_{2nm}

.
.
.

Time p

Fig. 10. Data matrix of object scores (X_{ijk}).

X_{411} (not shown) would be correlated with entries $Y_{111}, Y_{211}, Y_{311}, Y_{411}$ from some other extended data matrix representing object valences. Such analyses were not possible in our studies, but they would provide, in some cases, particularly appropriate tests of the underlying rationales.

The results presented in Table 21 are averages (arithmetic means) of all within-subjects correlations computed among the properties of objects defined in Chapter 5. The mean correlations are very stable; each is based on two to four instruments (containing different samples of objects) and three different samples of subjects.

The results do not support the sole hypothesis advanced in Chapter 5 about relations among properties of cognitive objects, that object complexity would be positively associated with ambivalence. Instead, the mean correlation between these two object properties was significantly negative; only 6 of the 24 correlations on which the mean is based were positive. Assuming that a

Table 21. Mean Within-Subjects Correlations Among Properties of Objects (Numbers of correlations and standard deviation of correlations in parentheses)

Property	Complexity	Affect	Liking	Evaluation
Affect	.21* (36: .11)			
Liking	.21* (36: .11)	.28* (48: .27)		
Evaluation	.12* (24: .09)	.10 (24: .20)	.63* (24: .12)	
Ambivalence	−.10* (24: .12)	−.28* (36: .11)	−.21* (36: .15)	−.29* (24: .17)

*Mean correlations were based on correlations computed from a variable number of instruments, within four cognitive domains in three samples. Starred mean correlations are at least three times their standard errors estimated from the numbers of correlations indicated.

within-subjects, across-objects analysis is appropriate for testing this hypothesis, we must conclude that the reasoning on which it is based is erroneous. Before modifying that portion of the theory, however, the results of the domain level analysis must be considered.

The positive correlation of affect with liking reflects the fact that the samples of objects rated were, on the whole, favorably regarded by these respondents. Exceptions to this general trend occurred within the domain of family. Even within this domain, however, correlations from the *List and Compare* instruments were positive, indicating that when subjects generated their own lists of important family activities, the most extreme affect tended to be directed toward liked, rather than disliked, activities. Thus, it is safe to infer that, among these respondents, extreme affect tends to be favorable affect.

Complexity of an object was positively correlated with the three measures of affect and object valence. Liking and evaluation were, of course, substantially correlated, and all three measures were negatively correlated with ambivalence. It is apparent that better known objects tend to be better liked. This was less true for nations than for the other three types of objects. The mean correlation within the domain of nations was only .08, in contrast to the mean of .25 for all other domains combined. Also, less ambivalence was expressed, on the average, toward liked than toward disliked objects. These results require a different interpretation from that originally anticipated. Instead of increasing information leading from univalence to ambivalence, it appears that initially ambivalent attitudes toward little known objects come, with increasing information, to be replaced by more favorable and univalent attitudes. Perhaps the effect is circular, in that one tends to acquire more information about liked objects, and to filter it in such a way as to produce ever-increasing univalence. All such interpretations require, for clear verification, longitudinal analyses over different stages of acquaintance with objects. Meanwhile, our cross-sectional analyses suggest that having more elaborate views about objects tends to be associated with increasingly univalent liking for them.

RELATIONS AMONG PROPERTIES OF ATTRIBUTES
(ATTRIBUTE-LEVEL ANALYSIS)

Table 22 presents attribute-level analyses of relations among properties of attributes. Correlations are presented separately for the different domains, since little consistency appeared across domains. In the right-hand column appear mean within-subjects correlations between centrality and precision,

Table 22. Mean Intercorrelations Among Properties of Attributes

Property and domain	Ordinality[a]	Evaluation[ab]	Centrality[cd]
Evaluation[ab]			
Acquaintances	.49*		
Family	−.10		
Nations	.47*		
Self	−.10		
Centrality[cd]			
Acquaintances	.27*	.37*	
Family	.10	.12*	
Nations	−.04	−.01	
Self	−.07*	.28*	
Precision[d]			
Acquaintances	−	.12*	.30*
Family	−	.11	.34*
Nations	−	.21	.37*
Self	−	−.05	.36*

[a]Judged (as a dichotomous variable) from codes for *Free Description* and *Free Comparison* instruments.

[b]Judged (as a dichotomous variable) for attributes on *Grouping* instruments. Means are computed over varying numbers of correlations—3, 6, or 9—depending on the number of instruments which the two properties had in common.

[c]Scored from subjects' responses to *Free Description* and *Free Comparison* instruments.

[d]Scored from subjects' responses to *Grouping* instruments. Correlations were computed over attributes within each subject, then averaged over subjects.

*Mean correlation is at least 3 times its standard error (estimated from standard deviation of correlations).

computed over sets of 10 attributes included on *Grouping of Objects* within each domain and sample. The ordinality and evaluation of attributes included on the *Grouping, Free Description*, and *Free Comparison* instruments were treated as a priori, dichotomous variables, and therefore no within-subject analysis was possible. Instead, these a priori values were correlated with the mean centrality and precision scores obtained from respondents in each sample for each cognitive domain. These mean point-biserial correlations (averaged across samples) are also reported in Table 22.

The only significant relations which appeared in all cognitive domains (and in all three samples) were between centrality and precision. Although these results come from a single instrument (*Grouping* of objects), they confirm the prediction developed in Chapter 5 that attributes most useful for describing objects are those which permit the finest degrees of discrimination. Partial confirmation of the predicted relation between attribute evaluation and centrality appears in the significant mean correlations found in three cognitive domains. The single exception occurs within the domain of nations, and may reflect a peculiar characteristic of that domain, or at least of the manner in which our samples viewed it. Many of its most widely learned attributes—such as topography, climate, ethnicity, and religion—are nonevaluative, yet susceptible to very fine subdivisions. In the other three cognitive domains, we found the expected result that evaluative attributes tend to be more central than neutral attributes.

One of the remaining three predictions about inter-attribute relationships (that ordinality and precision would be positively associated) could not be tested on the present data, and the other two predictions yielded generally nonsignificant results. Ordinality and centrality were not consistently related. There was only one significant mean correlation between evaluation and precision, and it was in the direction opposite to prediction.

RELATIONS AMONG STRUCTURAL PROPERTIES AND PROPERTIES OF COGNITIVE ELEMENTS

In this section we examine the formal properties of cognitive elements as they apply to an entire domain. For this domain-level analysis we have averaged scores for an object property over all objects in the domain to yield a single score for a respondent—for instance, mean ambivalence toward objects in the domain. Similarly, we have averaged attribute properties over all attributes in the domain to yield, for example, a mean score on attribute precision. This mode of analysis ignores differences among objects and among attributes.

The domain-level analysis of the formal properties of cognitive elements yields scores comparable to the structural properties, in that there is one score for each subject for each domain. With these domain scores, it is thus possible to test predictions about relations of object and attribute properties to each other and to the structural properties. Furthermore, the relations among

Table 23. Mean Intercorrelations Among Properties of Objects, Attributes, and Structural Properties (standard deviations of correlations in parentheses; mean reliabilities in diagonal brackets)

Property	Mean object complexity	Mean affect	Mean object liking	Mean object evaluation	Mean object ambivalence	Use of ordinal attributes	Mean attribute precision
Mean object complexity	.67 [.07]						
Mean affect	.21* (.10)	.76 [.09]					
Mean object liking	.03 (.13)	.33* (.19)	.78 [.08]				
Mean object evaluation	.01 (.11)	.20* (.14)	.61* (.12)	.55 [.14]			
Mean object ambivalence	.19* (.17)	−.17 (.20)	−.23* (.25)	−.35* (.23)	.49 [.10]		
Use of ordinal attributes	.16 (.20)	.07 (.11)	−.01 (.14)	.00 (.13)	−.01 (.18)	.41 [.23]	
Mean attribute precision	.21* (.12)	.09* (.09)	−.08 (.12)	−.14* (.15)	.05 (.13)	−.11* (.11)	.33 [.13]
Evaluative centrality	.18* (.16)	.60* (.11)	.24* (.20)	.17* (.17)	−.19 (.24)	.07 (.11)	.07 (.16)
Image comparability	.46* (.15)	.16* (.08)	.03 (.16)	.01 (.12)	.09 (.16)	.14 (.17)	.13* (.09)
Centralization	.21* (.10)	.12* (.07)	.04 (.09)	.06 (.10)	.01 (.09)	.07 (.12)	.05 (.10)
Affective-evaluative consistency	−.04 (.17)	.13* (.14)	.02 (.24)	.04 (.16)	−.27* (.15)	.07 (.08)	.11* (.11)
Affective balance	−.11 (.14)	.15* (.12)	.05 (.16)	.04 (.16)	−.20* (.14)	.07 (.14)	.10* (.09)
Dimensionality	.38* (.16)	.00 (.09)	−.06 (.14)	−.10* (.11)	.28* (.10)	.06 (.13)	.23* (.11)

Note. Table entries represent means and standard deviations of 12 correlations (3 samples × 4 cognitive domains). These are based on multitrait-multimethod correlations (see p. 143) from which the spurious component due to identical instruments has been removed. Right-hand continuation appears in Table 20. An asterisk signifies that the mean correlation is at least three times its standard error (estimated from the standard deviation of correlations). Reliabilities are estimated from Cronbach's (1951) coefficient alpha.

object properties and among attribute properties which have been considered at the level of individual elements can also be examined at the domain level. It must be noted, however, that the meaning of domain-level scores is rather different from that of object- or attribute-level scores. Relations that apply at the level of individual objects or attributes may not hold at the domain level, where the variables provide characterizations of people in terms of the types of images they tend to form or the manner in which they tend to use attributes. The characteristics of a single image which a person holds tell no more about the person than about the object conceived, but generalizing across a series of images is informative about the manner in which that particular individual tends to view the world.

The results of the domain-level analyses are summarized in Table 23, which presents mean correlations computed within each of four cognitive domains for each of three samples (see p. 113), together with their standard deviations. When these mean correlations are at least three times their estimated standard errors $(s_r / \sqrt{12})$, we will judge them significantly different from zero.

Object Complexity

Considering first the predicted relationship between mean object complexity and mean object ambivalence, we find that this prediction is confirmed at the domain level, though generally opposite results obtained for the object-level analyses of Table 21. People who hold complex views of objects within a particular domain tend to appraise those objects more ambivalently than do people who hold simple views of the objects. This relationship depends on differences among people, rather than on differing reactions of the same person to better-known and less-known objects. People who are well informed about a particular class of objects, in that they offer lengthy descriptions of the objects, also tend to evaluate those objects, as a group, in a complex way. The more an individual has to say about any particular object, however, the more likely he or she is to feel univalently positive about it. If this finding is not an artifact of the particular measures employed, it suggests that individual differences in ambivalence are based on different processes than are inter-object differences in ambivalence for any particular person. We shall return to this problem in the final chapter.

Of the three relationships between mean object complexity and structural properties hypothesized in Chapter 5, one was confirmed by the present data while two were not. The predicted negative relationships of complexity to balance and to affective-evaluative consistency were both nonsignificant by the criterion chosen.

As predicted, the more complex people's views of objects within a domain, the more likely they are to hold a multidimensional conception of it. A large amount of information about objects is generally associated with a complex perspective, which includes many distinct attributes for appraising them. It is noteworthy also that mean object complexity is correlated with mean attribute precision and that both are correlated with dimensionality. These three aspects of differentiation—an elaborate view of objects, many distinct attributes for viewing them, and precisely articulated attributes that permit fine distinctions—all tend to be found together in a particular cognitive domain. Thus, cognitive differentiation tends to be consistently displayed in various ways and with regard to different types of objects. It will be noted later, however, that dimensionality and attribute precision correlate differently with some other cognitive variables.

Object complexity correlates substantially with image comparability, the tendency to use a large number of common attributes in appraising a class of objects. It is clear from these results that when objects of a domain are profusely described, this tends to be done repeatedly with the same set of attributes.

The unexpected correlation between object complexity and evaluative centrality suggests that use of evaluative attributes is associated with complex views of objects, even though the perspective may not be multidimensional (see Table 20). Again, it must be noted that this result is perhaps attributable to our particular respondents. For subjects displaying their cognitions about a domain in which they have expert knowledge, such a correlation might not be observed.

Object Valence

Liking and evaluation, the two measures of mean directional valence, were highly correlated, and both were significantly correlated with nondirectional affect (mean extremity of object ratings). In some respects, these three variables showed similar correlates—negative association with mean object ambivalence and positive association with evaluative centrality. In other respects, however, their patterns of correlation were quite different. Affective extremity was positively correlated (as predicted, p. 72) with centralization, affective balance, and affective-evaluative consistency, while mean object liking and mean object evaluation were not. In addition, affect was positively correlated with mean attribute precision and image comparability, while mean object evaluation was negatively correlated with mean attribute precision.

This pattern of results indicates that extreme affect is more commonly associated with extreme liking and favorable evaluation than with extreme dislike and unfavorable evaluation. The result may depend on the particular samples of objects presented, but it is more likely attributable to a general Pollyanna set within the cultures studied: People tend to express their positive feelings more openly and strongly than their negative feelings (see Boucher & Osgood, 1969; Johnson, 1966).

The differing correlates of directional valence and nondirectional affect suggest that strength of feeling has implications for cognitive processes that simple liking for objects does not. Balanced cognitive states and evaluatively consistent views of objects tend to be found not just when objects are liked, but when feelings are strong in either direction. The correlation of mean affect with centralization was predicted on the ground that domination of images by a single attribute is most likely to occur when the attribute is evaluative. The unexpected finding that mean affect also correlates with image comparability can be explained, with hindsight, by the recognition that image comparability itself was positively correlated with centralization, due to the low range of image comparability scores obtained in these samples.

The correlation between affect and mean attribute precision was also unexpected. One possible interpretation of this finding would be that this kind of differentiation is facilitated by sufficient involvement in the domain to generate extreme affect.

Object Ambivalence

Turning next to correlates of mean object ambivalence, we have already noted that this property is positively correlated with the mean level of object complexity, and negatively correlated with mean object liking and evaluation. Additionally, as predicted from the structural model (p. 74), mean object ambivalence shows a positive correlation with dimensionality, and negative correlations with affective balance and affective-evaluative consistency.

Attribute Precision

We have no good test of the predicted relation between attribute ordinality and precision (see p. 71) because the available measures of precision were all taken on ordinal attributes. Nevertheless, the data of Table 23 do offer an indirect test of this expectation in that people who make greater use of ordinal attributes show greater precision in employing them. The relationship is very small, however (even though significant by the present criterion), and should perhaps not be emphasized.

A positive relation between mean attribute precision and image comparability was predicted on the ground that attributes with many categories most readily accommodate new objects. This prediction was supported. In addition, mean attribute precision was positively correlated with affective balance and affective-evaluative consistency. This is quite a different pattern of correlates than that obtained for dimensionality (Table 20), even though dimensionality and mean attribute precision are positively correlated.

Our results indicate that the various modes of cognitive differentiation—object complexity, attribute precision, and dimensional complexity—have different implications for other structural properties. While all three modes are associated with image comparability, only object complexity is associated with centralization. Although attribute precision is positively correlated with affective balance and affective-evaluative consistency, dimensionality is negatively correlated with these modes of cognitive integration. It is not enough to ascertain that cognitive objects are elaborated and differentiated; one must also know how this is accomplished in order to appreciate the implications for cognitive organization. When object differentiation occurs by subdividing a small number of attributes into refined categories, the accompanying cognitive organization is likely to be affectively dominated. When differentiation occurs though gross distinctions made on a large number of independent attributes, the accompanying cognitive organization shows greater distinction between liking for objects and judgments made about them.

Figure 11 summarizes the joint relationship of dimensionality and precision to affective balance. A very similar picture appears for affective-evaluative consistency. The highest levels of affective balance and affective-evaluative consistency are ˙found when dimensionality is low but precision is high. Conversely, the lowest levels of affective balance and affective-evaluative consistency occur under conditions of high dimensionality and low precision. This relationship obtains within each of the three samples and within each of the four cognitive domains.

SUMMARY

A summary of the major findings concerning relations among properties of objects, attributes, and cognitive structure appears in Table 24, which is

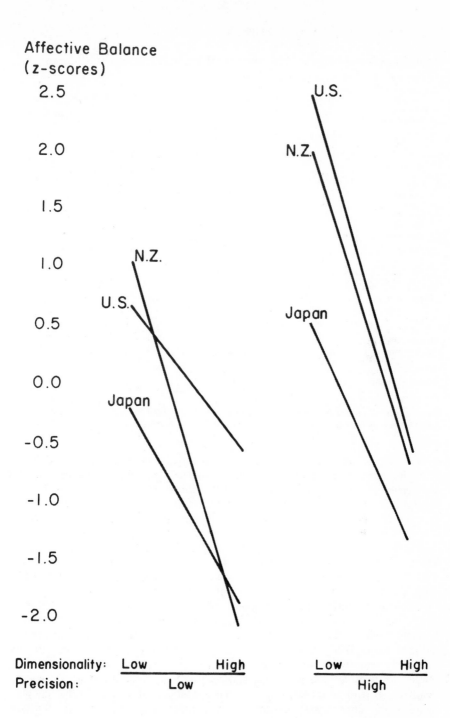

Fig. 11. Joint relation of dimensionality and precision to affective balance.

Table 24. Obtained Intercorrelations Among Variable Properties

	1	2a	2b	2c	3	4	5	6	7	8	9	10	12	13
Object properties														
1. Complexity														
2. Valence:														
a. Affect	+ (+)													
b. Liking	(+)	+ (+)												
c. Evaluation	(+)	+	+											
3. Ambivalence	+ (−)	(−)	− (−)	− (−)										
Attribute properties														
4. Ordinality														
5. Evaluation	+	Def	+	+										
6. Centrality	+	+					+ (+)							
7. Precision	+	+		−		+		+ (+)						
Structural properties														
8. Evaluative centrality	+	Def	+	+			Def	+						
9. Image comparability	+	+					+	Def	+	+				
10. Centralization	+	+					+	+			+			
12. Affective-evalua- tive consistency		+			−		+		+	+				
13. Affective balance		+			−		+		+	+			+	
14. Dimensionality	+			−		+		+	+		+		−	−

Note. Variable 11 (from Table 5) is omitted because no measure of dissonance was included in this study. Parenthesized signs refer to within-subjects correlations (over objects or attributes). Other signs refer to between-subjects correlations (referring to structural properties, mean object properties, or mean attribute properties). When signs are absent, the obtained relationship did not differ significantly from zero.

constructed to parallel the theoretical predictions displayed in Table 5 (p. 70). For the most part, predictions made from the structural model have been confirmed in this study of four cognitive domains in three cultures. Major exceptions occur with respect to relations among properties of attributes. A number of results not predicted by the model are also summarized in Table 24.

There are positive correlations among mean object complexity, mean attribute precision, dimensionality, and image comparability. These variables may be considered as aspects of cognitive differentiation, which is associated with a systematic, abstract view of objects in the domain.

Though dimensionality is positively correlated with mean object ambivalence, mean attribute precision and image comparability are not. Furthermore, though mean object complexity is correlated with mean ambivalence across subjects, complexity and ambivalence of particular objects tend to be negatively correlated within any particular subject. The interpretation we suggest is twofold: (1) that increasing elaboration of the image of an object tends to go with an increasingly univalent evaluation of it, but (2) that people with large dimensional capacity tend, more than others, to express ambivalence toward all objects in the domain.

Affective balance and affective-evaluative consistency are closely related ways of organizing cognitive objects. Both properties tend to be associated with a high level of evaluative centrality—i.e., with a tendency to view objects in affective terms. Both styles of cognitive organization are positively correlated with mean attribute precision, negatively correlated with dimensionality, negatively correlated with mean object ambivalence, and not consistently correlated with mean object complexity. In other words, precision and dimensionality, two different ways of distinguishing among objects, have different implications for affective organization: Precise distinction within each attribute of a small set is associated with balance and affective consistency, whereas crude distinction within each attribute of a larger set is associated with a more emotion-free, nonevaluative appraisal of objects.

Centralization and image comparability are positively correlated in the present samples. This result suggests that, to the extent the basis for object appraisal is abstract, rather than concrete and object-specific, images will be composed of a limited number of attributes, used repeatedly. Both modes of cognitive organization tend to be found where images are complex and affect-dominated, but they differ in that image comparability is positively correlated with mean dimensionality and mean attribute precision, while centralization is not.

Our information about relations among properties of attributes is quite scanty but suggests that ordinality and centrality are unrelated: The attributes on which people most rely are just as likely to be nominal as ordinal. Evaluation and centrality tend to be positively correlated, both within and between persons: Evaluative attributes are more likely to be used extensively than neutral attributes, and people who use evaluative attributes more than average show higher levels of image comparability. Within subjects, precisely subdivided attributes are more likely than crudely categorized attributes to be used frequently in describing objects, and subjects with generally high levels of image comparability also tend to display fine distinctions on all attributes.

For the samples of objects studied here—and these were quite extensive and representative of their respective domains—there was a positive correlation between extremity and favorability of affect, both within and between subjects. These respondents tended to feel more strongly about the objects they liked than about those they disliked. This association between direction and extremity was not, however, a factor in relations with the structural properties, for it was generally extremity of affect, rather than direction, that was correlated with such structural properties as affective balance, affective-evaluative consistency, image comparability, and centralization.

Chapter 12

MEAN STRUCTURAL SCORES AND DIFFERENCES AMONG COGNITIVE DOMAINS

In this chapter, two rather different questions are considered. First, to what degree was the goal of fundamental measurement achieved? Second, did mean scores differ between domains in ways that might reasonably be expected? The data with which these questions were answered came from samples *a* through *e* described on p. 113.

UNITS OF MEASUREMENT

A number of our structural properties were defined with units of measurement which were interpretable independently of the various instruments by which they were assessed. If we were successful in defining and operationalizing these properties, then the scores yielded by different measures of the same property should be approximately the same. It is somewhat difficult to decide just what degree of similarity is satisfactory, since properties with upper and lower limits, such as ambivalence, probably demand different criteria than those with only lower limits, such as dimensionality. Nevertheless, it is our sense, based on the data to be reviewed below, that the objective of fundamental measurement has been occasionally approached but certainly not achieved.

The index of dimensionality, D, varied substantially over the three instruments from which it was assessed: The mean score from *Rating* instruments was 2.0, from *Grouping* instruments 2.5, and from *Checklist* instruments 6.3. A comparable index, *H*, computed from *List and Compare* instruments had a mean of 2.87. If one were to interpret these scores in the absolute sense intended—as the number of dimensions-worth of information yielded by the respondent's cognitive display—one would have to conclude that dimensionality depends mainly on the kind of display required. This is not a satisfactory state of affairs if one aspires to measures that are invariant over instruments.

A similar circumstance obtains for the indices of attribute precision, which were intended to represent the number of categories-worth of distinctions displayed by the subject. The mean index, *P*, from the *Rating* instruments was 3.1, while the mean number of groups formed on the *Grouping* instruments was 2.4.

Substantially better results were obtained for measures of evaluative centrality and ambivalence. It will be recalled that the index of evaluative centrality was intended to represent the respondent's relative preference for evaluative over neutral attributes, also conceived as the mean centrality of evaluative attributes relative to the centrality of neutral attributes. Mean indices were .54, .50, and .48 for *Free Description*, *Checklist Description*, and *Rating* instruments, respectively, which suggests that their scales of measurement are roughly comparable. More persuasive data come from the mean scores computed within each domain for each of the three samples. These show an intra-class correlation of .46, indicating substantial agreement among the three instruments in displaying means for the 12 occasions (4 domains, 3 samples each). By contrast, the intra-class correlation attributable to instruments was −.79, indicating that there were no consistent differences among instruments in mean scores on this variable.

Mean scores on ambivalence were .32, .31, and .30 from *Free Description*, *Checklist Description*, and *Rating* instruments, respectively. The intra-class correlation reflecting the consistency with which mean ambivalence scores are measured within the 12 sample-domain instances is .40; the intra-class correlation reflecting the magnitude of instrument effects is .53. Thus, there is some main effect of instrument on the ambivalence scores obtained, but these still show substantial consistency for a particular domain and sample of respondents.

Measures of affective balance were substantially affected by the particular instrument used. The three instruments which required subjects to construct groups (*List and Compare*, *Grouping*, and *Constructing Sets*) yielded balance scores which averaged around zero, while the two instruments which asked subjects explicitly to consider the similarities of listed objects (*Similarity of Paired Objects* and *Most Similar Pairs*) yielded mean balance scores around .30. Although the intra-class correlations computed between pairs of similar instruments were .71 and .51, their metrics were so discrepant as to yield a combined intra-class correlation of −.71. From these results one would infer that the two different approaches to measuring cognitive balance need to be reconciled before a preferred index can be selected. It is quite possible that the discrepancies between these measures resulted from calling subjects' attention to their organizational principles in the *Similarity of Paired Objects* and *Most Similar Pairs*, a procedure which might be expected to increase tendencies toward balanced cognitions.

Affective-evaluative consistency scores from the four instruments showed means varying between .51 and .70. The four instruments measuring centralization yielded means ranging from .33 to .43. The six instruments measuring image comparability yielded mean scores from .08 to .61. Within the last set similar instruments yielded similar scores, but the free-response and checklist instruments were quite discrepant, and both of these scores were substantially lower than those computed from *Grouping* and from *List and Compare* instruments.

The conclusion from these analyses is that, except for evaluative centrality and ambivalence, we do not yet have satisfactory metrics for representing the variables in any absolute sense. One can only resort to the familiar device of conversion to standard scores in constructing composite indices. This we have done throughout the following analyses (as well as those in the other chapters).

DIFFERENCES AMONG DOMAINS

The object domains were chosen with a view toward eliciting a wide range of cognitive content, from nations to role relationships. This was done for two reasons: to assure that the structural variables and measures were applicable to various kinds of objects and to permit some exploration of inter-domain differences in structural properties. It was expected, for example, that cognitive domains acquired in a formal, didactic way would be organized more abstractly, and less emotionally than domains acquired through direct personal experience, without any explicit teaching. Nations constitute an example of a remote domain acquired didactically. Family relationships and self-roles are examples of domains acquired through direct experience, which are less likely to be verbally described in abstract terminology. Acquaintances constitute a domain of intermediate concreteness. Although one experiences people directly, rather than through abstract words, one tends—especially if one is a psychology student, as our subjects were—to apply some abstract standards of comparison simply because people are frequently, often simultaneously, confronted.

Thus, two experimental variables are posited as hypothetical bases for differences in cognitive organization: immediacy (vs. remoteness) of the object domain and availability of the objects for simultaneous comparison. It is proposed that the more remote a domain from everyday experience, the more likely it is to be acquired in abstract language, which imposes a culturally common structure that is fairly complex and systematic. Conversely, the closer the objects are to personal experience, the more the learning process is idiosyncratic, and the more the domain is emotion-laden and significant to the self. Also, it is proposed that when objects are experienced or contemplated

Table 25. Mean Scores on Properties of Objects, Attributes, and Cognitive Structure

Property		Domain				Mean
		Acquaintances	*Family*	*Nations*	*Self*	
Object complexity	U.S.	5.98_a	4.32_e	5.10_{bc}	4.49_{cd}	4.97
	Japan	4.40_{de}	3.90_f	5.20_{bc}	4.72_{cd}	4.56
	N.Z.	5.48_b	2.93_g	5.64_a	4.35_d	4.60
Mean		5.29_{st}	3.72_u	5.31_s	4.52_t	4.71
Dimensionality	U.S.	3.67_a	3.13_{de}	3.50_b	3.50_b	3.45
	Japan	3.28_c	3.21_{cd}	3.40_b	3.34_{bc}	3.32
	N.Z.	3.75_a	3.07_e	3.73_a	3.48_b	3.51
Mean		3.57_s	3.14_t	3.54_s	3.44_s	3.42
Attribute precision	U.S.	2.83_{bc}	2.76_{bc}	2.71_c	2.57_d	2.72_y
	Japan	2.84_{bc}	2.72_c	2.72_c	2.49_d	2.69_y
	N.Z.	3.02_a	2.82_{bc}	2.93_{ab}	2.81_{bc}	2.90_x
Mean		2.90_s	2.77_s	2.79_s	2.62_t	2.77
Evaluative centrality	U.S.	$.62_a$	$.49_d$	$.50_{cd}$	$.55_b$	$.54_x$
	Japan	$.51_c$	$.42_e$	$.43_e$	$.45_e$	$.45_y$
	N.Z.	$.62_a$	$.46_e$	$.52_c$	$.52_c$	$.53_x$
Mean		$.58_s$	$.45_u$	$.49_t$	$.51_t$	.51
Object valence (affect)	U.S.	1.94_a	1.64_c	1.35_d	1.61_c	1.64_x
	Japan	1.42_d	1.36_d	1.07_e	1.15_e	1.25_y
	N.Z.	1.80_b	1.57_c	1.35_d	1.59_c	1.58_x
Mean		1.72_s	1.52_t	1.26_u	1.45_t	1.49
Object liking	U.S.	5.28_a	4.29_f	4.46_{de}	4.97_b	4.75_x
	Japan	4.63_c	3.97_g	4.34_{ef}	4.32_{ef}	4.32_y
	N.Z.	5.26_a	4.30_f	4.52_{cd}	4.97_b	4.76_x
Mean		5.06_s	4.19_u	4.44_t	4.75_t	4.61
Object evaluation	U.S.	$.43_{bc}$	$.27_{de}$	$-.03_g$	$.71_a$	.35
	Japan	$.40_{bc}$	$.28_{de}$	$.27_{de}$	$.37_{cd}$	.33
	N.Z.	$.52_{ab}$	$.30_{cd}$	$.11_e$	$.72_a$	.41
Mean		$.45_s$	$.28_t$	$.12_u$	$.60_s$	.36
Object ambivalence	U.S.	$.27_f$	$.28_{ef}$	$.33_c$	$.29_{def}$	$.29_y$
	Japan	$.29_{def}$	$.31_{cde}$	$.36_b$	$.32_{cd}$	$.32_x$
	N.Z.	$.27_f$	$.31_{cde}$	$.39_a$	$.30_{def}$	$.32_{xy}$
Mean		$.28_t$	$.30_t$	$.36_s$	$.30_t$	.31
Affective balance	U.S.	$.19_{bc}$	$.29_a$	$.04_{fg}$	$.15_{cd}$	$.17_x$
	Japan	$.11_{cde}$	$.22_b$	$-.04_h$	$.07_{ef}$	$.09_y$
	N.Z.	$.09_{def}$	$.30_a$	$.02_g$	$.16_{bc}$	$.14_{xy}$
Mean		$.13_t$	$.27_s$	$.01_u$	$.13_t$	.13

Table 25. (contd)

Property		Domain				Mean
		Acquaintances	*Family*	*Nations*	*Self*	
Affective	U.S.	$.70_a$	$.71_a$	$.70_a$	$.63_{bc}$	$.69_x$
evaluative	Japan	$.63_{bc}$	$.62_{bc}$	$.55_d$	$.51_d$	$.58_y$
consistency	N.Z.	$.65_{ab}$	$.66_{ab}$	$.60_c$	$.55_d$	$.62_y$
Mean		$.66_{st}$	$.66_s$	$.62_t$	$.56_u$	$.63$
Image	U.S.	$.24_a$	$.20_c$	$.23_{ab}$	$.19_{cd}$	$.22_x$
comparability	Japan	$.18_d$	$.10_e$	$.20_c$	$.17_d$	$.16_y$
	N.Z.	$.22_{ab}$	$.17_d$	$.21_{bc}$	$.19_{cd}$	$.20_x$
Mean		$.21_s$	$.16_t$	$.21_s$	$.18_t$	$.19$
Centralization	U.S.	$.43_a$	$.41_{ab}$	$.42_{ab}$	$.38_{bc}$	$.41_x$
	Japan	$.34_d$	$.36_{cd}$	$.40_{ab}$	$.35_{cd}$	$.36_y$
	N.Z.	$.41_{ab}$	$.39_{bc}$	$.43_a$	$.36_{cd}$	$.40_x$
Mean		$.39_{stu}$	$.39_t$	$.42_s$	$.36_u$	$.39$

Note. Composite scores were computed by weighting a particular measure of a property inversely proportional to its average standard deviation (computed over all domains and all samples), adding these weighted scores, and dividing by the sum of weights. Within each subtable the subscripts a through h are used to indicate significant differences among cell means. If two cells have a subscript letter in common, their means are *not* significantly different, at $p < .05$, by the Newman-Keuls test (Winer, 1971, p. 191). The subscripts s through u are similarly used to indicate significant differences among domain means (pooling the three samples), based on the Newman-Keuls test and, additionally, on consistent directions of difference within all three samples. The subscripts x and y are similarly used to indicate significant differences among sample means (pooling all four domains), based on the Newman-Keuls test and, additionally, on consistent directions of difference within all four domains.

simultaneously, standards of appraisal are developed to facilitate abstract comparison among them. Conversely, when objects are experienced successively and no demands for inter-object comparison are imposed, one tends to comprehend them in a more concrete manner.

The sample of domains available is far too small to represent adequately even one of these hypothetically determining variables. Any differences among domains may well be attributable to characteristics quite different from those proposed. Therefore, these analyses must be considered suggestive, rather than definitive. In order to avoid seduction by chance findings, we shall confine our interpretations to inter-domain differences that appear consistently in all three samples. For the same reason, we have chosen a conservative, a posteriori test of significance, the Newman-Keuls test (Winer, 1971, p. 191), even though many of the differences could be anticipated a priori.

Table 25 reports all mean scores for the four cognitive domains from each sample as well as composite means for each domain and for each sample. All components of a score are equally weighted (as standard scores) in the composite, but a sense of the metric is preserved by averaging the raw-score means, rather than converting them to zero, in the standard-score transformation.

Differentiation

One can readily see that the four domains differ in the degree of cognitive elaboration, with nations typically described more fully than the self, and these two domains, as well as acquaintances, generally described more fully than family relationships. These differences appeared in all three samples. It may be noteworthy that nations are especially elaborated in New Zealand, where students typically learn a great deal of world geography and history; acquaintances are especially elaborated in the U.S. sample (from a university long noted for its emphasis on interpersonal relations); and family relationships are *least* elaborated in New Zealand, where joint parent-child activities are uncommon.

The patterns of inter-domain difference displayed for dimensionality and attribute precision may be seen as complementary in generating the differences in object complexity just reported. Family relationships show the lowest level of dimensionality in all three samples, while the domain of self shows the least precise articulation of attributes. Nations and acquaintances are moderate to high on both these variables. Although the measures were not constructed to assure this interpretation, one might view object complexity as a joint function of dimensionality and attribute precision, as the two latter variables together predict object complexity better than either of them alone. The most highly elaborated cognitive domains tend to be those for which dimensionality and attribute precision are both high.

Affective Variables

The domain of acquaintances is the most affect-laden of the four domains studied here. These objects tend to be best liked and to have the most extreme affect expressed toward them, especially in the U.S. sample. The self tends to rank second in these respects, while family and nations alternate in third place. The exceptionally low level of liking accorded to family relationships by Japanese respondents may reflect a society-wide intergenerational conflict. The average liking for all family activities is approximately at the mean (neutral point) of the rating scale, which implies a relatively large number of distasteful family contacts for these Japanese subjects.

Of the four domains, only nations show a consistently elevated level of ambivalence, especially in the New Zealand sample. Even this level is not high in absolute terms (mean Am = .36); it appears to reflect detachment from, rather than emotional involvement in, the objects, for the mean nondirectional affect score for nations is lowest of the four domains.

Integrative Styles

Two of the integrative styles may be regarded as affect-dominated: balance and affective-evaluative consistency. Family relationships show the highest mean level of affective balance, while family and acquaintances are tied for first rank in affective-evaluative consistency. The domain of nations has the lowest mean level of affective balance, while the domain of self has the lowest mean level of affective-evaluative consistency.

The other two integrative styles, image comparability and centralization, were intended to differ from the first two in relying on abstract cognitive (informational) standards of appraisal, rather than on liking for the objects. Repeated use of the same attributes for describing objects was interpreted as reflecting a concern for abstract qualities which might be sought in all objects of the domain. Additionally, centralization and image comparability were intended to reflect different degrees of stereotypy applied to this abstract judgment. Centralization implies repeated use of a single attribute, while image comparability implies repeated use of a large number of attributes. However, the mean image comparability score was just .08 for the *Free Description* instruments and only .27 for the *Checklist Descriptions*, implying that the subjects typically employed any given attribute for only a small minority of their object-descriptions. There were very few high scores on these instruments, with the result that relatively "high" image comparability within the present range reflected considerably more stereotypy of attribute use than might be the case for more sophisticated respondents. The highest mean levels of image comparability were found within the domains of nations and acquaintances. The highest mean level of centralization appeared in the domain of nations, and the lowest level in the domain of self.

Putting together this fragmentary information from just four cognitive domains, we may say that our expectations concerning inter-domain differences in integrative styles were generally confirmed. The most abstractly organized domains (nations and acquaintances) are those for which the objects are often experienced simultaneously, either directly or symbolically. The least abstractly organized domains (self-roles and family relationships) are those that are experienced consecutively, and are rarely brought in reflection to simultaneous comparison.

The most affectively balanced domain is that of family relationships, which are typically acquired in a direct, unverbalized, affect-laden way. The least affectively balanced domain (nations) is almost never experienced by these subjects in a direct self-relevant way, and many of the attributes acquired at a distance are affectively neutral in tone. These considerations also apply substantially to inter-domain differences in affective-evaluative consistency, but they do not explain the low levels found for the domain of self-roles. It is possible that, for these psychology students, the self was once organized in a predominantly affective way, but that a more detached view is being acquired—a view which has not yet, however, resulted in very abstract dimensions of appraisal.

DIFFERENCES AMONG SAMPLES

It 'may be noted from Table 25 that there were certain consistent differences among the three samples which appeared in all four cognitive domains. For example, the Japanese students tended to display lower levels of object liking and lower levels of affect, image comparability, and centralization than did American and New Zealand subjects. Although these might reflect differences in nationwide cognitive styles, we hestitate to interpret them in these terms without further information. The three samples of students were chosen in such different ways that we cannot even be confident that they reflect equivalently their own university populations. This lack of standardization is not particularly critical for interpreting inter-domain differences, for these were treated as dependable only when they appeared consistently within all three samples. A comparable consistency among domains does not lend the same assurance to inter-sample differences, for these could all result from the same variation in sampling procedures combined with individual consistencies in style across domains. When a particular inter-domain difference has been exaggerated in one of the samples, we have noted it, but the result should be treated more as an anecdote than as a dependable conclusion.

SUMMARY

Although the several measures of each property show reasonable degrees of intercorrelation, they are not necessarily scaled with a common unit of measurement. The only properties for which fairly dependable units have been demonstrated are evaluative centrality and ambivalence. The unit of measurement for evaluative centrality is the proportion of object descriptions that are evaluative in tone. The unit of measurement for ambivalence is the number of object descriptions that are of opposite evaluation, expressed as a proportion of the total number of evaluative descriptions (and with appropriate constants added to the numerator and denominator).

Among the four cognitive domains studied in all three cultures, the highest levels of object complexity appeared for nations and the lowest for family relationships. The highest levels of affective involvement appeared for acquaintances and the lowest for nations or family relationships. The highest level of ambivalence occurred consistently within the domain of nations, but this must be interpreted as reflecting detachment more than stressful conflict. The most abstractly organized cognitive domains (those with the highest mean levels of image comparability) were nations and acquaintances. The most affectively organized domain (showing the highest levels of affective balance and affective-evaluative consistency) was that of family relationships. These differences were tentatively interpreted as resulting from the differing circumstances in which ideas about these domains are typically acquired.

Chapter 13

INFORMATION AND COGNITIVE DIFFERENTIATION

One area for which it would be reasonable to expect correlates of the variables defined in our conceptual model is the amount of information a person possesses about a domain. Though the accuracy of views plays no role in our structural model of cognition, certain structural features are likely to be compatible with increased knowledge. In particular, we have hypothesized that information level will be positively associated with cognitive differentiation. Our reasoning is that structural elaboration of a cognitive domain allows a person to represent information with less simplification and hence less distortion than in a structurally simple domain. Among the cognitive domains we have investigated, factual accuracy can be readily assessed only for nations. For the other domains, a high degree of acquaintance (for persons) or substantial involvement (in roles and family relationships) provides presumptive conditions for the accumulation of facts about the domain, and should therefore be associated with the complexity of the conceptual structures relevant to them.

We have divided cognitive differentiation into three manifestations: object complexity (the number of attributes on which an object is projected), attribute precision (the number of categories into which an attribute is subdivided), and dimensionality (the number and distinctness of the attributes available to the person). Although the association of information with object complexity is patent, it is by no means certain that increasing information will automatically expand the dimensionality and precision of the conceptual apparatus which utilizes it. These are matters for empirical inquiry; there are presumably differences in persons and circumstances which contribute to variable effects of information on the conceptual structure.

We may speculate about some of these in the absence of systematic empirical evidence. It is to be expected that information acquired as rote catechism, in which multiple characteristics are assigned to a particular object, will have less impact on precision and dimensionality of the conceptual space than will information that presents multiple objects for comparison. It may also be expected that the initial level of cognitive dimensionality will affect the utilization and distribution of incoming information. An habitual capacity to utilize incoming information is an essential ingredient of intelligence, so it would not be surprising to find higher dimensionality and precision in a variety of cognitive domains among persons of high than of low intelligence.

Our explorations on these matters have been limited in the three international samples described on p. 113, and it will be necessary to refer to earlier studies for pertinent data.

DIMENSIONALITY AND INFORMATION

Five studies using a variety of subjects and measures have correlated dimensionality of nations with information about them. In the first of these, 167 undergraduate students at Northwestern University were given an abbreviated version of the "Tulane Data Test," which assesses knowledge of geography, world politics, and recent international events. They also grouped a standard list of 20 nations according to the procedures described on p. 86 for *Listing and Grouping*, and H was computed from these groupings (see p. 105) as a measure of dimensionality. The correlation between information score and H was .31 ($p < .001$).

In the second study, 107 adults selected from the Evanston, Illinois area by students of the senior author were administered interviews which incorporated *Listing and Grouping of Nations* utilizing, first, the respondent's own free list of 20 "most important" nations and, second, a standard list of 20 nations provided by the interviewer. An information score was assigned as the number of government heads known by the respondent for nations on the standard list. This score correlated .37 ($p < .001$) with H calculated for groups formed from the respondent's own list of nations, and .47 ($p < .001$) with H calculated for groups formed from the standard list.

The third study included a measure of information about nations within a battery of cognitive structure tests administered in 1966 to 104 students at the University of Colorado. The information test required subjects to name the premiers and capitals of 20 specified nations, and also to estimate their populations and geographical sizes by checking from a range of categories provided. This 80-item information test correlated .58 ($p < .001$) with the measure of dimensionality, D, calculated from *Rating of Nations* (p. 243), .20 ($p < .05$) with D calculated from *Grouping Nations on Specified Attributes* (p. 238), and .19 ($p < .05$) with H calculated from *Listing and Grouping Nations* (p. 233).

A fourth study used the same instruments as the preceding; these were administered to 54 Boulder (Colorado) high school students and to 67 of their parents. The correlations of information about nations with the three measures of dimensionality were .40, −.20, and .33. The first and third of these were significantly greater than zero (at $p < .001$), but the second (with *Grouping of Nations*) was opposite to the expected direction.

The fifth study, performed by Mania Seferi (1968), utilized a measure of factual accuracy which was broadened to include degree of exposure to information about nations. This was done in order to develop a parallel measure for the domain of acquaintances, in which factual accuracy could not be readily ascertained by the investigators. Thirty-five introductory psychology students at the University of Colorado were asked to list the names of 20 nations important in world affairs. Then, for each nation listed, they indicated: (a) how often they came across information or opinions about it, (b) in what different contexts (e.g., media) they had encountered that information, (c) the name of its prime minister, and (d) its capital. Measure (b) was scored for the number of different sources reported, and all measures were combined into an equally weighted composite. Their average intercorrelation (within subjects, over the 20 nations) was .34, yielding a composite within-subjects reliability of .67.

This index of familiarity correlated .26 ($p < .07$) with H calculated from a grouping measure like that described on p. 105. In addition, H was calculated separately for the 8 nations the subject knew best and for the 8 least known nations. The mean H for best known nations was 2.74, and for least known nations 2.50. The difference between these (correlated) means was significant at $p < .01$.

Another study by Seferi (1968) included parallel analyses for the domain of acquaintances. Seventy subjects each listed the initials of 20 persons well known to them, and for each person they indicated (a) that person's role relation to S (coded into a 5-point scale of familiarity), activities performed together (coded for (b) number and also for (c) degree of intimacy), and (d) whether they usually saw that person in private or in the presence of other people. These four indices showed an average intercorrelation (within subjects, over the 20 acquaintances) of .42, yielding a composite within-subjects reliability of .74. The composite index correlated .54 with H computed from *Listing and Grouping Acquaintances* (p. 86). H was also calculated separately for the 10 best known and the 10 least known of the acquaintances. The mean Hs for these objects were 3.12 and 3.08, which are significantly different (at $p < .01$) by the t-test for correlated variables. It is noteworthy that both these mean dimensionality scores are higher than those for well and poorly known nations, a result which was corroborated in a later study of subjects from the same population (see p. 174).

The implication of these six studies is that a high level of familiarity with objects in a domain is associated, both between subjects and within subjects (between different sets of objects), with relatively high levels of dimensional complexity. Whether familiarity is measured by a factual test or by the degree of self-reported contact (physical or symbolic) with the domain, a similar relationship appears. This was also investigated in two studies of the effect of information on dimensionality. One of these assessed the domain of nations in a pre- and post-test design conducted on volunteers from two university classes in comparative government. The index of dimensionality, D, was computed from a *Rating of Nations* completed by 26 students at the beginning and end of the 4-month course; 20 nations were rated twice on each of 19 attributes suggested by the lecturers as relevant to the course content. The mean D (corrected for unreliability of ratings, see p. 109) at the beginning was 1.94, and at the end 2.13.

The other study assigned volunteer subjects randomly to experimental and control groups which met in three 1-hour sessions, spread over a 3-week interval, either to receive information about psychological and ability tests (experimental group) or to take a sample of factual tests on psychology (control group). At the beginning of the experiment, subjects rated 20 tests (set A or set B) on 12 bipolar attributes; at the end of the experiment, they rated the same 20 tests plus 20 others (both sets A and B) on the same bipolar attributes. The additional sample of 20 tests was included on the posttest to ascertain the generality of experimental effects, and required counterbalancing within the experimental group of the presented information.

The experimental group showed a significant increase in dimensionality from pretest (mean $D = 3.07$) to posttest (mean $D = 3.46$), an increase which differed significantly from the change in mean D score of the control group. The inference to be drawn from these two studies is that the dimensionality of a cognitive domain can be increased by providing specific information about a range of objects within it, and that this increased dimensionality is not confined to the particular objects described, but generalizes to the entire domain.

Considered together, these several experimental and correlational studies serve to validate two of the measures of dimensionality which were included in our composite index for the study of three cultures. Perhaps the only surprising result in them was the single failure of the predicted relationship to appear in the sample of high school students and their parents responding to *Grouping of Nations*. The most likely reason for this failure, juding from the reactions of these subjects, is that the instrument was not very clear to them: Many of the less informed subjects constructed quite random groups, and the procedure for scoring this instrument provides no way of correcting for randomness, as is done with *Rating of Nations*. In other studies of nonuniversity subjects, we have encountered some difficulty in having the questionnaires understood in their self-administered form. Our cautionary recommendation at this time is that, when subjects are unaccustomed to filling out questionnaires, the instruments should be administered in a face-to-face interview, where instructions can be clarified.

INFORMATION IN RELATION TO ATTRIBUTE PRECISION
AND OBJECT COMPLEXITY

The relation of information about nations to the mean precision of attributes for appraising them and to the mean complexity of object views was assessed in one study of university students and another study of high school students and their parents (see p. 113). Attribute precision was measured from *Grouping Nations* (p. 238) and from *Rating of Nations* (p. 243). Mean object complexity was assessed only from *Free Description and Rating of Nations* (p. 234).

Level of information (knowledge of premiers, capitals, population, and size) correlated, on the average, .29 with mean attribute precision and .36 with mean object complexity. These correlations are of roughly the same magnitude as the correlations between information and dimensionality of nations obtained in the same two studies.

INTELLIGENCE AND DIFFERENTIATION

In two studies at the University of Colorado, we have had access to scores on the Scholastic Aptitude Test routinely administered by the university to incoming students. This test provides separate scores for verbal and quantitative aptitudes; In our two samples, they correlated .52 and .47 with each other. Results of the studies are summarized in Table 26. The mean

Table 26. Mean Correlations of Academic Aptitude with Measures of Cognitive Differentiation

Cognitive property	Aptitude score and sample			
	Verbal		Quantitative	
	C.U. 1966	C.U. 1970	C.U. 1966	C.U. 1970
Object complexity	*	.30	*	.19
Attribute precision	.22	.34	.22	.29
Dimensionality	.15	.27	.08	.17

Note. Mean correlations are based on four cognitive domains each. In the 1966 study these were acquaintances, celebrities, nations, and self; in the 1970 study they were acquaintances, family, nations, and self.

*No separate measure of object complexity was computed in the 1966 study.

correlation of aptitude scores with object complexity is .24, with attribute precision .27, and with dimensionality .17. The last correlation is significantly smaller than the second, if the variance of the mean r is estimated from the standard deviation of the 16 computed correlations (2 studies × 4 cognitive domains × 2 indices of aptitude). The mean correlation computed from verbal aptitude scores is not significantly larger than that from quantitative aptitude scores.

The mean correlation of the two aptitude scores with the three complexity scores was .38 for the domain of nations, but only .22 for the three other domains (acquaintances, celebrities, and self) combined. The difference is significant ($p < .01$) if the variance among computed correlations is used as a basis for the error estimate. The higher correlation for nations was expected, considering that this domain is acquired in an indirect, abstract way, presumably facilitated by general intelligence to a greater degree than is the acquisition, through direct experience, of knowledge about intimate objects, such as the self and other people.

The general conclusion to be drawn from these results is that measures of academic aptitude (quantitative and verbal intelligence) correlate with measures of cognitive complexity in a manner to be expected from the conception of cognitive complexity. Although the mean correlation computed from the six studies of information (or familiarity) and complexity is .31, compared to a mean of .22 from the two studies of academic aptitude, these means are not significantly different with the small number of studies considered; in any case, the samples were not comparable. So it will take a study designed for that purpose to test the reasonable expectation that specific acquaintance with a particular domain should be more highly correlated than general intelligence with the dimensionality of that domain.

SUMMARY

A variety of measures of information and familiarity with three different cognitive domains have been quite consistently correlated with various measures of cognitive differentiation in these domains, thus lending support to the construct validity of the differentiation measures. In addition, measures of verbal and quantitative intelligence show consistently positive correlations with object complexity, attribute precision, and dimensionality within five different domains, especially in the domain of nations. There is tentative evidence that intelligence may be more highly correlated with attribute precision than with dimensionality.

Chapter 14

CORRELATES OF POLITICAL IDEOLOGY

Long before the present effort to describe cognitive representation in terms of objects and attributes, these cognitive elements were assessed with instruments designed to measure knowledge, beliefs, attitudes, and values. These constructs have been among the most fundamental in social psychology. Although it is possible to conceptualize them within the terms of our model (see Chapters 5 and 16), they have typically been measured at rather different levels. Our focus has been on a domain of objects, but measures of these other constructs usually have either a narrower or a broader focus.

The measures which have been most frequently framed with reference to a cognitive domain, in our sense, are tests of knowledge. They are intended to assess the degree of factual accuracy in a person's beliefs about a population of objects—such as nations, anatomical features, or psychological processes—which have certain attributes in common.

Beliefs and attitudes are usually assessed with reference to a particular object or limited class of objects, such as the Soviet Union, Jews, or one's mother. There is a sense in which each object is a world unto itself, and might be considered a separate domain if examined in detail (as in our treatment of self as a domain). Nevertheless, this is not often the case in attitude and belief assessment. Rather than attempting to ascertain the framework of attributes for appraising an entire domain, these procedures usually ascertain how people apply a given set of attributes to a particular object or set of objects.

Constructs such as value and ideology have a supra-domain status, in that they encompass attitudes and beliefs about widely diverse objects, from the self to the universe. A value has been defined (e.g., Kluckhohn, 1951; Rokeach, 1969; Scott, 1965b) as a person's conception of an ideal state of affairs against which actual objects are appraised. An ideology has been defined (Newcomb, 1950b, p. 274) as a cluster of beliefs and values organized around a dominant societal value or institution.

Within the realm of political ideology, a dimension that has attracted great attention from psychologists is liberalism-vs.-conservatism. Broadly speaking, this dimension is intended to represent a fundamental orientation toward political, economic, and social change; the liberal welcomes changes of diverse sorts and the conservative opposes them. Particular measures of liberalism and conservatism are typically much narrower than this, focusing on some more limited class of objects, such as labor-management relations (as in Newcomb, 1943, and in Centers, 1949) or government services (as in Wright & Hicks, 1966). This has led, on occasion, to overgeneralization of restricted results, implying liberalism in the comprehensive sense, rather than a pro-union viewpoint (in an era of management dominance) or an internationalist viewpoint (in an era of isolationism).

A number of studies reported by Harvey and his associates (reviewed by Harvey, 1966) have shown substantial negative correlations between the California F-scale and Harvey's measure of conceptual abstractness. One tempting interpretation of these findings is that ideological conservatives have less abstract thought processes, which are more dependent on authoritative sources, than is true for ideological liberals.

Two cautions must be raised against such an interpretation, however. First, it will be recalled that the classification of cognitive types by Harvey's "This I Believe" test (see p. 118) depends in part on finding appeals to authority or negative references to authority in subjects' replies; hence, F-scale and cognitive scores are conceptually overlapping. Second, although, F-scale scores are typically associated with ideological conservatism within American samples, there are grounds for suspecting that this depends on particular cultural influences operating on typical subjects, rather than on any intrinsic relation between ideology and the kind of dogmatic rigidity generally attributed to high authoritarians (e.g., Rokeach, 1960).

Our measures permit a clear separation of cognitive structure from ideological content; they can be applied to objects and attributes that are fixed, mixed, or random in regard to almost any substantive variable, including liberalism-vs.-conservatism. Therefore, they offer a reasonably clear way of ascertaining the relation between formal properties of cognition and political ideology. We investigated this topic by including abbreviated measures of several structural properties (object complexity, object evaluation, ambivalence, evaluative centrality, and dimensionality) in three community studies of public attitudes toward societal groups. (Some of these results also appear in Scott & Rohrbaugh, 1975).

COMMUNITY SURVEYS

Representative samples of adult residents were chosen in Boulder, Colorado; Kyoto and Otsu, Japan; and Wellington, New Zealand. The Boulder residents were chosen by a two-stage probability sample of dwelling units (see Kish, 1965); a respondent of age 18 or over was randomly picked from within each selected household (see Kish, 1949). Complete interviews were obtained from 205 respondents. These constituted 78% of the designated sample; the remaining 22% either refused or could not be found at home, even with repeated call-backs.

In Wellington, respondents were selected by name from lists of eligible voters in two of the city's four districts. These electoral rolls proved to be somewhat out of date, but designated respondents who had moved out of the district by the time of the interview were replaced by a person of the same sex and, if possible, a similar age, currently residing at the same address. Altogether, 200 (74%) of the designated respondents, or their substitutes at the same address, completed interviews.

Respondents in Japan were selected from files in the city office of Otsu and in two ward offices of Kyoto. Following random starts, systematic samples of listed dwelling units were selected, and within each household an adult was picked from a predetermined pattern based on age and sex. There was considerable difficulty in obtaining interviews with the designated respondents, due both to refusals (especially among older females) and to out-of-date listings. The resulting sample of 137 completed interviews included only about half the originally designated respondents.

The Boulder and Wellington samples were subsequently augmented by training interviews (39 and 72, respectively), after preliminary analyses indicated that these were not different on the measured variables from their respective probability samples. Despite limitations of locale and availability, these samples may be regarded as much more representative of their respective societies than subjects typically obtained from universities. Although 77% of the Boulder respondents had attended a college or university, this was true of only 24% and 7% of respondents in Kyoto/Otsu and Wellington, respectively. Even respondents without much education experienced little difficulty coping with the necessary instruments in the context of a personal interview.

Interviews lasted about 40 minutes, on the average, and included the following tasks: (a) naming groups of people considered harmful to the country, (b) giving descriptions of those harmful groups, (c) selecting from a list of 50 or 60 societal groups those the respondent deemed harmful to the country, (d) giving checklist descriptions of several groups specified identically for all respondents, (e) responding to items measuring conservatism (vs. liberalism) adapted from Wilson and Patterson's (1968) instrument, and (f) providing demographic information.

Description of Groups

Checklist description instruments were used to assess variable properties of cognition for the domain of societal groups. These instruments appeared in two contexts. In the first, respondents described groups they had named as harmful to the country; in the second context, all respondents described a standard set of groups.

Table 27. Checklist Description of Groups (from Community Interview Surveys)

1. all alike	21. helpful	41. oppressive
2. all different	22. hypocritical	42. out for themselves
3. afraid	23. idealistic	43. parasitic (hangers-on)
4. ambitious	24. ignorant	44. poor appearance
5. antisocial	25. immature	45. power-seeking
6. authoritarian	26. immoral	46. prejudiced
7. closed-minded	27. impolite	47. radical
8. childish	28. inconsiderate	48. restrictive
9. conservative	29. informed	49. rigid
10. cruel	30. insecure	50. selfish
11. deceitful	31. insincere	51. sloppy
12. destructive	32. intelligent	52. subversive
13. dirty	33. lazy	53. trouble-makers
14. dishonest	34. leftist	54. undemocratic
15. disloyal	35. liberal	55. unhappy
16. they don't give a damn	36. lying	56. uninformed
17. drop-outs	37. maladjusted	57. unpatriotic
18. easily led	38. mean	58. violent
19. good intentions	39. neurotic	59. well dressed
20. hardworking	40. oppose progress	60. well mannered

The checklist consisted of 60 adjectives which were identical for the three samples. They appear in Table 27. (The Japanese checklist was a direct translation of the English checklist.) The checklist was developed from a pilot survey previously conducted on a random sample of Boulder residents. In this pilot study, some 200 respondents were asked to name and describe five groups that were helpful to the community and five groups that were harmful. Characteristics most frequently attributed to helpful and harmful groups were

Table 28. Major Types of Groups Named as Dangerous and Their Exemplars in Three Communities

Group type	U.S.	N.Z.	Japan
Left-wing	Communists	Communists	Radical Democrats
Right-wing	John Birch Society	Large industrial enterprises	Ultranationalists
Ethnic protest groups	Black militants	(omitted)	(omitted)
Other protestors	Student protesters	Progressive Youth Movement	All-Japan Student League
Criminal deviants	Criminals	(omitted)	(omitted)
Traditional institutions	The Establishment	Trade unions	Big business
Drop-outs	Hippies	Hippies	Hippies

intercorrelated, to identify major clusters. Adjectives representing these clusters were arranged alphabetically to form the list used in the present study.

Respondents first gave checklist descriptions of groups they had freely named as harmful to the country. The number of groups described depended on the number they had named. The sets of specified groups were developed from the pilot study mentioned above. From the harmful groups most frequently named in that survey, seven major types (see Table 28) were identified by cluster analysis, and represented by one group each in the Boulder survey.

Groups specified for checklist description in Wellington were determined after consultation with university informants (from psychology, sociology, and political science departments) to ascertain instances of the clusters previously identified in Boulder. Only five pertinent groups were included, as no equivalent to militant minorities existed in New Zealand at that time, and criminals were deemed insufficiently controversial for the purpose. Equivalent groups in Japan were identified by the translator[5] in consultation with resident academic informants.

Conservatism Scale

Items from Wilson and Patterson's (1968) conservatism scale were used as a starting point for developing a cross-culturally comparable measure. A separate item analysis was conducted for each sample. Items were retained if they showed positive correlations with the total scale in all three samples and a significant item-total correlation in at least one sample. These common items appear in Table 29. The common scale was considerably less homogeneous in Japan and New Zealand than in the U.S. sample. A "culturally specific" scale in Japan was substantially more homogeneous (with a reliability of .83 and an average inter-item correlation of .26), but even an optimal set of items in the New Zealand sample showed relatively low homogeneity (reliability of .72 and mean inter-item correlation of .16), indicating that conservatism-liberalism is less unidimensional in this culture (see also Boshier, 1972).

Within each sample, the scales could be validated by their correlations with certain demographic variables, such as age, political preference, and religious affiliation, and also by the respondent's choice of harmful groups from a list presented. (The list contained 60 groups in Boulder, 50 in Wellington, and 52 in Kyoto/Otsu.) The groups on these lists were formed into clusters. Choice of a group as harmful was treated as a dichotomous variable (1 if chosen, 0 if not) and these variables were intercorrelated. A group was included in a particular cluster if it correlated at least .15, on the average, with all other groups in the cluster, and if its mean intra-cluster correlation was at least .05

[5]We are indebted to Professors Shigeo Imamura, Okichi Endo, and Satoru Inomata for collaboration in the Japanese studies reported here and earlier.

Table 29. Conservatism Scale (after Wilson & Patterson, 1968)

Item	Item-total correlation[a]		
Sample:	*U.S.*	*Japan*	*N.Z.*
1. death penalty	.30	.23	.08
−2. legalized abortion	.46	.17	.37
3. sabbath observance[b]	.44	.46	.32
−4. sex before marriage	.58	.50	.47
5. church authority[c]	.39	.36	.43
−6. women judges	.31	.10	.02
−7. mixed marriage[d]	.46	.19	.17
8. censorship	.37	.36	.28
9. "Are you conservative or liberal?"	.61	.24	.21
Mean inter-item correlation	.26	.14	.13
Scale reliability	.76	.59	.57

Note. Instructions for the first eight items were: "I am going to read some items that refer to various matters that people have differing opinions about. As I read each one, would you please tell me whether you generally believe in it, or generally don't believe in it." A response of "don't know" or "neither" was recorded as an intermediate category. The last common item (9) appeared in a different form: "Do you regard yourself generally as a conservative or a liberal, politically?"

[a]Each item was excluded from the total score with which it was correlated. Negative items (−) were reverse-scored in the scale total.

[b]Translated into Japanese as "paying respect to shrines."

[c]Translated into Japanese as "religious authority."

[d]Translated into Japanese as "international marriage."

higher than its mean correlation with items of any other cluster. Groups which correlated equally well with two or more clusters were excluded, in order to reduce inter-cluster overlap.

This procedure yielded fairly independent cluster scores of reasonably high homogeneity. They correspond fairly well with clusters identified from the Boulder pilot study, using free responses, rather than checklists (see Table 28). In each of the samples, it was possible to designate clusters of both pro- and anti-establishment groups against which scores on the conservatism scale could be compared (see Table 30).

The validity of the scale was supported by these analyses in all three samples (see Table 31). Liberals were most likely to pick right-wing radicals, conservatives, and establishment groups as harmful, while conservatives were most likely to pick protestors, alienated, and anti-establishment groups. In all three cultures, ideological conservatism was associated with conservative political and religious affiliations. Among the notably consistent correlates is age; young people were generally more ideologically liberal than their elders in all three cultures. There was a small tendency for female respondents to be

Table 30. Clusters of Groups Picked as "Harmful"

		r_{tt}
Establishment groups		
U.S.:	big business, bureaucrats, capitalists, merchants, the military, National Guard, right-wingers	.77
Japan:	bureaucrats, capitalists, industrial monopolists, large industrial enterprises, local government officials	.85
N.Z.:	The Establishment, churches, the military, police, Roman Catholics, Rugby Union	.58
Right-wing radicals		
U.S.:	Fascists, John Birch Society, Ku Klux Klan, Minutemen, Nazis, vigilantes	.79
Japan:	The Establishment, Fascists, ultra-nationalists, right-wingers	.81
N.Z.:	Country Party, news media, Returned Services Association, right-wingers, Security Service	.57
Conservative groups		
Japan:	shrines and temples, conservatives, Nazi party, police, private guards	.77
N.Z.:	capitalists, censors, conservatives, industrial monopolists	.51
Alienated groups		
U.S.:	people who don't contribute to society, people who don't work, unemployed people, welfare recipients, women's liberation	.65
Japan:	motorcycle gangs, hippies, homosexuals, urban migrants from rural areas, people who disturb the peace, people who don't contribute to society	.74
N.Z.:	criminals, drug peddlers, drug users, motorcycle gangs, hippies, homosexuals, juvenile delinquents, people who disturb the peace, people who don't contribute to society, sex perverts, unemployed people	.79
Protesting groups		
U.S.:	Black militants, Black Panthers, extremists, left-wingers, militants, people who advocate violence, Students for a Democratic Society, subversives	.77
Japan:	anti-government demonstrators, Communists, All-Japan Student League, protesters	.54
N.Z.:	protesters, university students, young people	.37
Anti-establishment groups		
U.S.:	anti-government demonstrators, Communists, drug pushers, drug users, hippies, juvenile delinquents, Negro rioters, people who break laws, people who disturb the peace, protesters, rioters	.85

Note. The nearest equivalents appear under a common heading to identify clusters in Table 31, but cluster names should be taken lightly, as it is apparent that they often have different operational meanings within the three cultures.

r_{tt} is Cronbach's (1951) coefficient alpha.

Table 31. Correlates of Ideological Conservatism

	Sample		
	U.S.	Japan	N.Z.
	(N = 244)	(N = 137)	(N = 272)
Establishment groups are harmful	−.30*	−.45*	−.34*
Right-wing radicals are harmful	−.19*	−.46*	−.20*
Conservative groups are harmful	†	−.37*	−.14*
Alienated groups are harmful	.35*	.12	.25*
Protesting groups are harmful	.27*	.24*	.18*
Anti-establishment groups are harmful	.51*	†	†
Conservative religious affiliation[a]	.46*	.46*	.33*
Frequency of religious observance[b]	.47*	.30*	.39*
Conservative political party preference[c]	.44*	.25*	.23*
Age	.39*	.45*	.35*
Sex (female scored high)	.08	.17*	.15*
Education	−.33*	−.47*	−.11

*$p < .05$ (two-tailed test).

†No such cluster in this sample (see Table 30).

[a]Order of categories was: (U.S.) Roman Catholic, conservative Protestant, liberal Protestant, non-Christian or non-sectarian, none; (Japan) Shinto, Buddhist, Christian or non-sectarian, none; (N.Z.) Roman Catholic, Church of England, other Christian, non-Christian, none.

[b]Frequency was scored into four categories, ranging from "every week" to "almost never." Religious observance was defined as follows: (U.S.) "attend religious services"; (Japan) "shrine-visiting, church attendance, or other religious observance"; (N.Z.) "church attendance."

[c]Order of categories in the code was: (U.S.) Republican, neither, Democratic; (Japan) Democratic-Liberal and other right-wing, Komeito and other intermediate (or none), socialist and other left-wing; (N.Z.) National, neither, Labour.

more conservative than males in Japan and New Zealand. And there was a substantial tendency for better educated respondents to be more liberal in Boulder and Kyoto/Otsu, but not in Wellington.

Consistency of Cognitive Measures

The consistency of cognitive measures over different samples of objects may be judged by comparing scores computed from checklist descriptions of the standard set of specified groups with scores computed from separate checklist descriptions of one or more groups which the respondent had personally identified as harmful.

A maximum of five harmful groups was considered in the descriptions, but few respondents named that many groups as harmful. The mean number described was just 2.8 in Boulder, 2.2 in Kyoto/Otsu, and 1.8 in Wellington.

Table 32. Correlations Between Cognitive Properties Assessed From Volunteered and Specified Groups

Property	Sample		
	U.S.	*Japan*	*N.Z.*
N:	225	115	181
Mean object complexity	.69*	.76*	.78*
Mean object evaluation	.31*	.25*	.23*
Mean object ambivalence	.38*	.25*	.23*
Evaluative centrality	.42*	.06	.31*

Note. Based on the subsamples of respondents who named and described at least one harmful group, in addition to describing the specified groups posed to all respondents. Hence, these *N*s are less than the total sample sizes.

*p < .05 (one-tail test).

Few respondents named enough harmful groups to yield a meaningful measure of dimensionality, so this property was measured only from descriptions of specified groups. Thus, inter-instrument consistency was ascertained for four of the properties measured by checklists: mean object complexity, mean object evaluation, mean ambivalence, and evaluative centrality. As Table 32 shows, there was a significant degree of consistency in every case except for evluative centrality in the Japanese sample. The highest agreement between descriptions of volunteered and specified groups appeared for the property of mean object complexity, but at least part of this must be discounted because it is contaminated by an instrument-specific response set to pick many or few adjectives from the list. (Image comparability was not treated separately, because its scores on the checklist instrument are necessarily correlated with mean object complexity.)

Correlates of Cognitive Properties

Ideological and demographic correlates of selected cognitive properties are reported in Table 33. Sex is omitted because it showed no significant correlates, and frequency of religious observance is omitted because it showed a pattern of results identical to that for conservative religious affiliation. Only the five cognitive properties which could be scored from the checklist description are represented. Data are presented separately for descriptions of volunteered groups and descriptions of specified groups. In both cases measures are limited to one instrument type and one domain, so the results must be regarded as tentative. They are important, however, because they are based on heterogeneous public (i.e., nonuniversity) samples in three quite different cultures.

Table 33. Ideological and Demographic Correlates of Selected Cognitive Properties

Cognitive property	Conservative ideology		Conservative religion		Conservative politics		Age		Education	
	Vol.	Spec.	Vol.	Spec.	Vol.	Spec.	Vol.	Spec.	Vol.	Spec.
Mean object complexity										
U.S. (N = 225 & 244)[a]	−.01	.01	.01	.06	−.03	.04	−.10	−.06	.08	.06
Japan (N = 115 & 137)	−.19*	−.20*	−.14*	−.04	−.13	−.13	−.05	−.02	.20*	.16*
N.Z. (N = 181 & 272)	.12	.15*	.00	.03	.00	.09	.05	.02	.07	.13*
Mean object evaluation										
U.S.	−.17*	−.35*	−.15*	−.17*	−.04	−.15*	−.16*	−.30*	.10	.15*
Japan	.01	.00	−.11	−.09	−.06	−.25*	.10	−.03	−.01	.06
N.Z.	−.08	−.13*	−.04	−.08	−.12	−.08	−.05	−.15*	.03	−.01
Mean object ambivalence										
U.S.	−.17*	−.44*	−.17*	−.25*	−.10	−.16*	−.17*	−.31*	.12	.23*
Japan	−.04	.06	−.10	−.07	−.08	−.11	.02	.00	−.06	.03
N.Z.	−.03	−.13*	−.05	.00	−.15*	−.02	−.02	−.20*	.07	.24*
Evaluative centrality										
U.S.	.27*	.39*	.14*	.23*	.05	.19*	.21*	.29*	−.10	−.28*
Japan	.11	.15*	.14*	.21*	−.05	−.07	.09	.09	.09	−.09
N.Z.	.18*	.22*	−.01	.20*	.02	.07	.12	.12	−.04	−.34*
Dimensionality										
U.S.	b	−.12*	b	−.01	b	.02	b	−.04	b	.03
Japan	b	−.22*	b	−.02	b	.06	b	−.10	b	.18*
N.Z.	b	−.13*	b	.01	b	.16*	b	−.22*	b	.23*

*$p < .05$ (two-tail test).

[a]First N is the number of respondents who voluntarily named and described harmful groups (vol. columns); second N is the total number of respondents who described the specified groups.

[b]Dimensionality was not measured for volunteered harmful groups due to insufficient objects.

It is evident that the three samples differ considerably, so it would not be wise to generalize widely about cognitive differences between liberals and conservatives. There are, however, differences that appear consistently: Conservatives tend to use more evaluative attributes in describing societal groups (i.e., they score higher on evaluative centrality) than do liberals, while idological liberals tend more than conservatives to use the various attributes independently in describing the groups—i.e., they have higher dimensionality scores, on the average. (In this analysis, each characteristic on the checklist was treated as a distinct attribute, rather than collapsing antonyms into bipolar attributes, as is recommended in Chapter 7. The distortion should not be great, since there were only six strictly antonymic pairs in the list.) From this result, one could infer that, in these samples, a conservative ideology is associated with a relatively evaluative orientation toward all the designated societal groups, while a liberal ideology is associated with a relatively broad perspective for comprehending differences among them.

In Japan and New Zealand, dimensionality of societal groups was correlated with level of education, but not in the U.S. sample. The latter failure may reflect the generally higher level of education in Boulder, which means that very few persons were grossly ignorant in this domain.

In the Boulder and Wellington samples, more ambivalence toward the specified groups was expressed by respondents with high education and liberal ideology. Also, liberals in these two communities tended to evaluate the specified groups more favorably than did conservatives. These correlations were substantially reduced, however, when volunteered harmful groups were used as bases for the cognitive measures. It is quite likely that these associations are due, in part, to the preponderance of anti-establishment groups among those designated for description by all respondents (see Table 28). Within the Boulder sample, the association between liberalism and ambivalence toward societal groups is maintained even when attention is restricted to groups named as harmful by the respondent, but this is not true in Wellington. The ideological correlates of object complexity are inconsistent from one sample to another.

Although this one cognitive domain is too limited to be a base for firm conclusions, societal groups of pro- and anti-establishment stance must certainly be central to conservative and liberal ideology. If consistent correlations between conservatism and structural properties are to be found within any cognitive domain, it will most probably be in this area. Structural correlates of conservatism are unlikely to be higher in any other cognitive domain. Our results suggest small correlations with two structural properties: evaluative centrality and dimensionality. The remaining three properties are either not consistently correlated with conservatism from one sample to another, or else their correlations may be artifactually created by the kinds of groups (anti-establishment) which predominated in the standard list presented to all respondents.

SUMMARY

Interview surveys were conducted with heterogeneous samples of adults in Boulder, Colorado; Kyoto and Otsu, Japan; and Wellington, New Zealand. The ideological dimension of conservatism-vs.-liberalism was measured by a standard set of items from Wilson and Patterson's scale. Five properties of cognition, referring to objects, attributes, and cognitive structure, were assessed from checklist descriptions of various societal groups and of groups regarded by the particular respondent as harmful to the country. Ideological conservatives tended, in all three communities, to score higher than liberals on evaluative centrality and lower than liberals on dimensionality.

It is inappropriate to generalize these findings to other cognitive domains, and the small size of correlations within this most pertinent of domains (societal groups) makes one suspect that ideology and cognitive structure bear no general relationship outside the particular cognitive domain represented in the measuring instruments. Furthermore, results presented in Chapter 15 show interpersonal adjustment to be correlated with structural properties only within interpersonally relevant domains. Findings from other studies concerning a relationship between ideology and general cognitive style might be attributable to a confounding of style and content in the measures utilized, but our data show some limited relationship even when the variables are conceptually and operationally independent.

Chapter 15

COGNITIVE CORRELATES
OF INTERPERSONAL
ADJUSTMENT

The relevance of cognition for interpersonal adjustment is widely accepted by psychologists. The success of individual human adaptation can be judged by various criteria, as diverse as reproductive capacity, role performance, cultural contribution, and subjective adequacy. One important task of psychology is to discover determinants and correlates of adaptive success, however defined. The fact that criteria vary with time and place, depend on the values of the appraiser, and may be mutually incompatible does not vitiate the enterprise, but rather makes the search longer, and tentative answers more complex. There was a time, for example, when intelligence was viewed as a generalized predictor of adaptive success. This imperialistic view has since been replaced with the more restricted interpretation that intelligence tests predict success in school—which is exactly what they were designed to do in the first place. Research on interpersonal adjustment is likely to uncover an equivalent degree of situation-specificity in any correlates that may be found.

CRITERIA OF PERSONAL ADJUSTMENT

Three related ways of measuring personal adequacy have occupied the attention of personality and social psychologists for several decades. These are subjective reports, professional appraisal, and social appraisal. Though these approaches assess only a portion of what is meant by human fulfillment, they at least offer the advantages of specific operational definitions.

Subjective well-being has been the most readily operationalized, and a multitude of self-report tests exist for appraising happiness, neurotic tendencies, anxiety, and personal adequacy. Typically, these different self-assessments correlate quite highly with each other, suggesting that a common underlying disposition is being measured. Doubt is sometimes cast on their meaning because they also correlate substantially with "lie scales," "social desirability response set," and tendencies toward "sensitization-vs.-repression." But such results do not seriously challenge the prima facie interpretation that subjective well-being is the primary ingredient of such test scores, for the alternative (response-set) interpretation has not led to any seriously competing predictions, and one can therefore question whether the "lie scales" themselves have been appropriately named.

Professional psychiatric judgment offers a seemingly preferred, albeit more expensive, alternative to subjective report of personal adequacy. After some initially discouraging attempts to achieve agreement between independent diagnosticians, standardized procedures have been developed (e.g., Wing, 1974) which permit high levels of agreement, provided identical questions are asked in the same sequence by both examiners. Professional ratings of psychological functioning, obtained in this way, or even in less standardized fashion, usually correlate significantly with subjective adequacy, measured by self-report instruments. This convergence of methods may, however, be illusory. In standardized methods the professionals' judgment relies heavily on subjects' reports of well-being, just like the paper and pencil tests do. Small wonder the two are correlated; they are thoroughly confounded, rather than independent.

Psychologists' systematic attention to social appraisal of personal adjustment has developed within the sociometric tradition, and hence has been predominantly focused on likability and social acceptance. Such acceptance is certainly an aspect of personal adjustment, but more precise and situation-specific judgments can also be made, with fair levels of inter-observer agreement. It is quite possible to develop reliable measures of role performance and social adequacy based on the judgments of other actors. The value of such judgments has been recognized in the area of job performance, but they have been less appreciated in the sphere of emotional adjustment— perhaps due to ethical considerations or to the belief that only expert judgment can be valid. Recognizing the fallibility of expert judgment and the degree to which it depends on subjective self-report, one becomes more appreciative of lay opinion. There is good reason for thinking that the reactions of lay persons to the subject should be embodied in the concept of adjustment itself. In our research we have used both self-report and peer judgments of personal well-being in exploring the implications of cognitive variables for adjustment.

DETERMINANTS OF ADJUSTMENT

Since the independent variables we are studying come from the cognitive-personality sphere, we sought determinants of personal adequacy in the individual's view of himself and the surrounding world—particularly the interpersonal world. It seemed reasonable to believe, with George Herbert Mead, that subjective adequacy and interpersonal appraisals interact, that one's feeling of well-being (or the opposite) both affects and is affected by the way significant others appraise one. We expected, first, that self-evaluation would correlate with peer evaluation, specifically with reference to personal adequacy. Second, we expected that judged adequacy of the self would correlate with some descriptive features of the self-concept embodied in our measures for the domain of self-roles. Third, we expected self-adequacy to correlate with one's view of other people, on the ground that an acceptable self concept arises out of, and helps to perpetuate, satisfactory interpersonal relations. Finally, we focused on the family of orientation as a significant source of self appraisal, in the light of both interpersonal (Meadian) and psychoanalytic (Freudian) views that family relations are likely propotypes of subsequent interpersonal relations, influencing the type of acquaintance patterns chosen and the direction that one gives to them.

Our search for cognitive correlates of adjustment was, at first, no more specifically focused than this, for we had no a priori basis for identifying appropriate and inappropriate structural properties. In defining our properties of cognition we had specifically rejected an evaluative conception of intergration in preference for a more descriptive definition of several varieties of integration, any of which might be adaptive or maladaptive, depending on the circumstances. Although a high degree of differentiation seemed, intuitively, to favor adaptation within any domain of objects, early findings quickly disabused us of this notion.

SOME PRELIMINARY FINDINGS

One study of students at the University of Colorado (Scott, 1969) yielded the results summarized in Table 34. The measure of adjustment combined self-ratings with records of attendance at the University Counseling Center (taken to indicate maladjustment). The structural measures were earlier versions of those reported in Section II (Chapters 6-10). Four cognitive domains were studied: self, acquaintances, nations, and celebrities. The last of these included currently well known persons, appraised on attributes similar to those used in the acquaintance instruments (see Chapter 6).

The measures of differentiation (dimensionality and precision) showed no consistent correlations with adjustment, except for precision concerning the domain of self, and here the direction of relationship was opposite to what common sense might have suggested: If anything, students with more precisely defined dimensions for appraising themselves showed more maladjustment

Table 34. Correlations Between Maladjustment and Structural Properties (104 University of Colorado Students, 1966)

Properties	Cognitive domain			
	Self	*Acquaintances*	*Celebrities*	*Nations*
Dimensionality	.09	.03	.14	.19
Precision	.23*	.14	.05	.16
Evaluative centrality	−.33*	−.25*	−.14	−.04
Affective-evaluative consistency	−.30*	−.24*	−.19	−.16
Affective balance	−.18	−.04	−.11	−.07
Ambivalence	.45*	.32*	.15	.14

*$p < .05$ (two-tail test).

than students who used grosser categories on the same attributes. These results differ from those reported by Reker (1974) and by Hayden, Nasby, and Davids (1977), all of whom claimed that emotionally disturbed young boys showed less differentiation among people than did comparison groups of "normal" boys. In addition to noting the obvious difference between their populations and ours, one may question the measures of differentiation they employed. Hayden et al. computed both a measure of complexity (dimensionality) and a measure of discrimination capacity (precision) from ratings of 10 photographs; no other tasks were used to permit convergent validation. While Reker used two different tasks, he provided no information about the correlation between their measures of differentiation, and at least one of the measures appears faulty: Purportedly based on a procedure developed by Scott (1962) (described on p. 105), it does not appear actually to have followed that procedure—employing only one object-sort, and miscalculating the index of complexity (H).

Though our own results were certainly not expected, they provide evidence that complexity and adjustment are unrelated—evidence that is at least as convincing as the positive relationships reported by Reker and Hayden. It seems that replication is required to settle the question.

Three additional results from our own study are worthy of note. Maladjusted university students tended to show a higher level of ambivalence and lower degrees of evaluative centrality and affective-evaluative consistency within the domains of self and acquaintances than did the better adjusted respondents. Evidently, one concomitant of maladjustment is a tendency to view the self and others in a detached, nonevaluative, and affectively inconsistent way. Correlations within the domains of celebrities and nations were nonsignificant, suggesting that thoughts about such remote domains are less relevant for personal adjustment than are thoughts about immediately experienced personal objects.

When self-report and counseling center attendance were considered separately as measures of adjustment, essentially the same pattern of correlations appeared for both. The degree of inter-matrix similarity was .55 over the 24 correlations represented in Table 34. The level of correlations was generally higher (in absolute magnitude) for the self-report criterion than for counseling center attendance.

A TENTATIVE INTERPRETATION

These results led us to reformulate our thinking about the relevance of structural properties for interpersonal adjustment (Scott, 1974a). This new interpretation, which is described below, was applied to data from university students in three different countries, using improved measures of all variables. The data base has since been expanded to a fourth country, with essentially similar results.

We interpret these results as showing that interpersonal adjustment depends, in large part, on confirming the rather simplistic expectations of one's peers. Associates are likely to be most comfortable when they can predict what one is going to do. Complexity as such is not valued; indeed, a diplomatic way of describing disliked people of high status is to say that they are complex. From this perspective, univalent attitudes are generally preferred to ambivalent ones, especially attitudes concerning the self and other. Ego wants to be univocally praised and to feel univocally reassured that alter is an admirable person.

Among fortunately socialized persons, univalently favorable attitudes about oneself and significant others are acquired within the family of orientation and subsequently generalized to personal objects that are culturally valued. Thus arises the well known Pollyanna set to see, hear, and speak no evil (Johnson, 1966; Boucher & Osgood, 1969). Though apparently quite shallow, this set is likely to be genuine, because it is reinforced and is interpersonally adaptive. People without sufficient reason to see their interpersonal world as rosy may nevertheless choose to describe it so in conversations, because this is an interpersonally rewarding way to elicit favorable appraisals from others. What is at first sheer opportunistic expression may get converted, by delayed internalization, into genuine Pollyanna feelings of interpersonal warmth.

It follows that people who are most happy, and so viewed by others, are likely to be practiced Pollyannas, especially in the field of interpersonal relations. They are likely to describe themselves and valued others in warm, affective tones. Toward objects that are culturally defined as undesirable they will tend to express univalently negative sentiments, so as not to confuse their associates with mixed signals or arouse suspicions of disloyalty.

It should be stressed that this is a simplified recipe, intended to apply only to interpersonal adaptation. It is not intended to predict success in coping with impersonal objects, or even administrative coping with people, when one's goal is to influence behaviors rather than elicit affection. It is not even certain that the recipe applies to interpersonal adjustment outside the university student culture, for we have yet to gather systematic data from a wider range of settings. At present, it should be viewed as a tentative framework for anticipating the analyses that follow.

MEASURES OF PERSONAL INADEQUACY

In most of this research, personal inadequacy was assessed from three different self-report instruments and from two friends' ratings. Exceptions to this general pattern will be noted. In samples (a) through (e) described on p. 113, the self-report instruments consisted of:[6]

> (a) a 20-item version of Taylor's (1953) Manifest Anxiety Scale, to which the subject answered "generally true" or "generally false" to items like: "I have sometimes felt that difficulties were piling up so high that I could not overcome them" and "I believe I am no more nervous than most others" (see Scott & Scott, 1979). Seven of the 20 items were worded in an "adjusted" direction and 13 in a "maladjusted" direction.
>
> (b) a 15-item measure, "Satisfaction with Self," in which subjects rated, on a 5-point scale (from "very satisfied" to "very dissatisfied"), aspects of their self-concepts (e.g., appearance, self-confidence, personality, ability to make friends).
>
> (c) a 9-item instrument, "My Effect On Others," in which subjects indicated, on a 5-point rating scale, the degree to which various first-person descriptions applied to them (e.g., "I am seen as the type of person who can be confided in" and "I make people uncomfortable quite often").

In a sample of 133 introductory psychology students at the Australian National University, tested in 1978, only two self-report measures of personal inadequacy were used: (a) the 20-item Manifest Anxiety Scale described above and (b) a composite score obtained from two administrations (separated by a one-week interval) of Goldberg's (1972) General Health Questionnaire (30-item version).

In all four countries, friends' ratings of subjects were obtained on an "Acquaintance Rating Form" (Scott & Scott, 1979), consisting of 15 statements about various behaviors indicating adjustment or maladjustment (e.g., "Does he get upset easily?" and "Does he get along with people easily?"). Each statement was rated from 0 to 4, indicating the degree to which it applied to the subject. Two copies of this form were given to each subject, with instructions to take them to close acquaintances. The informants were asked to fill out the questionnaire honestly and confidentially, and to

---

[6]In previous reports (Scott, 1969, 1974) a fourth instrument, "Liking for Roles," was included in the self-report composite. To avoid confounding measures of adjustment with measures of cognitive properties in the present analyses (see Table 36), however, this instrument was not included here.

Table 35. Correlations Among Measures of Personal Inadequacy

	1	2	3	4
1. Manifest anxiety				
United States (N = 88)	(.81)			
Japan (N = 80)	(.84)			
New Zealand (N = 411)[a]	(.78)			
Australia (N = 133)	(.78)			
2. Self-dissatisfaction				
United States	.47*	(.87)		
Japan	.61*	(.77)		
New Zealand	.53*	(.81)		
Australia[b]	.46*	(.92)		
3. Poor impression[c]				
United States	.28*	.40*	(.76)	
Japan	.36*	.55*	(.65)	
New Zealand	.28*	.41*	(.66)	
4. Acquaintance ratings				
United States	.30*	.37*	.19*	(.67)
Japan	.23*	.32*	.34*	(.61)
New Zealand	.40*	.33*	.15*	(.61)
Australia	.46*	.29*	c	(.76)

Note. Parenthesized figures on the diagonal are scale reliabilities estimated from Cronbach's (1951) coefficient alpha.

*$p < .05$ (one-tail test).

[a]Includes 24 subjects who did not complete cognitive structure questionnaires.

[b]In the Australian sample a different measure was used: the mean of two 30-item versions of Goldberg's (1972) *General Health Questionnaire*, administered one week apart.

[c]"My effect on others" was not administered to the Australian sample.

return it directly to the investigator, in a self-addressed envelope, without letting the subject see the ratings. Occasionally only one rating form was returned for a particular subject, in which case the item scores were doubled for use in subsequent analyses. Subjects without friends' ratings are excluded from the analyses reported here, but self-reports from this group were not noticeably different.

Correlations among these measures of personal inadequacy are reported in Table 35. Scale reliabilities are substantial, and all correlations are significantly greater than zero, averaging .44 among the self-report measures and .31 between self-report and acquaintance ratings. A single criterion of adjustment was formed in such a way that subjective and externally judged adequacy were equally weighted in the total adjustment score: An equally weighted composite of self-report measures was combined with an equally weighted composite of acquaintances' ratings.

Table 36. Cognitive Correlates of Personal Inadequacy

Domain	Acquaintances				Family				Nations				Self				
Sample	U.S.	Japan	N.Z.	Mean	U.S.	Japan	N.Z.	Mean	U.S.	Japan	N.Z.	Mean	U.S.	Japan	N.Z.	Aus.	Mean
N	88	80	129		88	80	122		88	80	136		88	80	136	133	
Object complexity	.03	.04	-.07	-.01	-.03	.18	.09	.08	.04	.17	.00	.06	.06	.12	.07	.00	.06
Object valence	-.19	-.16	-.04	-.12*	-.04	-.17	-.02	-.07	.05	-.09	-.10	-.05	-.26*	.00	-.17*	-.05	-.12*
Object liking	-.26*	-.28*	-.17*	-.23*	-.29*	-.35*	-.27*	-.30*	-.29*	-.26*	.07	-.13*	-.42*	-.57*	-.23*	-.14	-.31*
Object evaluation	-.18	-.34*	-.23*	-.24*	-.31*	-.37*	-.38*	-.36*	-.11	.01	.10	.02	-.40*	-.55*	-.33*	-.38*	-.40*
Object ambivalence	.22*	.18	.22*	.21*	.22*	.20	.34*	.26*	-.13	.18	.11	.06	.46*	.42*	.33*	.34*	.37*
Attribute precision	.04	-.22*	.10	.00	-.06	-.14	.09	-.02	.16	-.01	-.09	.00	.18	-.06	.05	a	.06
Evaluative centrality	-.06	-.25*	-.08	-.12*	-.10	-.03	-.02	-.05	.06	-.04	-.05	-.02	-.19	-.03	-.19*	-.12	-.14*
Affective-evaluative consistency	-.15	-.16	-.09	-.13*	-.16	-.22*	.04	-.09*	.00	.03	.01	.01	-.07	-.11	-.28*	-.03	-.13*
Affective balance	-.03	-.06	-.04	-.04	-.04	-.17	.08	-.03	-.17	-.01	-.06	-.08	.00	-.03	-.04	a	-.03
Dimensionality	-.03	.05	-.05	-.02	.01	.01	.03	.02	.08	-.15	-.05	-.04	.11	.00	.01	.16	.07
Image comparability	-.01	.11	-.13	-.03	.02	.14	.06	.07	.02	.20	-.09	.02	-.06	.11	-.11	.02	-.02
Centralization	.08	.03	-.08	.00	.08	.04	.10	.08	-.01	-.05	.08	.02	.05	.06	.10	.01	.05

Note. Mean correlations are based on Fisher's z transformations, weighted by sample sizes. Significance levels of mean correlations were ascertained by multiplying the separate significance levels and referring $\log_e$ of the doubled product to the χ^2 distribution (Fisher, 1941, pp. 97–98).
*p < .05 (two-tail test).

PERSONAL INADEQUACY AND COGNITIVE PROPERTIES

Table 36 shows correlations of the composite measure of maladjustment (i.e., high scores imply poor adjustment) with each of the cognitive variables of every domain, calculated separately for each sample. Note, first, that correlations of maladjustment with measures of cognitive complexity are generally not significant. This applies to object complexity, attribute precision, and dimensionality. There is certainly no evidence that cognitive complexity concerning people is interpersonally adaptive in this setting.

The findings in Table 36 also indicate that ambivalence toward personal objects (self, family, and acquaintances) is consistently associated with maladjustment in all three main samples and also in Australia for the single domain (self) assessed there. No such correlation obtains within the domain of nations, indicating once again that the obtained relationship is specific to those objects that are most relevant to personal adjustment.

Correlations of maladjustment with evaluative centrality and affective-evaluative consistency are quite variable over the four samples. The general trend replicates previous findings (Table 34) that maladjustment is associated with less affective involvement in others and less affective determination of interpersonal cognitions. Nevertheless, acceptable significance levels are attained only from the composite sets of results within acquaintances and self domains (combining three or four samples by Fisher's (1941) formula); results within each sample considered separately are generally not significant.

Finally, among the variables most closely associated with maladjustment are dislike and negative appraisal of objects. This finding confirms that adjustment tends to be associated with a general Pollyanna tendency in regard to a range of cognitive objects. The magnitudes of these correlations are generally less within the domain of nations than within the personal domains. If different types of objects within the personal domains are considered, it appears that adjustment is most particularly associated with a preference for close (as distinct from distant) objects (see Scott & Peterson, 1975).

Since liking for objects is correlated with several of the other cognitive variables, it is appropriate to inquire if the correlations of maladjustment with ambivalence, evaluative centrality, and affective-evaluative consistency are still maintained when the common variance due to Pollyannaism is partialed out. Table 37 shows that this is generally the case for ambivalence and, to some extent, for affective-evaluative consistency. Controlling for Pollyannaism, however, eliminates the relation of maladjustment to evaluative centrality. Hence, we conclude that cognitions concerning the self and others are associated with adjustment and maladjustment primarily through affective responses to interpersonal objects. Complex appraisals and systematic appraisals of others (via centralization or image comparability) are not associated with either increased or reduced levels of adjustment. Rather, it is favorable, univalent, and affectively consistent appraisals that are associated with interpersonal adjustment.

Table 37. Selected Cognitive Correlates of Maladjustment, With Object Liking Partialled Out

Domain	Acquaintances				Family				Nations				Self				
Sample	U.S.	Japan	N.Z.	Mean	U.S.	Japan	N.Z.	Mean	U.S.	Japan	N.Z.	Mean	U.S.	Japan	N.Z.	Aus.	Mean
N	88	80	129		88	80	122		88	80	136		88	80	136	133	
Ambivalence	.15	.12	.17*	.15*	.08	.07	.27*	.16*	−.07	.12	.10	.06	.33*	.19	.27*	.31*	.28*
Evaluative centrality	.16	−.15	−.01	−.03	−.02	.04	.05	.03	.06	−.03	−.06	−.02	.03	.02	−.10	−.09	−.05
Affective-evaluative consistency	−.25*	−.16	−.10	−.16*	−.03	−.11	.12	.01	−.11	.01	.03	−.02	−.05	.03	−.26*	−.05	−.10*

Note. Mean correlations are based on Fisher's z transformations, weighted by sample sizes. Significance levels of mean correlations were ascertained by multiplying the separate significance levels and referring $\log_e$ of the doubled product to the χ^2 distribution (Fisher, 1941, pp. 97–98).
*$p < .05$ (two-tail test).

VIEWS OF SELF AND OTHERS

Explanations for these relations between cognitive properties and maladjustment might be sought in the kinds of expectations that significant others hold, as suggested above, or they might be sought in intra-psychic processes, such as the strain of maintaining complex, ambivalent interpersonal attitudes. We have no data bearing on such interpretations, but instead will pursue another line of inquiry to which some of our instruments are applicable, namely, the similarity in descriptions of self and others. These analyses arose out of unpublished work by Donovan (1972).

The degree to which the self is seen as similar to other persons may be ascertained from two checklist description instruments, one pertaining to the self and one pertaining to acquaintances.[7] These two checklists have 43 adjectives in common (see p. 91 and p. 237). Though the data base is limited, these results are sufficiently clear to suggest that a more thorough appraisal of self-other similarity would merely strengthen the obtained relationships.

Measures

Self-concept. The subject's total self-picture was operationalized as the frequency with which each of the 43 common adjectives was used across the 10 roles included in *Checklist Description of Self.* This scoring was based on the assumption that traits displayed most frequently by a person in the several circumstances constitute the most important features of the "self" conceived as a stable entity.

Conceptions of liked and disliked others. The respondent's liking for each person identified on the *Checklist Description of Acquaintances* was ascertained on the last page of that instrument by means of a 7-point rating scale. It was thus possible, with most respondents, to distinguish liked others (rated 7, 6, or 5) from disliked others (rated 1, 2, or 3). Conceptions of liked

[7]These analyses could not be performed for subjects in New Zealand, as separate samples were used for the self and acquaintance domains. Consequently, the analyses reported here are restricted to the U.S. and Japanese samples.

and disliked others in terms of the 43 common adjectives were assessed separately in the same manner as the self-concept. If there were no liked persons, or (more commonly) no disliked persons, that category was unavailable for description.

Self-other similarity. Perceived similarity between self and liked others was operationalized as the product-moment correlation over the 43 common adjectives between summated scores for all 10 self-roles and summated scores for liked acquaintances. A corresponding score was also computed representing each respondent's perceived similarity between self and disliked others.

Overall Similarity

The mean similarity index between conceptions of self and liked acquaintances was .37 in the U.S. sample and .23 in the Japanese sample; by contrast, the mean similarity indices between conceptions of self and disliked acquaintances were −.06 and .03, respectively, in the two cultures. Among the 68 U.S. respondents who described one or more disliked persons on a checklist, 65 described these persons as less similar to the self than were their liked acquaintances. In Japan, of the 54 subjects who described both liked and disliked acquaintances on checklist instruments, 41 described the disliked persons as less similar to the self than were the liked persons. Both of these proportions are significantly greater than chance ($p < .001$, by binomial test), and confirm the expectation that liked persons are generally seen as more similar to the self than disliked persons. This result is important primarily in showing that our limited measure of self-other similarity is sufficiently valid for present purposes.

Cognitive Correlates of Self-Other Similarity

In both samples similarity of self to liked acquaintances was positively correlated with image comparability for the domain of acquaintances, but not consistently for other domains. This result suggests that the tendency to describe acquaintances with respect to a common set of attributes may reflect, in part, a view of them as similar to the self.

The correlations obtained between self-other similarity and the affective variables of this study depend quite markedly on whether liked others or disliked others are being described. In general, the patterns of correlations for these two classes of acquaintances are exactly opposite. The first four columns of Table 38 show results within two cognitive domains (acquaintances and self) for those cognitive properties that have a major affective component. In both samples, similarity between self and liked acquaintances is positively correlated with liking for self, favorable evaluation of self, and evaluative centrality, negatively correlated with ambivalence regarding the self. By contrast, similarity between self and disliked acquaintances is negatively correlated with liking for self in both samples. The Japanese sample shows a negative correlation with evaluation of self and a positive correlation with

Table 38. Correlations of Selected Cognitive Properties With Self-Other Similarity and Maladjustment

Domain and property	Similarity to				Maladjustment (composite score)	
	Liked acquaintances		Disliked acquaintances			
	U.S.	Japan	U.S.	Japan	U.S.	Japan
N:	88	78	68	54	88	80
Acquaintances						
Liking	.37*	.01	−.08	−.28*	−.26*	−.28*
Evaluation	.49*	.12	.16	−.22	−.18	−.34*
Ambivalence	−.27*	−.22*	−.03	.28*	.22*	.18
Evaluative centrality	.19	.16	−.05	−.27*	−.06	−.25*
Affective-evaluative consistency	−.13	.18	−.13	−.13	−.15	−.16
Affective balance	−.10	.12	.06	−.18	−.03	−.06
Self						
Liking	.33*	.24*	−.25*	−.35*	−.42*	−.57*
Evaluation	.50*	.29*	−.20	−.35*	−.40*	−.55*
Ambivalence	−.33*	−.29*	.17	.39*	.46*	.42*
Evaluative centrality	.33*	.27*	−.22	−.24	−.19	−.03
Affective-evaluative consistency	−.08	.20	−.06	−.15	−.07	−.11
Affective balance	−.18	−.05	.10	−.25	.00	−.03
Maladjustment composite score	−.17	−.15	.25*	.25		

*p <.05 (two-tail test).

ambivalence regarding the self. Within the acquaintance domain, the patterns are also opposite for the two classes of acquaintance, though individual correlations are generally of lower absolute magnitude than within the self domain. It is possible to represent the contrast between correlates of the two types of similarity by a coefficient of correlation computed over the entries in columns 1 and 3 (for the U.S.) and over the entries in columns 2 and 4 (for Japan). These correlations are, respectively, −.45 and −.84.

For purposes of comparison, columns 5 and 6 of Table 38 are repeated from Table 36. These show that, in general, the correlates of similarity between self and disliked acquaintances are roughly the same as the correlates of maladjustment. The similarity between corresponding columns is .69 for the U.S. sample, .86 for the Japanese. The pattern of correlates for liked acquaintances (cols. 1 and 2) is quite the opposite of that for maladjustment (cols. 5 and 6), with similarity indices of −.82 for the U.S. and −.78 for the Japanese sample.

Although maladjustment scores and self-other similarity scores are correlated only marginally and at generally nonsignificant levels, the similar patterns of correlation with cognitive variables suggest that self-other conceptions and interpersonal adjustment are functionally related. In general, the conception that liked others are similar to the self tends to be associated with univalent, favorable views of both self and others, while the conception that disliked others are similar to the self tends to be associated with negative, ambivalent views of the self and (in Japan) with detached, ambivalent views of other people.

The interpretation of these results can only be speculative, as the analyses were more exploratory than guided by theory. Tentatively, we may suggest that among the concomitants of interpersonal adjustment are not only favorable attitudes toward oneself and others, but also a tendency to emphasize one's similarities to valued persons and differences from disliked persons. This appraisal of self-other relationships by assimilation or contrast is most commonly found among people who express affective, favorable, univalent views of themselves and others.

SUMMARY

Two aspects of interpersonal relations have been investigated: judged similarity between self and others, and personal adequacy. Judged self-other similarity was assessed separately for liked and disliked acquaintances. Personal adequacy was assessed both from the standpoint of the subject and from the standpoint of two close acquaintances. Self-other similarity and personal adequacy were only marginally correlated with each other, but they bore similar relationships to certain variable properties of cognition that have been considered in previous chapters: Good personal adjustment and assumed similarity to liked acquaintances were both found most commonly among respondents who expressed univalently favorable attitudes toward themselves and others. Assumed similarity to disliked acquaintances was more commonly found among persons with unfavorable, ambivalent views of the self.

Personal adjustment was also associated with univalent, favorable views of relations within the family of orientation and—at marginal levels—with high affective-evaluative consistency within the personal domains of self, acquaintances, and family. Few of these relationships appeared within the domain of nations. Also, there was no indication that personal adjustment or assumed similarity to liked others is correlated with cognitive complexity in any of the four domains. Adjustment and maladjustment appear to be related to affective properties of cognition, more than to the varieties of differentiation and integration measured here.

Chapter 16

NEXT STEPS:
A SUMMARY AND EXTENSION

The structural model proposed in Chapter 5 is a consolidation and extension of theories about cognition growing out of the work of Kurt Lewin, Fritz Heider, Solomon Asch, George Kelly, and others. It has led to some new concepts and measures on which the research reported in subsequent chapters was based. While many of the outcomes were in accord with the model, some of them were not, and other predictions could not be tested with available measures. It is time to summarize what we have found and take advantage of unexpected findings to alter the model. Also, we will attempt some extensions to accommodate the work of other investigators, generated from quite different perspectives.

SOME FINDINGS

This summary of findings is organized to consider, first, relations among cognitive properties defined within the model and, second, relationships with external variables, including differences among cognitive domains. For this purpose, the variable properties of cognition will be grouped into three categories according to whether they pertain to affect, differentiation, or integration.

Affective Variables

Affective variables include the traditional components of attitude measures, liking for objects and evaluation of them. On the average, these two components were highly correlated, both within and between subjects (see Tables 21 and 23). Any given respondent was likely to describe liked objects more favorably than disliked objects. Also, the more a person liked all objects of a domain, the more favorably were they described, on the average. Corrected for unreliability of measures, mean object liking correlated .93 with mean object evaluation; further, these two mean scores showed almost identical patterns of correlations over the other cognitive variables assessed here. We conclude that mean liking for objects and mean evaluation of them are virtually synonymous variables, when inter-person differences are considered with respect to a particular cognitive domain. *Within* any particular domain there were stable and consistent individual differences in the degree to which liking and evaluation of various objects correspond. These differences formed the basis for our measures of affective-evaluative consistency.

The mean liking and evaluation expressed toward objects within a domain were both negatively correlated with mean ambivalence concerning those objects. Thus, in considering these four domains (acquaintances, nations, role performances, and intra-family relations), most subjects did not show univalent dislike, but rather a mixture of positive and negative sentiments. Moreover, there is a generalized Pollyanna tendency along which people differ rather consistently in their expressed attitudes toward a variety of domains. When affect is expressed, it tends to be favorable more often than unfavorable, so a person low in the Pollyanna tendency is likely to display ambivalent, rather than negative, object-appraisals.

Differentiation

Cognitive differentiation was considered from three aspects: (a) object complexity, or the degree to which an object is assigned many characteristics; (b) attribute precision, or the degree to which an attribute is finely subdivided into distinct categories; and (c) dimensionality, or the degree to which many, independent attributes are brought to bear in describing all objects of a particular domain. All three of these variables were related. The correlation between mean object complexity and mean attribute precision was .21, on the average, over all four domains and all three samples. The corresponding correlation between mean object complexity and dimensionality was .38. Corrected for unreliability of measures, these two correlations were .47 and .93, which suggests that object complexity depends primarily on dimensionality, secondarily on attribute precision. (Mean attribute precision correlated, on the average, .23 with dimensionality; corrected for unreliability, the mean r would be .76.)

Both dimensionality and mean object complexity were positively correlated with average object ambivalence, while mean attribute precision was not. One interpretation of these findings is that increasing object complexity via dimensionality (the most common way) leads to ambivalent views of objects, while increasing object complexity via subdivision of attributes helps preserve univalence. This interpretation is weakened by our failure to find any positive correlation, within subjects, between the complexity and ambivalence of single objects; in fact, the correlation was, on the average, negative. We shall return to this problem later, but may anticipate an explanation by suggesting that multiple dimensions of appraisal lead to complex, ambivalent views of the total object domain; however, within a person's given level of dimensionality, knowledge of objects is positively correlated with liking for them, and hence negatively with ambivalence.

Integration

Four varieties of cognitive integration were investigated and they turned out not to be independent. Affective-evaluative consistency and affective balance were quite highly correlated (particularly in relation to their reliabilities), as were image comparability and centralization. It is reasonable to conclude that people who think of similarly liked objects as similar in substance do so by appraising the objects similarly on evaluative attributes. Both affective balance and affective-evaluative consistency were negatively correlated with mean object ambivalence, indicating that clear evaluative differences across objects are associated with evaluative consistency within objects.

Image comparability and centralization were, contrary to expectation, positively correlated in the present samples. This finding suggests that when people think of objects abstractly (describing them with comparable attributes) rather than concretely (describing each object with unique attributes), they tend to do so only with a very small number of attribtues. The tendency to think about objects in a highly abstract way was rare in the present sample.

Affect and Differentiation

Complex views of objects are commonly found among persons who are most affectively oriented toward the domain (with either positive or negative attitudes). Although this finding was not predicted within the model, it may be interpreted, post hoc, as indicating that affective involvement facilitates the acquisition of information about a domain. Nevertheless, affect was not correlated with dimensionality and only slightly with mean attribute precision, so any impact of involvement on knowledge of particular objects does not automatically expand the cognitive frame of reference within which these objects are viewed.

There were small negative correlations of dimensionality and mean attribute precision with object evaluation, and a substantial positive correlation between mean ambivalence and dimensionality, suggesting that the most complex frameworks for evaluating objects tend to generate attitudes that are not uniformly favorable.

Affect and Integration

As expected, affective balance and affective-evaluative consistency were most commonly found in affect-dominated structures. More surprisingly, evaluative centrality was also positively correlated with image comparability. Of course, we cannot safely generalize to integrative styles not investigated here, but these results may suggest that affective involvement in a domain facilitates integration as well as object differentiation. The integration may presumably be complex or simple, depending in part on the kind of information acquired.

Differentiation and Integration

High image comparability is most commonly found in structures of high object complexity, high attribute precision, and high dimensionality. The latter two of these relationships were predicted from the model, but the first relationship turned out to be the strongest of the three. This suggests that complex views of objects tend to result from repeated utilization of the same attributes (with different combinations of categories), rather than from unique, object-specific sets of attributes.

Affective balance and affective-evaluative consistency were positively correlated with mean attribute precision, but negatively correlated with dimensionality, and not significantly related to mean object complexity. Combining these findings with those preceding, it appears that an abstract integrative style is facilitated by both affective involvement and substantial information leading to an enlarged perspective on the domain. In contrast, an affectively balanced and evaluatively consistent integrative style is facilitated by affective involvement and careful attention to certain attributes, in conjunction with a limited number of independent dimensions for appraising objects.

Differences Among Cognitive Domains

The domain of nations was characterized by relatively high levels of object complexity, object ambivalence, image comparability and centralization, and by relatively low levels of object valence, object evaluation, and affective balance. Such a detached, informed, and abstract perspective is what one would expect for a cognitive domain that is acquired indirectly through systematic instruction, rather than through direct, personal experience. By contrast, the domain of acquaintances was characterized by relatively high levels of evaluative centrality, object liking, and image comparability. The first two of these properties reflect positive emotional involvement, while the third suggests an abstract appraisal derived from repeated experience with objects.

Interpersonal relations within the family of orientation were characterized by relatively high levels of affective balance and affective-evaluative consistency, and by low levels of object complexity, evaluative centrality, and object liking. This was a domain of little current involvement for these subjects, although their tendency to organize it along affective lines could reflect their intimate involvement of the past. Finally, the domain of self displayed relatively high levels of object evaluation, and relatively low levels of centralization and affective-evaluative consistency. In other words, most subjects (with the notable exception of Japanese students) tended to display a favorable self-regard, but with no pronounced mode of organization, either abstractly or affectively based.

Information and Differentiation

In one cognitive domain (the domain of nations) where objective measures of knowledge are readily available, the level of information was positively correlated with mean object complexity, mean attribute precision, and dimensionality. We do not know for sure that similar relations would appear in other cognitive domains, but inferential support for this expectation came from a study of the acquaintance domain, in which dimensionality was found to be higher for people well known to the subject than for little known people.

There is also evidence from two studies that intelligence is positively correlated with all three aspects of cognitive differentiation in the several domains considered—especially within the domain of nations. The inference to be drawn from these findings is that cognitive differentiation reflects both general intellectual capacity and specific knowledge about the domain, but we cannot yet say anything about their relative contributions.

Political Ideology and Structural Properties

We have collected fragmentary data on relationships between the contents of attitudes and the cognitive structure within which they are embedded. For three different samples of community residents, questioned about various groups within their societies, there were consistent tendencies for persons of conservative ideology to display higher levels of evaluative centrality than liberals, while liberals tended to display higher levels of dimensionality than conservatives. If similar results appear for other cognitive domains, one might be tempted to speculate that conservatism reflects relatively greater emotional involvement in the domain, while liberalism reflects a relatively more complex perspective within which the objects are viewed. Such a speculation is only preliminary, however, as too few cognitive domains have been assessed, and we are not very confident about the generality of liberal or conservative ideology over various cognitive domains.

Interpersonal Processes and Cognitive Properties

The tendency to view the self as similar to liked acquaintances is associated with high evaluative centrality, low ambivalence, and favorable regard for the self, and also with low ambivalence toward acquaintances. A high level of personal adjustment, both in one's own eyes and in the judgment of close acquaintances, is similarly associated with high evaluative centrality, low ambivalence, and favorable regard for both self and acquaintances, and with high affective-evaluative consistency concerning self and acquaintances. Personal adjustment is also associated with univalent, favorable appraisal of relations within one's family of orientation.

NEEDED IMPROVEMENTS IN MEASURES

In some respects, our contribution to measurement of these cognitive variables represents an advance over previous work: We have employed multiple measures of each construct and revised them to the point where a modicum of inter-measure agreement has been achieved. This has been accomplished within three different cultures, utilizing two very different languages, thereby offering some promise of cross-cultural generality. There are, however, serious defects remaining in our measures, which can only be remedied by closer attention to the kinds of tasks required of subjects and to the ways in which their responses are combined into appropriate indices.

The measures that are currently most satisfactory, in the sense of showing high reliability, are those describing mean characteristics of objects—complexity, affect, and liking—averaged over all objects within a domain. The large number of objects contributes to their reliability, but so may certain irrelevant response-sets, such as verbosity and use of extreme ratings. Though good enough for their purpose, these measures are not particularly novel, and do not even aim at fundamental concepts for which fundamental measures can be developed.

Among the fundamental structural properties, those most satisfactorily measured are evaluative centrality and mean object ambivalence. Although the reliabilities of these measures are not high by traditional standards, this is due chiefly to the small numbers of instruments (three each) from which they are derived. The mean inter-instrument correlations are well above .20, indicating that reliabilities could be raised substantially by adding similar instruments. Equally important, their units of measurement appear consistent from one instrument to another, so that scores can be interpreted in absolute terms as representing high or low levels of the intended variables.

The concepts of dimensionality and attribute precision both require additional measures and greater attention to their metric. At present, different instruments do not yield comparable scores. The concepts of centralization and image comparability should be redefined algebraically to distinguish their measures better and to yield more consistent metrics. The properties of affective balance and affective-evaluative consistency should probably be merged into one superordinate construct and their respective measures combined after appropriate algebraic redefinitions. Evidently, an entirely new approach to measuring attribute centrality is required to supplement the generally satisfactory results from checklists. Instruments that allow more natural responses, without at the same time being distorted by individual differences in vocabulary and verbosity, would be most appropriate. Finally, it would be useful to develop rational metrics for the object properties of complexity, valence, liking, and evaluation in the hope that the generally high reliabilities achieved with these instruments for total domains can also be demonstrated for individual objects.

ELABORATION OF THE GEOMETRIC MODEL

The geometric model presented in Chapter 5 contained few psychological assumptions. Some of those it did contain have turned out to be wrong and need to be corrected. We can also add some assumptions based on our findings, which serve to make the model more useful in accounting for the development of cognitions.

Affect and Liking

Extrapolating from four cognitive domains assessed within a limited population of respondents, we infer that affect toward objects in familiar domains tends to be favorable. This may reflect social norms to "speak no evil," a generalized Pollyanna tendency, or an inclination to consider thoroughly only those domains that are attractive. Whatever the reason, extreme affect expressed toward objects tends to be favorable affect—including liking and positive evaluation. Less favorable affect is likely to be expressed in neutral terms, rather than in outright condemnation of an object. Certainly there are exceptions to this generalization—for instance, with respect to enemy nations or venomous reptiles—but, by and large, we may assume that objects within any cognitive domain are more apt to be liked than disliked by people familiar with them.

In terms of the geometric model, this implies that correlations among attributes may be importantly affected by rare objects—those that are disliked—more than by the vast majority of objects the person knows well, which typically range in valence from neutral to well liked. Herein lies a basis for the development of stereotypes in which an unusual combination of characteristics affects inter-attribute associations—hence generalizations—more than it should.

Affect and Complexity

A second assumption that appears warranted by our findings is that affect and complexity are positively correlated, both within subjects (over objects) and across subjects. For a given individual, better known objects tend to be better liked than little known objects. This probably reflects a general tendency to approach benign objects and avoid malevolent ones. Since liking carries more affect than disliking, there will be a correlation within subjects between affective intensity and object complexity. The between-subjects correlation obtains for mean affective intensity, but not for mean liking of objects. That is, the more people "know" (or think they know) about a class of objects, the more intensely they feel about them; whether they like these objects better or worse, as a result, we cannot say.

Differentiation and Ambivalence

The major sources of ambivalence appear to be different within subjects (across objects) than between subjects. Within an individual, high ambivalence tends to be associated with low object complexity, implying an impoverished image. Additional information tends to support a univalent image (either favorable or unfavorable), perhaps because it is apt to come in clusters from just a few sources, who attempt to impart an affectively consistent view. The result is that a particular person is likely to feel ambivalently (perhaps tentatively) about little known objects, but more univalently (and with greater certainty) about well known objects. Considering all a person's cognitions about a domain, however, a large number of ambivalently viewed objects are apt to be found in structures of high dimensionality; this condition is associated with high object complexity. Conversely, a low average level of ambivalence implies low dimensionality, with attendant simple views of objects. It is as if the level of dimensionality predisposes one toward a given level of average object ambivalence; given that, the more information one acquires about a particular object, the more univalent becomes one's view of it.

The implications of these assumptions for the geometric model are partly dynamic and partly structural. Structurally, they help explain the lack of negative correlation between mean object complexity, on the one hand, and both affective balance and affective-evaluative consistency, on the other. The expectation of a negative relationship depended on the assumption that increasing object complexity leads to increasing object ambivalence, which is not true. Dynamically, these assumptions suggest at least two directions of development within cognitive structures: A continued striving toward univalent views of particular objects may be accompanied by an increased tolerance for ambivalence within the object class as a whole. More generally, one may suggest that not only do cognitions about particular objects determine the relative positions of attributes (as proposed on p. 60), but that, once established, the increasingly independent (i.e., orthogonal) relations among attributes enable more ambivalent views of objects than had been admitted when the domain was less rich in distinct attributes.

Properties of Attributes

Except for the predictions that central attributes tend to be more evaluative and more precise than noncentral attributes, our expectations about relations among attributes, for an individual cognizer, were largely unsupported. Nevertheless, the evidence at this time is not sufficiently clear or persuasive to warrant any modification in the model. First, we need better measures of the centrality of particular attributes. Next, we need to incorporate a larger number of attributes in each instrument than was managed here. Finally, the same set of attributes must appear in two different instruments so that instrument-specific relations can be discounted. In our studies, these aims were neglected because of our desire to randomize objects and attributes over instruments so that structural properties could be measured in as general a way as possible. It will take another series of studies to investigate adequately the variable properties of particular attributes.

Complexity and Image Comparability

We may assume that complex views of objects emerge through the repeated use of one or more attributes more often than through unique combinations of attributes that are object-specific. This leads to positive correlations of mean object complexity with image comparability and centralization. In other words, a rich view of objects results most commonly from an abstract, rather than a concrete, use of available attributes. New objects are likely to be defined on preexisting attributes, rather than on entirely new attributes. This implication is, of course, psychologically reasonable, even though not implicit in the original model.

Evaluative Centrality and Image Comparability

Somewhat less expected is the finding that mean affect, or mean intensity of object valence (which is synonymous with evaluative centrality), is positively correlated with image comparability, as well as with affective balance and affective-evaluative consistency (as predicted). Although image comparability was initially viewed as a more "abstract" than "affective" mode of conceptual organization, these results suggest that affective involvement may facilitate other integrative styles besides those specifically identified as affective. In a way, this is implicit in one of the two predicted relations among attribute properties that was confirmed—i.e., that evaluative attributes are likely to be more central than nonevaluative attributes. It follows that people who make extensive use of evaluative attributes will show a high level of mean attribute centrality, which is the essence of image comparability as we have defined it.

Image Comparability and Centralization

These two theoretically distinct modes of cognitive organization should have been empirically distinct, but were not. It has been noted that the confounding may result from a generally low level of image comparability encountered in the present samples. Nevertheless, it would be desirable to distinguish these two variable properties within ranges typically encountered, and further effort in this direction seems warranted. This undertaking may require both algebraic redefinition and instruments less contaminated by the specific response sets which checklists and free descriptions often attract. Failing an improved distinction through better methodology, it would be appropriate to recognize the implied limit on abstraction: Perhaps the "range of convenience" of most attributes is too narrow to accommodate the majority of objects recognized by most people. This would mean that whatever abstraction occurs is likely to be based on a small number of attributes, instead of many.

The Representation of Values

Our model is intended to represent cognized objects and attributes. Although only real objects have been included in the instruments, there is no reason why ideal objects could not be included, as well. This would allow the representation of valued states. Respondents could be asked, for example, to describe family relationships as they would like them to have been, or to define ideal interaction patterns for their own families of procreation. Appropriate analyses of such instruments could yield several new scores, such as the degree of correspondence (or confusion) between real and ideal structures.

Generalized ideologies, such as liberalism and conservatism, might be represented as structures of ideal objects from several domains that the person ordinarily distinguishes in viewing actual objects. If our tentative finding from the domain of societal groups were replicated and extended, one might propose that the high level of evaluative centrality which characterizes a conservative ideology reflects an affective investment in the currently perceived reality, while the high level of dimensionality that characterizes a liberal ideology reflects an appreciation of the diversity inherent in present reality, which encourages a more favorable view toward change.

The Representation of Factual Accuracy

Our model makes no distinction between attributions that are correct and those that are incorrect. Nevertheless, the positive correlations of information with object complexity, dimensionality, and attribute precision that were obtained within the domain of nations suggest that in some domains, at least, elaboration tends to be in the direction of consensually recognized "fact." It is tempting to speculate that this is true for all domains, including those, such as the self, where consensus of external observers is not entirely dependable. To the extent that a consensual reality can be established for a domain of objects, it would be possible to compare inter-object and inter-attribute relations cognized by a particular observer with those defined as "true," in terms of some of the variable properties (such as affective balance) we have considered. The implications of various discrepancies for personal adjustment, for coping with the objects, and for persuading ignorant or informed others of one's view could then be investigated.

The correlations we have found between measures of intelligence and measures of differentiation within several different cognitive domains suggest that general intellectual capacity helps set the framework within which views of objects become simple or complex through experience. This interpretation is consistent with current views of intelligence. Moreover, it points to certain aspects of intellectual development which have less to do with "capacity" than with affective organization of ideas—such as ambivalence and affective-evaluative consistency.

Inter-Domain Comparability and Similarity

It was initially suggested (p. 60) that a cognitive domain is identified primarily by the kinds of attributes applied to objects within it. Two domains are overlapping or identical to the extent that the same attributes are applied to their objects. It seems quite reasonable to take the next step and propose that inter-domain similarity in structural properties depends on their similarity in attributes. For all cognizers, one would expect various domains of person-objects (for example, acquaintances and fictional characters) to be more similar in their structural properties than domains of people and inanimate objects; this is because similar sets of attributes are ordinarily applied to objects that are similarly classified. When individuals differ in the degree to which they apply similar attributes to two different domains (say, nations and people), one would expect them to differ correspondingly in the consistency of their structural properties between the two domains.

Testing such propositions would be arduous, since the appropriate research would require large samples of domains, as well as large samples of tedium-proof subjects. Nevertheless, some such grandiose undertaking is necessary in order to clarify further the question of domain-generality vs. domain-specificity, which was barely touched in Chapter 10.

It is necessary to distinguish between the comparability of domains and inter-domain similarity of objects. Comparability means that similar attributes are used (hence the domains are overlapping for the subject), whereas similarity means that the same categories of the attributes are applied to certain classes of objects. In an affectively balanced structure, liked objects are described similarly, and so are disliked objects. Subjects in our samples—especially well adjusted subjects—tended to show something like affective balancing *between domains*: Liked acquaintances were described as more like the self than disliked acquaintances. This result encourages a cognitive definition of one kind of adjustment—i.e., the perceived similarity of self to valued objects that are culturally defined as appropriate models. To the extent that this self-image is validated by the appraisals of relevant others, it becomes extended and stabilized, increasingly immune to transient perceived discrepancies. There are, of course, other kinds of adjustment and other kinds of adaptation having little to do with the person's own view of self and others. Whether these are related to our cognitive definition of interpersonal adjustment is a question that invites study.

Associative and Implicative Relations Between Attributes

Our model represents relations among attributes, based on similarities and differences between views of objects, but in no case have we introduced the sort of directional inference process that underlies the theories and technologies of implicative relations. We infer a nondirectional relationship between attributes A and B on the basis of a respondent's report that combinations A_1B_1 and A_2B_2 are more prevalent in cognized objects than are combinations A_1B_2 and A_2B_1, for example. We do not ask whether B depends on A, as in the trait-implication method (p. 43), nor do we manipulate A to produce an effect on B, as is done in experiments by Anderson and Hammond (see p. 45 and 47). Were we to do so, any of several outcomes might ensue with just two attributes: (a) The implicative relationship might be symmetrical and consistent with that found in conceptions of actual objects: A affects B, B affects A in the same way, and known objects display the same association; (b) the relationship might be symmetric, but different from that implicit in known objects; (c) the relationship might be asymmetric and consistent with real-object associations: A affects B in a manner found in known objects, but B has no effect on A; (d) the relationship might be asymmetric and inconsistent with that implicit in known objects.

Other possibilities exist and their number increases as more predictor attributes are considered. We may confine attention to these four at the moment. Outcomes (b) and (d), in which implicative relationships established experimentally do not correspond to inter-attribute associations derived from descriptions of known objects, would require one to consider at least two different cognitive structures: one inferred for previously known objects and one inferred for objects newly presented in the experimental situation. In addition, it would be possible, via the trait-implication method (see p. 43), to generate a third cognitive structure, that inferred by the subjects themselves. The relative utilities of these structures for predicting responses to old and new objects might be compared, or an attempt might be made, to influence one structure by confronting the subject with data about another. (The latter manipulation has been undertaken by Hammond, 1971, in his investigations of cognitive feedback.)

Outcome (a) would require no alteration in the geometrical model. Outcome (c) merits special attention, as it is a plausible result with potential application to the judgment of real-world objects. An example might be that intelligent persons are judged to be desirable employees, but not the reverse.

Algebraic representation of asymmetry would be preferable to geometric representation by "directed graphs," as proposed by Harary et al. (1965), because it would more readily relate to other quantified variables defined in the preceding chapters. One might expect, for instance, that an asymmetrical implication would generate a weaker associative bond than a symmetrical implication. That is, if A_1 implies B_1 but B_1 does not imply A_1, then one would expect the correlation between attributes A and B to be smaller than if the implication were bidirectional. Accordingly, the dimensionality of a cognitive space incorporating asymmetric implications should be larger than one with all-symmetric implications for the same attributes. This circumstance should generate more ambivalent objects and a lower level of affective-evaluative consistency. From a reverse standpoint, the higher the dimensionality, the greater is the likelihood that the person will recognize asymmetric implications, since the meanings of attributes are more distinct than in structures of low dimensionality.

The introduction of additional cue variables entails differential weighting, which may be additive (as implied by Hammond's formulation) or interactive (as implied by Anderson's). Additive weighting is entirely compatible with our geometric model, as the multiple regression coefficients are affected by intercorrelations among the cue variables, which may be interpreted as cosines of angles between attributes in multidimensional space. Complications would arise if each different judgment variable implied a different configuration among cue variables. It is not clear whether this circumstance is implied by Hammond's model. But it certainly is by Anderson's. Also, Anderson's interactions, entailing a change in the effective weight of one cue, depending on what other cues appear with it, are very difficult to represent with a stable geometric model like ours.

Other Structural and Dynamic Variables

It is possible to represent other structural properties from psychological theories in terms of the geometric model. We shall merely suggest some directions of approach here; serious elaboration would depend on the sorts of results that accrue from empirical studies with preliminary measures. The notion of *rigidity* (Cattel & Tiner, 1949; Scott, 1966) could be represented as resistence to change in the relation between attributes in the face of persuasive information about objects that is incompatible with the accepted relationship. An example would be failure of a person who believes that competence requires education to accept contradictory evidence supplied in the form of a competent worker of low education. As commonly used, rigidity refers, not just to a two-attribute relationship, but to a state of the total person, or at least of an entire cognitive domain. The generality of rigidity could be investigated, given adequate measures. If it proved to be pervasive, then one way of representing structural rigidity within the model might be to weight objects differentially, by temporal priority or some other biasing strategy, in treating their effect on the intercorrelations among attributes.

A way of incorporating the concept of *field dependence* (Witkin, Dyk, Faterson, Goodenough, & Karp, 1962) might be developed along the following lines: Field dependence occurs when judgment about an object is influenced by attributes other than those defined as relevant to the task. Examples would be judging the horizontality of a line with reference to one's own body orientation, rather than with reference to a gravitational upright, or judging the social status of other people by contrast to one's own status (see Scott & Cohen, 1978). In field dependence, the person, in attending to irrelevant cues, evidently defines the domain inappropriately (including the wrong objects and attributes) or represents inter-attribute relations inaccurately. If some external standard of cue validity is available, one can represent quantitatively the degree to which a subject's cue utilization is inappropriate (see Hammond, Stewart, Brehmer, & Steinmann, 1975).

Intolerance of ambiguity might be defined in a restricted way within the model. According to Frenkel-Brunswik (1949, 1954), this trait is manifest in *premature closure*, the tendency of a person to supply, by inference, information about an object which is neither provided directly nor sufficiently justified in the data given. For example, a subject infers with certainty that a newly encountered person, dapper and well groomed, is also of high social status, because this association of attributes has been well established in the subject's previous encounters. Just how much justification for an inference is sufficient, and how much certainty about it is warranted, are matters that would have to be specified by reference to some external standards of cue validity, which might vary from one culture to another, or from one actor's world to another. Thus, one can expect considerable difficulty developing measures that are widely applicable to diverse subjects and circumstances.

In considering these three variables, we have ventured onto the boundary separating structural properties (relatively enduring traits) from dynamic (relatively transient) processes. Differences between them depend largely on the span of time over which responses must be observed to infer the variable. A structural variable, such as ambivalence, may be inferred from a single cross-sectional view. A dynamic variable, such as rigidity, requires two or more cross-sectional views, separated in time, to infer a change in state.

It is not much of a step to inferences about noncognitive structural properties from long-continuing behavior dispositions. An incompatibility or conflict between two motives might be inferred, for example, from the observation over time that activities which gratify one tend to thwart the other. We have deliberately confined out structural model to cognitive events known to the person, though recognizing that these offer only a limited picture of the total personality. In principle, however, it would be possible to insert noncognitive elements into our structural model. We hope that our efforts on the limited task might encourage others to measure more precisely structural relations among additional personality components which have heretofore been treated only metaphorically. The task of conceptualization has been well advanced through several generations of theory. The more demanding task of precise measurement should begin.

REFERENCES

Abelson, R. B., Aronson, E., McGuire, W. J., Newcomb, T. M., Rosenberg, M. J., & Tannenbaum, P. H. (Eds.). *Theories of cognitive consistency.* Chicago: Rand McNally, 1968.

Allport, G. W. Attitudes. In C. M. Murchison (Ed.), *Handbook of social psychology.* Worcester, Mass.: Clark University Press, 1935, pp. 798–844.

Allport, G. W. *Pattern and growth in personality.* New York: Holt, Rinehart, & Winston, 1961.

Anderson, N. H. Likableness ratings of 555 personality-trait words. *Journal of Personality and Social Psychology*, 1968, 9, 272–279.

Anderson, N. H. Integration theory and attitude change. *Psychological Review*, 1971, 78, 171–206.

Anderson, N. H. Looking for configurality in clinical judgment. *Psychological Bulletin*, 1972, 78, 93–102.

Asch, S. E. Forming impressions of personality. *Journal of Abnormal and Social Psychology*, 1946, 41, 258–290.

Asch, S. E. *Social psychology.* New York: Prentice-Hall, 1952.

Attneave, F. *Applications of information theory to psychology.* New York: Holt-Dryden, 1959.

Bannister, D. (Ed.). *New perspectives in personal construct theory.* New York: Academic Press, 1977.

Bannister, D., & Mair, J. M. M. *The evaluation of personal constructs.* New York: Academic Press, 1968.

Bieri, J. Cognitive complexity-simplicity and predictive behavior. *Journal of Abnormal and Social Psychology*, 1955, 51, 263–268.

Bieri, J. Cognitive complexity and personality development. In O. J. Harvey (Ed.), *Experience, structure, and adaptability.* New York: Springer, 1966, pp. 13–37.

Blake, R. R., & Ramsey, G. V. (Eds.). *Perception: An approach to personality.* New York: Ronald, 1951.

Bonarius, J. C. J. Research in the personal construct theory of George A. Kelly. In B. Maher (Ed.), *Progress in experimental personality research* (Vol. 2). New York: Academic Press, 1965.

Boshier, R. To rotate or not to rotate: The question of the conservatism scale. *British Journal of Social and Clinical Psychology,* 1972, **11,** 313–323.

Boucher, J., & Osgood, C. E. The Pollyanna hypothesis. *Journal of Verbal Learning and Verbal Behavior,* 1969, 8, 1–8.

Brigham, J. C., & Cook, S. W. The influence of attitude on the recall of controversial material: A failure to confirm. *Journal of Experimental Social Psychology,* 1969, **5,** 240–243.

Brigham, J. C., & Cook, S. W. The influence of attitudes on judgments of plausibility: A replication and extension. *Educational and Psychological Measurement,* 1970, **30,** 283–292.

Bruner, J. S., Goodnow, J. J., & Austin, G. A. *A study of thinking.* New York: John Wiley & Sons, 1956.

Bruner, J. S., Shapiro, D., & Taguiri, R. The mean of traits in isolation and in combination. In R. Tagiuri & L. Petrullo (Eds.), *Person perception and interpersonal behavior.* Stanford: Stanford University Press, 1958, pp. 277–288.

Bruner, J. S., & Tagiuri, R. The perception of people. In G. Lindzey (Ed.), *Handbook of social psychology.* Cambridge, Mass.: Addison-Wesley, 1954, pp. 634–654.

Brunswik, E. *Wahrnehmung und Gegenstandswelt.* Leipzig: Deuticke, 1934.

Brunswik, E. Organismic achievement and environmental probability. *Psychological Review,* 1943, **50,** 255–272.

Brunswik, E. *Perception and the representative design of experiments.* Berkeley, Calif.: University of California Press, 1956.

Burgoyne, P. H. *Conceptual structure and social interaction.* Unpublished doctoral dissertation. University of Sussex, 1975.

Campbell, V. N. *Assumed similarity, perceived sociometric balance, and social influence.* Unpublished doctoral dissertation, University of Colorado, 1960.

Carlson, E. Attitude change through modification of attitude structure. *Journal of Abnormal and Social Psychology,* 1956, **52,** 256–261.

Carroll, J. D., & Chang, J. J. Analysis of individual differences in multidimensional scaling via an N-way generalization of "Eckart-Young" decomposition. *Psychometrika,* 1970, **35,** 283–319.

Cartwright, D., & Harary, F. Structural balance: A generalization of Heider's theory. *Psychological Review,* 1956, **63,** 277–293.

Cattell, R. B., & Tiner, L. G. The varieties of structural rigidity. *Journal of Personality,* 1949, **17,** 321–341.

Centers, R. *The psychology of social classes.* Princeton, N.J.: Princeton University Press, 1949.

Cook, S. W., & Selltiz, C. A multiple-indicator approach to attitude measurement. *Psychological Bulletin,* 1964, **62,** 36–55.

Cox, G. B. *Cognitive structure: A comparison of two theories and measures of integrative complexity.* Unpublished doctoral dissertation, Duke University, 1970.

Crabbe, J. *Measuring attribute articulation.* Unpublished report, University of Colorado, 1969.

Cronbach, L. J. Coefficient alpha and the internal structure of tests. *Psychometrika*, 1951, **16**, 297–334.

Cronbach, L. J. Processes affecting scores on "understanding of others" and "assumed similarity." *Psychological Bulletin*, 1955, **52**, 177–193.

D'Andrade, R. G. Trait psychology and componential analysis. *American Anthropologist*, 1965, **67**, 215–228.

Dawes, R. M. *Fundamentals of attitude measurement.* New York: John Wiley & Sons, 1972.

Dean, D. Alienation: Its meaning and measurement. *American Sociological Review*, 1961, **26**, 753–758.

Donovan, J. *Liking for others, cognitive structure, and similarity of self-other descriptions.* Unpublished report, University of Colorado, 1972.

Du Preez, P. The application of Kelly's personal construct theory to the analysis of political debates. *Journal of Social Psychology*, 1975, **95**, 267–270.

Erikson, E. H. Growth and crises of the "healty personality." In C. Kluckhohn, H. A. Murray, & D. M. Schneider (Eds.), *Personality in nature, society, and culture.* New York: Knopf, 1955, pp. 185–225.

Estes, W. K. (Ed.). *Handbook of learning and cognitive processes* (Vols. 1–5). Hillsdale, N.J.: Erlbaum, 1975–1978.

Feather, N. T. Organization and discrepancy in cognitive structures. *Psychological Review*, 1971, **78**, 355–379.

Festinger, L. *A theory of cognitive dissonance.* Evanston, Ill.: Row, Peterson, 1957.

Fishbein, M. A consideration of beliefs, and their role in attitude measurement. In M. Fishbein (Ed.), *Readings in attitude theory and measurement.* New York: John Wiley & Sons, 1967, pp. 257–266.

Fisher, R. A. *Statistical methods for research workers* (8th ed., rev.). Edinburgh: Oliver & Boyd, 1941.

Flament, C. *Applications of graph theory to group structure.* Englewood Cliffs, N.J.: Prentice-Hall, 1963.

Fransella, F., & Bannister, D. *A manual for repertory grid technique.* New York: Academic Press, 1977.

Frenkel-Brunswik, E. Intolerance of ambiguity as an emotional and perceptual personality variable. *Journal of Personality*, 1949, **18**, 108–143.

Frenkel-Brunswik, E. Further explorations by a contributor to the "Authoritarian Personality." In R. Christie & M. Jahoda (Eds.), *Studies in the scope and method of "The Authoritarian Personality."* Glencoe, Ill.: Free Press, 1954, pp. 226–275.

Gardiner, G. S., & Schroder, H. M. Reliability and validity of the Paragraph Completion Test: Theoretical and empirical notes. *Psychological Reports*, 1972, **31**, 959–962.

Gardner, R. W. Cognitive styles in categorizing behavior. *Journal of Personality*, 1953, **22**, 214–233.

Goldberg, D. P. *The detection of psychiatric illness by questionnaire.* London: Oxford University Press, 1972.

Goldstein, K. M., & Blackman, S. *Cognitive style: Five approaches and research.* New York: John Wiley & Sons, 1978.

Green, B. F., & Goldfried, M. R. On the bipolarity of semantic space. *Psychological Monographs*, 1965, **79** (Whole No. 599).

Guilford, J. P. *Psychometric methods* (2nd ed.). New York: McGraw-Hill, 1954.

Hall, C. S., & Lindzey, G. *Theories of personality* (2nd ed.). New York: John Wiley & Sons, 1970.

Hamilton, D. L. The structure of personality judgments: Comments on Kuusinen's paper and further evidence. *Scandinavian Journal of Psychology*, 1970, **11**, 261–265.

Hammond, K. R. Computer graphics as an aid to learning. *Science*, 1971, **172**, 903–908.

Hammond, K. R. Inductive knowing. In J. R. Royce & W. N. Rozeboom (Eds.), *The psychology of knowing*. London: Gordon & Breach, 1972.

Hammond, K. R., Stewart, T. R., Brehmer, B., & Steinmann, D. O. Social judgment theory. In M. F. Kaplan & S. Schwartz (Eds.), *Human judgment and decision processes: Formal and mathematical approaches*. New York: Academic Press, 1975.

Harary, F., Norman, R. Z., & Cartwright, D. *Structural models: An introduction to the theory of directed graphs*. New York: John Wiley & Sons, 1965.

Harvey, O. J. System structure, flexibility, and creativity. In O. J. Harvey (Ed.), *Experience, structure, and adaptability*. New York: Springer, 1966, pp. 39–65.

Harvey, O. J., Hunt, D. E., & Schroder, H. M. *Conceptual systems and personality organization*. New York: John Wiley & Sons, 1961.

Hayden, B., Nasby, W., & Davids, A. Interpersonal conceptual structures, predictive accuracy, and social adjustment of emotionally disturbed boys. *Journal of Abnormal Psychology*, 1977, **86**, 315–320.

Hays, W. L. An approach to the study of trait implications and trait similarity. In R. Tagiuri & L. Petrullo (Eds.), *Person perception and interpersonal behavior*. Stanford: Stanford University Press, 1958, pp. 289–299.

Heider, F. Attitudes and cognitive organization. *Journal of Psychology*, 1946, **21**, 107–112.

Heider, F. *The psychology of interpersonal relations*. New York: John Wiley & Sons, 1958.

Heider, F. On Lewin's methods and theory. *Psychological Issues*, 1959, **1**, 123.

Holland, R. George Kelly: Constructive innocent and reluctant existentialist. In D. Bannister (Ed.), *Perspectives in personal construct theory*. New York: Academic Press, 1970.

Johnson, R. C. Word affect and word frequency in written English. *Journal of General Psychology*, 1966, **75**, 35–38.

Jordan, N. Behavioral forces that are a function of attitudes and of cognitive organization. *Human relations*, 1953, **6**, 273–287.

Kaplan, K. J. On the ambivalence-indifference problem in attitude theory and measurement: A suggested modification of the Semantic Differential technique. *Psychological Bulletin*, 1972, 77, 361–372.

Katz, E. Experimental studies of Negro-White relationships. In L. Berkowitz (Ed.), *Advances in experimental social psychology* (Vol. 5). New York: Academic Press, 1971.

Kelly, G. *The psychology of personal constructs*. New York: Norton, 1955.

Kelly, G. A brief introduction to personal construct theory. In D. Bannister (Ed.), *Perspectives in personal construct theory*. New York: Academic Press, 1970.

Kenny, D. T., & Ginsberg, R. The specificity of intolerance of ambiguity measures. *Journal of Abnormal and Social Psychology*, 1958, **56**, 300–304.

Kish, L. A procedure for objective respondent selection within the household. *Journal of the American Statistical Association*, 1949, **44**, 380–387.

Kish, L. *Survey sampling*. New York: John Wiley & Sons, 1965.

Kluckhohn, C. Values and value-orientations in the theory of action: An exploration in definition and classification. In T. Parsons & E. A. Shils (Eds.), *Toward a general theory of action*. Cambridge: Harvard University Press, 1951.

Kounin, J. S. Experimental studies of rigidity: I. Measurement of rigidity in normal and feeble-minded persons. II. Explanatory power of the concept of rigidity as applied to feeble-mindedness. *Character and Personality*, 1941, **9**, 251–282.

Krech, D., & Crutchfield, R. S. *Theory and problems of social psychology*. New York: McGraw-Hill, 1948.

Kruskal, J. B. Multidimensional scaling by optimizing goodness of fit to a nonmetric hypothesis. *Psychometrika*, 1964, **29**, 1–27.

Kuusinen, J. Factorial invariance of personality ratings. *Scandinavian Journal of Psychology*, 1969, **10**, 33–44.

Le Bach, J., & Scott, R. *Structural properties of cognition for the domains of family and occupation*. Unpublished report, University of Colorado, 1969.

Levy, L. H. *Conceptions of personality: Theory and research*. New York: Random House, 1970.

Lewin, K. *A dynamic theory of personality*. New York: McGraw-Hill, 1935.

Lewin, K. *Principles of topological psychology*. New York: McGraw-Hill, 1936.

Lewin, K. *Resolving social conflicts*. New York: Harper, 1948.

MacLeod, R. B. The phenomenological approach to social psychology. *Psychological Review*, 1947, **54**, 193–210.

Middleton, R. Alienation, race, and education. *American Sociological Review*, 1963, **28**, 973–977.

Miller, G. A. The magical number seven, plus or minus two: Some limits on our capacity for processing information. *Psychological Review*, 1956, **63**, 81–97.

Mischel, W. *Personality and assessment*. New York: John Wiley & Sons, 1968.

Morrissette, J. An experimental study of the theory of structural balance. *Human Relations*, 1958, **11**, 239–254.

Murphy, G. *Personality: A biosocial approach to origins and structure*. New York: Harper, 1947.

Neisser, U. *Cognitive psychology*. New York: Appleton-Century-Crofts, 1967.

Newcomb, T. M. *Personality and social change*. New York: Dryden, 1943.

Newcomb, T. M. Role behaviors in the study of individual personality and of groups. *Journal of Personality*, 1950, **18**, 273–279. (a)

Newcomb, T. M. *Social psychology*. New York: Dryden, 1950. (b)

Nisbett, R. E., & Wilson, T. D. On telling more than we can know: Verbal reports on mental processes. *Psychological Review*, 1977, **84**, 231–259.

Noble, C. E. An analysis of meaning. *Psychological Review*, 1952, **59**, 421–430.

Norman, W. T. Toward an adequate taxonomy of personality attributes: Replicated factor structure in peer nomination personality ratings. *Journal of Abnormal and Social Psychology*, 1963, **66**, 574–583.

Nunnally, J. *Psychometric theory*. New York: McGraw-Hill, 1967.

Osgood, C. E., Suci, G. J., & Tannenbaum, P. H. *The measurement of meaning*. Urbana: University of Illinois Press, 1957.

Osgood, D. W. *A comparison of cognitive style in impression formation and in existing views about people*. Unpublished doctoral dissertation, University of Colorado, 1977.

Parsons, T., & Shils, E. A. (Eds.). *Toward a general theory of action*. Cambridge, Mass.: Harvard University Press, 1951.

Passini, F. T., & Norman, W. T. A universal conception of personality structure? *Journal of Personality and Social Psychology*, 1966, **4**, 44–49.

Peterson, L., & Peterson, M. J. Short-term retention of individual verbal items. *Journal of Experimental Psychology*, 1959, **58**, 193–198.

Peterson, C., & Scott, W. A. Generality and topic specificity of cognitive styles. *Journal of Research in Personality*, 1975, **9**, 366–374.

Pettigrew, T. F. The measurement and correlates of category width as a cognitive variable. *Journal of Personality*, 1958, **26**, 532–544.

Piaget, J. *The child's conception of physical causality.* London: Routledge & Kegan Paul, 1927.

Piaget, J. *The moral judgment of the child.* London: Routledge & Kegan Paul, 1932.

Piaget, J. *The origins of intelligence in children.* New York: International Universities Press, 1952.

Piaget, J. *Genetic epistemology.* New York: Norton, 1971.

Reker, G. T. Interpersonal conceptual structures of emotionally disturbed and normal boys. *Journal of Abnormal Psychology*, 1974, **83**, 380–386.

Rokeach, M. *The open and closed mind.* New York: Basic Books, 1960.

Rokeach, M. *Beliefs, attitudes, and values: A theory of organization and change.* San Francisco: Jossey-Bass, 1969.

Rosenberg, M. J. Cognitive structure and attitudinal affect. *Journal of Abnormal and Social Psychology*, 1956, **53**, 367–372.

Rosenberg, S., & Jones, R. A method for investigating and representing a person's implicit theory of personality: Theodore Drieser's view of people. *Journal of Personality and Social Psychology*, 1972, **22**, 372–386.

Rosenberg, S., & Sedlak, A. Structural representations of implicit personality theory. In L. Berkowitz (Ed.), *Advances in experimental social psychology* (Vol. 6). New York: Academic Press, 1972.

Rotter, J. B. *Social learning and clinical psychology.* Englewood Cliffs, N.J.: Prentice-Hall, 1954.

Rozin, P., & Kalat, J. W. Specific hungers and poison avoidance as adaptive specializations in learning. *Psychological Review*, 1971, **78**, 459–486.

Schroder, H. M., Driver, M. J., & Streufert, S. *Human information processing.* New York: Holt, Rinehart, & Winston, 1967.

Scott, W. A. Measures of test homogeneity. *Educational and Psychological Measurement*, 1960, **20**, 751–758.

Scott, W. A. Cognitive complexity and cognitive flexibility. *Sociometry*, 1962, **25**, 405–414.

Scott, W. A. *Measures of cognitive differentiation.* Unpublished report, University of Colorado, 1964.

Scott, W. A. *Progress report: Structural properties of cognition.* Unpublished report, University of Colorado, 1965. (a)

Scott, W. A. *Values and organizations: A study of fraternities and sororities.* Chicago: Rand McNally, 1965. (b)

Scott, W. A. Flexibility, rigidity, and adaptation: Toward a clarification of constructs. In O. J. Harvey (Ed.), *Experience, structure, and adaptability.* New York: Springer, 1966. (a)

Scott, W. A. Measures of cognitive structure. *Multivariate Behavioral Research*, 1966, **1**, 391–395. (b)

Scott, W. A. Attitude measurement. In G. Lindzey & E. Aronson (Eds.), *Handbook of social psychology* (Rev. ed., Vol. 2). Reading, Mass.: Addison-Wesley, 1968, pp. 204–273.

Scott, W. A. Structure of natural cognitions. *Journal of Personality and Social Psychology*, 1969, **12**, 261–278.

Scott, W. A. *Cognitive concomitants of successful and unsuccessful psychotherapy.* Unpublished report, University of Colorado, 1972.

Scott, W. A. Cognitive correlates of maladjustment among college students in three cultures. *Journal of Consulting and Clinical Psychology*, 1974, **42**, 184–195. (a)

Scott, W. A. Varieties of cognitive integration. *Journal of Personality and Social Psychology*, 1974, **30**, 563–578. (b)

Scott, W. A., & Cohen, R. D. Sociometric indices of group structure. *Australian Journal of Psychology*, 1978, **30**, 41–57.

Scott, W. A., Kline, J. A., Faguy-Coté, E., & Peterson, C. Centrality of cognitive attributes. *Journal of Research in Personality*, 1979, in press.

Scott, W. A., & Peterson, C. Adjustment, Pollyannaism, and attraction to close personal relationships. *Journal of Consulting and Clinical Psychology*, 1975, **43**, 872–880.

Scott, W. A., & Scott, R. Acquaintance ratings as criteria of adjustment. *Australian Psychologist*, 1979, in press.

Scott, W. A. Rohrbaugh, J. Conceptions of harmful groups: Some correlates of group descriptions in three cultures. *Journal of Personality and Social Psychology*, 1975, **31**, 992–1003.

Scott, W. A., & Wertheimer, M. *Introduction to psychological research.* New York: John Wiley & Sons, 1962.

Seferi, M. M. L. *International and interpersonal cognitions.* Unpublished report, University of Colorado, 1968.

Selltiz, C., & Cook, S. W. Racial attitude as a determinant of judgments of plausibility. *Journal of Social Psychology*, 1966, **70**, 139–147.

Sherif, M., & Hovland, C. I. *Social judgment: Assimilation and contrast effects in communication and attitude change.* New Haven: Yale University Press, 1961.

Sloane, H. N., Gorlow, L., & Jackson, D. N. Cognitive styles in equivalence range. *Perceptual and Motor Skills*, 1963, **16**, 389–404.

Slovic, P., & Lichtenstein, S. Comparison of Bayesian and regression approaches to the study of information processing in judgment. In L. Rappoport & D. A. Summers (Eds.), *Human judgment and social interaciton.* New York: Holt, Rinehart, & Winston, 1973.

Sperling, G. The information available in brief visual presentations. *Psychological Monographs*, 1960, **74** (Whole No. 11).

Streufert, S., & Streufert, S. C. *Behavior in the complex environment.* Washington, D.C.: V. H. Winston & Sons, 1978.

Tajfel, H. Social and cultural factors in perception. In G. Lindzey & E. Aronson (Eds.), *Handbook of Social Psychology* (Rev. ed., Vol. 3). Reading, Mass.: Addison-Wesley, 1969, pp. 395–449.

Taylor, J. A. A personality scale of manifest anxiety. *Journal of Abnormal and Social Psychology*, 1953, **48**, 285–290.

Triandris, H. C. *Attitudes and attitude change.* New York: John Wiley & Sons, 1970.

Vannoy, J. S. Generality of complexity-simplicity as a personality variable. *Journal of Personality and Social Psychology*, 1965, **2**, 385–396.

Waly, P., & Cook, S. W. Attitude as a determinant of learning and memory: A failure to confirm. *Journal of Personality and Social Psychology*, 1966, **4**, 280–288.

Werner, H. *Comparative psychology of mental development* (3rd ed.). New York: International Universities Press, 1957.

Wilson, G. D., & Patterson, J. R. A new measure of conservatism. *British Journal of Social and Clinical Psychology*, 1968, **7**, 264–269.

Winer, B. J. *Statistical principles in experimental design* (2nd ed.). New York: McGraw-Hill, 1971.

Wing, J. K., Cooper, J. E., & Sartorius, N. *The measurement and classification of psychiatric symptoms.* London: Cambridge University Press, 1974.

Witkin, H. A., Dyk, R. B., Faterson, H. F., Goodenough, D. R., & Karp, S. A. *Psychological differentiation: Studies of development.* New York: Wiley, 1962.

Woodmansee, J., & Cook, S. W. Dimensions of verbal racial attitudes. *Journal of Personality and Social Psychology*, 1967, **7**, 240–250.

Wright, J. H., & Hicks, J. M. Construction and validation of a Thurstone scale of liberalism-conservatism. *Journal of Applied Psychology*, 1966, **50**, 9–12.

Wyer, R. S. *Cognitive organization and change: An information processing approach.* Hillside, N.J.: Erlbaum, 1974.

Zajonc, R. The process of cognitive turning in communication. *Journal of Abnormal and Social Psychology*, 1960, **61**, 159–164.

Zajonc, R. Cognitive theories in social psychology. In G. Lindzey & E. Aronson (Eds.), *Handbook of social psychology* (Vol. 1, 2nd ed.). Reading, Mass.: Addison-Wesley, 1968.

APPENDIX A

CONSTRUCTING INSTRUMENTS FOR THE DOMAINS OF FAMILY ACTIVITIES, NATIONS, AND SELF-ROLES

LISTING AND COMPARING OBJECTS

The only differences among domains of this instrument are the instructions on the first page and the substitution of appropriate terms for "acquaintance" or "person." The instructions for three other domains appear below.

LISTING AND COMPARING FAMILY ACTIVITIES

Think about the situations that occur in your immediate family (your parents and any sisters or brothers) and the activities you engage in with them. On the lines below please write down 20 of these situations and activities. Include both things you like and things you dislike. (If you are not now living with your parents, please reply as you recall from your youth.)

LISTING AND COMPARING NATIONS

In the spaces below please write the names of 20 nations that you think are particularly important in world affairs. In doing this, be your own judge of whether or not a particular nation is important.

LISTING AND COMPARING SELF-ROLES

Throughout their lives, people play a variety of different roles. For instance, during the average week or month, one might be a friend, housekeeper, artist, daughter (or son), tennis player, and conversationalist. Think about the various things you do, and the people you relate to, fairly regularly. These are the various "roles" that you play in life. Please write down 20 different roles or situations that you find yourself in quite often. Include both roles you enjoy and those you do not enjoy.

FREE DESCRIPTION OF OBJECTS

FREE DESCRIPTION OF FAMILY SITUATIONS

On the following pages specific family situations and activities are written at the top of a set of lines. Please think about yourself and your immediate family in each of them and, on the blank lines below, write down some descriptions of yourself in that situation—that is, how you tend to act, think, and feel in those circumstances. State each description in a word, phrase, or sentence and start each different description on a new line. You may use as many or as few lines as you wish for each situation, but try to list all those descriptions which you feel are important for understanding your reactions in that situation.

(If you are not now living with your parents, please reply as you recall from your youth, and indicate how long ago that was:)

_____ I am now living with my family (parents and siblings).

_____ I still live with my family (parents and siblings) a good deal of the time, but am not doing so at present.

_____ I have not lived with my family (parents and siblings) for _____ years.

Pages 2 through 6 designate two situations per page, each followed by 12 blank lines: Spending time along with my mother, Talking with my parents about sex, Showing affection toward my family, Being away from home, Discussing moral standards with my parents, Fighting with my sister or brother, Being criticized by my family, Telling my family about school, Visiting friends with my family, Going camping with my family.

Pages 7 and 8 contain appropriate instructions for rating of descriptions and situations, as in *Free Description of Acquaintances*, (p. 88).

FREE DESCRIPTION OF NATIONS

On the following pages appear the names of several nations, followed by sets of blank lines. On the blank lines below each name, would you please write down some descriptions of that country. State each description in a word, phrase, or sentence and start each different description on a new line. You may use as many or as few lines as you wish for each nation, but try to list all those descriptions you feel are *important* for understanding that country.

Pages 2 through 6 designate two nations per page, each followed by 12 blank lines: Australia, France, Greece, India, Israel, Japan, Mexico, Soviet Union (Russia), United Arab Republic (Egypt), United Kingdom (Britain).

Pages 7 and 8 contain appropriate instructions for rating of descriptions and nations, as in *Free Description of Acquaintances* (p. 89).

FREE DESCRIPTION OF SELF-ROLES

On the following pages, various situations in which you might find yourself are described at the top of a set of lines. Please think about yourself in each of them: Then, on the blank lines below, write down some of the characteristics which describe yourself in that situation. State each characteristis in a word, phrase, or sentence and start each different characteristic on a new line. You may use as many or as few lines as you wish for each situation, but try to list all those characteristics which you feel are *important* for understanding yourself in that situation. If you have never been in one of the situations, just do your best to imagine how you would act, think, or feel under the circumstances.

Pages 2 through 6 designate 2 roles per page, each followed by 12 blank lines: Myself as a student, Myself at a religious service, Myself alone, Myself as a friend to someone of the opposite sex, Myself living at home, Myself as a friend to someone of the same sex, Myself in trouble, Myself as a casual acquaintance, Myself as a (potential) parent, Myself as a (potential) husband (or wife).

Pages 7 and 8 contain appropriate instructions for rating descriptions and roles, as in *Free Descriptions of Acquaintances* (p. 89).

CHECKLIST DESCRIPTION OF FAMILY SITUATIONS

Writing a letter to my parents is:

1. central	25. friendly (+)	49. cruel (−)
2. peripheral	26. unfriendly (−)	50. kind (+)
3. broadening (+)	27. healthy (+)	51. reserved
4. narrowing (−)	28. unhealthy (−)	52. demonstrative
5. changing	29. hurried	53. fair (+)
6. constant	30. unhurried	54. unfair (−)
7. continual	31. reasonable (+)	55. rewarding (+)
8. occasional	32. unreasonable (−)	56. waste of time (−)
9. conventional	33. interesting (+)	57. serious
10. different	34. boring (−)	58. carefree
11. difficult	35. meaningful (+)	59. simple
12. easy	36. meaningless (−)	60. complex
13. time consuming	37. novel	61. reliable (+)
14. not time consuming	38. old-fashioned	62. unreliable (−)
15. scheduled	39. ordinary	63. genuine (+)
16. unscheduled	40. unusual	64. false (−)
17. emotional	41. sincere (+)	65. tense (−)
18. unemotional	42. deceitful (−)	66. comfortable (+)
19. appropriate (+)	43. planned	67. structured
20. inappropriate (−)	44. unplanned	68. unstructured
21. polite (+)	45. quiet	69. just (+)
22. rude (−)	46. boisterous	70. unjust (−)
23. frequent	47. pleasant (+)	71. warm (+)
24. infrequent	48. unpleasant (−)	72. cold (−)

(Evaluative codings of the adjectives, + and −, do not appear on the instrument. The following rating form appears on the last page:)

Please write a number from the following scale beside each activity below to indicate how much you like doing it.

SCALE

7 Enjoy it very much
6 Enjoy it considerably
5 Enjoy it for the most part, with some degree of dislike
4 Neither enjoy it nor dislike it
3 Dislike for the most part, with some degree of enjoyment
2 Dislike considerably
1 Dislike very much

_____ 1. Writing a letter to my parents
_____ 2. Introducing a close friend to my family
_____ 3. Discussing my friends with my parents
_____ 4. Being punished by my father
_____ 5. Being caught in a lie by my parents
_____ 6. Borrowing money from my parents
_____ 7. Eating meals with my family
_____ 8. Spending my leisure time with my family
_____ 9. Singing or playing music with my family
_____ 10. Going for a drive with my family

CHECKLIST DESCRIPTION OF NATIONS

Canada

1. aggressive	25. dry	49. purposeful (+)
2. unaggressive	26. rainy	50. aimless (−)
3. backward (−)	27. friendly (+)	51. peaceful (+)
4. progressive (+)	28. hostile (−)	52. warlike (−)
5. beautiful (+)	29. greedy (−)	53. religious
6. ugly (−)	30. unselfish (+)	54. nonreligious
7. bureaucratic	31. hardworking (+)	55. responsible (+)
8. nonbureaucratic	32. lazy (−)	56. irresponsible (−)
9. classless	33. high crime rate (−)	57. rural
10. stratified	34. low crime rate (+)	58. urban
11. cold	35. homogeneous	59. simple
12. hot	36. diverse	60. complex
13. conformist	37. honest (+)	61. slow acting
14. nonconformist	38. dishonest (−)	62. fast acting
15. cruel (−)	39. isolated	63. stable (+)
16. kind (+)	40. not isolated	64. unstable (−)
17. dangerous (−)	41. large	65. united (+)
18. trustworthy (+)	42. small	66. disunited (−)
19. democratic (+)	43. leisurely	67. traditional
20. totalitarian (−)	44. fast living	68. changing
21. densely populated	45. much freedom (+)	69. well educated (+)
22. sparsely populated	46. little freedom (−)	70. poorly educated (−)
23. dominating	47. neutral	71. young
24. dependent	48. partisan	72. old

(Evaluative codings, + and −, do not appear on the instrument. The last page contains a scale, like that used at the end of *Checklist Description of Acquaintances*, for rating the following nations which the respondent has just described with the checklist: Canada, China, Czechoslovakia, East Germany, Italy, Republic of South Africa, South Vietnam, Switzerland, Thailand, and West Germany.)

CHECKLIST DESCRIPTION OF SELF-ROLES

Myself giving advice:

1. sincere (+)	25. introvert	49. predictable
2. insincere (−)	26. extrovert	50. unpredictable
3. aggressive	27. good sense of humor (+)	51. responsible (+)
4. unaggressive	28. poor sense of humor (−)	52. irresponsible (−)
5. argumentative	29. hardworking (+)	53. restrained
6. compliant	30. lazy (−)	54. impulsive
7. brave (+)	31. honest (+)	55. shy
8. cowardly (−)	32. dishonest (−)	56. bold
9. considerate (+)	33. hurried	57. solemn
10. selfish (−)	34. unhurried	58. frivolous
11. cooperative (+)	35. imaginative (+)	59. self-confident (+)
12. uncooperative (−)	36. unimaginative (−)	60. insecure (−)
13. complex	37. kind (+)	61. tactful (+)
14. simple	38. cruel (−)	62. tactless (−)
15. conformist	39. dominant	63. talkative
16. nonconformist	40. submissive	64. quiet
17. changeable	41. neurotic (−)	65. trustworthy (+)
18. unchanging	42. well adjusted (+)	66. untrustworthy (−)
19. demanding	43. loyal (+)	67. dependable (+)
20. unassuming	44. disloyal (−)	68. undependable (−)
21. emotional	45. ordinary	69. religious
22. unemotional	46. unusual	70. nonreligious
23. forgiving (+)	47. possessive	71. wise (+)
24. spiteful (−)	48. unpossessive	72. foolish (−)

(Evaluative codings, + and −, do not appear on the instrument. On the last page is a scale like that used for rating family situations, followed by a list of those roles which the respondent has just described with the checklist: Myself giving advice, Myself as a sports participant, Myself as a lover, Myself as a winner, Myself as a gardner, Myself when I'm "high" (stoned), Myself as an ex-friend to someone of the same sex, Myself as a cook, Myself as a newcomer in a group, and Myself as a loser.)

GROUPING OF OBJECTS

GROUPING OF FAMILY SITUATIONS

An introduction similar to *Grouping Acquaintances* (see p. 94) presents the following list of family situations: Arguing with my father, Asking my parents for advice, Being caught in a lie by my parents, Being criticized by my family, Being given advice by my family, Being sick at home, Being nagged by my mother, Borrowing money from my parents, Chatting with a friend of my parents, Confiding in my mother, Getting in a family fight, Going on a picnic with my family, Spending time along with my mother, Discussing my friends with my parents, Eating meals with my family, Fighting with my sister or brother, Going to a movie with my family, Discussing moral standards with my parents, Having a dinner guest at home, Having my parents angry with me, Introducing a close friend to my family, Living at home with my parents, Discussing pot and drugs with my parents, Performing for my parents and their friends, Playing card games with my family, Showing my parents my school reports, Singing or playing music with my family, Spending time alone with my father, Going shopping with my mother, and Talking with my parents about sex.

Subsequent pages present the following attributes, two per page, each above one-half page of blank space: How enjoyable they are for me, How much I learn from them, How relaxing (or exciting) they are for me, How much the other person enjoys them, How close to my family they make me feel, How solemn (or carefree) they make me feel, How well I manage myself in them, How well the other person manages himself, How much I discuss them with other people, How much I worry about them.

GROUPING NATIONS

An introduction, similar to that used in *Grouping Acquaintances*, presents the following list of nations: Albania, Brazil, Canada, China, Congo, Japan, United States of America, Israel, Jordan, Kuwait, Laos, Malaysia, North Korea, North Vietnam, Pakistan, Panama, Peru, Philippines, Portugal, Rhodesia, Rumania, South Vietnam, Spain, Sweden, Saudi Arabia, Syria, Turkey, United Arab Republic (Egypt), Venezuela, and West Germany.

Subsequent pages presented the following attributes, two per page, each above one-half page of blank space: How militaristic they are, How materialistic they are, How powerful they are, How capitalistic they are, How nationalistic they are, How ambitious they are, How anti-American they are, How friendly you feel toward them, How competent they are, How trustworthy they are.

GROUPING SELF-ROLES

An introduction similar to that used in *Grouping Acquaintances* presents the following list of roles: Myself giving advice, Myself as a host or hostess, Myself taking orders from someone superior, Myself as a shopper, Myself as a conversationalist, Myself at a party, Myself as a lover, Myself as a work supervisor, Myself doing repetitive tasks, Myself as a leader, Myself as a neighbor, Myself when I'm caught doing something illegal (or against the rules), Myself as an opponent, Myself as a (potential) parent, Myself as a son (or daughter), Myself as a (potential) husband (or wife), Myself as a student, Myself as a patient (when I'm sick), Myself as a worker, Myself as an enemy, Myself as a club member, Myself as a dinner companion, Myself as a friend to someone of the opposite sex, Myself in an audience, Myself as a daydreamer, Myself when I'm high (stoned), Myself as an ex-friend to someone of the opposite sex, Myself in the nude, Myself as a card player, and Myself as a repairman.

Subsequent pages present the following attributes, two per page, each above one-half page of blank space: How competent you are in them, How enthusiastic you feel in them, How flexible (or rigid) you are in them, How temperamental you are in them, How independent you are in them, How mature you are in them, How popular you are in them, How introverted (or extroverted) you are in them, How much you like yourself in them, How relaxed (or tense) you are in them.

MOST SIMILAR PAIRS OF OBJECTS

MOST SIMILAR PAIRS OF FAMILY SITUATIONS (first page)

1. Confiding in my mother	12. Going to a family reunion
2. Celebrating my birthday	13. Asking a favor of my father
3. Being criticized by my family	14. Engaging in sports with my family
4. Going shopping with my mother	
5. Asking my parents for advice	15. Performing for my parents and their friends
6. Telling my family about school	
7. Working for a parent	16. Going to a movie with my family
8. Going camping with my family	17. Arguing with my mother
9. Chatting with a friend of my family	18. Visting friends with my family
	19. Going to a restaurant with my family
10. Living at home with my parents	
11. Being shown off to my parents' acquaintances	20. Fighting with my brother or sister

From the list above, please pick out two situations that bring out *very similar* reactions (thoughts, feelings, or behavior) in you. Write their *numbers* in the space beside *A*. To the right of the pair, please write the main way in which they are similar. Then pick out two other situations in which you react alike; write their numbers and the principal similarity in your reactions on line *B*. Do the same with *C*. You may use any situation more than once, but do not repeat the same pairs.

And so forth, as in *Most Similar Pairs of Acquaintances* (p. 96). The second page requires the respondent to rate the 20 situations listed, according to these instructions: "Beside each situation below, write a number from the following scale, indicating how much you like being in that situation." The rating scale is identical to that presented in *Most Similar Pairs of Acquaintances*.

MOST SIMILAR PAIRS OF NATIONS (first page)

1. Algeria	11. Ireland
2. Argentina	12. Indonesia
3. Austria	13. Jordan
4. Belgium	14. Lebanon
5. Bulgaria	15. Laos
6. Cambodia	16. Netherlands (Holland)
7. East Germany	17. North Vietnam
8. Finland	18. Pakistan
9. Hungary	19. South Korea
10. Haiti	20. Venezuela

From the list above, please pick out two nations that you feel are *very similar* to each other (on whatever basis you choose). Write their *numbers* in the spaces beside *A*. To the right of the pair, please write the main way in which they are similar.

And so forth, as in *Most Similar Pairs of Acquaintances* (p. 96). The second page requires the respondent to rate the 20 nations, according to these instructions: "Besides each nation listed below, write a number from the following scale, indicating how much you like that nation." The rating scale is identical to that presented in *Most Similar Pairs of Acquaintances*.

MOST SIMILAR PAIRS OF SELF-ROLES (first page)

1. Myself when I'm high (stoned)
2. Myself as an entertainer
3. Myself as a (potential) husband or wife
4. Myself in an audience
5. Myself when I have failed
6. Myself as a loser
7. Myself as a teacher
8. Myself as a club member
9. Myself as a public speaker
10. Myself as a tourist
11. Myself as a card player
12. Myself meeting someone of the opposite sex for the first time
13. Myself as a citizen
14. Myself taking orders from someone superior
15. Myself as a weekend guest
16. Myself as a collector
17. Myself as an enemy
18. Myself when I can't get what I want
19. Myself as a gardener
20. Myself as a patient (when I'm sick)

Look at the situations listed above and imagine yourself and what you are like in each of them. Pick out two situations in which you are *very much alike* (on whatever basis you choose). Write their *numbers* in the spaces beside *A*. To the right of the pair, please write the main way in which you are alike in the two situations.

And so forth, as in *Most Similar Pairs of Acquaintances* (see p. 96). The second page requires the respondent to rate the 20 roles according to these instructions: "Besides each situation listed below, write a number from the following scale, indicating how much you like yourself in that situation." The rating scale is identical to that presented in *Most Similar Pairs of Acquaintances* except that "myself" was inserted in each alternative after the word "like" or "dislike."

SIMILARITY OF PAIRED OBJECTS

SIMILARITY OF PAIRED FAMILY SITUATIONS (first page)

Below are descriptions of common family situations. Please think about how you react in each of them with your family. Then rate the similarity of your reactions (both thoughts and actions) in the two situations of each pair. Mark the column which best expresses the degree of similarity.

The pairs listed are: (1) Spending time alone with my father & Discussing pot or drugs with my family, (2) Having a dinner guest at home & Being nagged by my mother, (3) Having my parents angry with me & Having my parents lie to me, (4) Doing household chores & Playing games with my family, (5) Going on holiday with my family

& Going to religious services with my family, (6) Writing a letter to my parents & Asking my parents for advice, (7) Discussing politics with my parents & Discussing my career plans with my parents, (8) Asking a favor of my father & Arguing with my mother, (9) Telling my parents I'm in trouble & Being shown off to my parents' acquaintances, (10) Celebrating my birthday & Being sick at home, (11) Spending time alone with my father & Writing a letter to my parents, (12) Discussing pot or drugs with my family & Asking my parents for advice, (13) Having a dinner guest at home & Discussing politics with my parents, (14) Being nagged by my mother & Discussing my career plans with my parents, (15) Having my parents angry with me & Asking a favor of my father, (16) Having my parents lie to me & Arguing with my mother, (17) Doing household chores & Telling my parents I'm in trouble, (18) Playing games with my family & Being shown off to my parents' acquaintances, (19) Going on holiday with my family & Celebrating my birthday, (20) Going to church with my family & Being sick at home.

The last page requires the respondent to rate each of the 20 situations according to the same instructions used in *Most Similar Pairs of Family Situations* (p. 239).

SIMILARITY OF PAIRED NATIONS (first page)

Please rate the following pairs of nations according to how similar you feel they are. Check the column which best expresses your opinion.

The 20 pairs listed are: Iran and Nigeria, Norway and United Kingdom (Britain), Iraq and Yugoslavia, China and Taiwan (Nationalist China), France and Hungary, Australia and Turkey, Kenya and Switzerland, Republic of South Africa and Rhodesia, Poland and Netherlands (Holland), Peru and Syria, China and Nigeria, France and United Kingdom (Britain), Australia and Yugoslavia, Kenya and Taiwan (Nationalist China), Republic of South Africa and Hungary, Netherlands (Holland) and Turkey, Peru and Switzerland, Syria and Norway, Iran and Poland, Iraq and Rhodesia.

The second page requires the respondent to rate each of the 20 nations, according to the same instructions used in *Most Similar Pairs of Nations* (p. 240).

SIMILARITY OF SELF-ROLES

Below are pairs of situations in which you might find yourself at one time or another in your life. Please think about yourself in the two situations. Then rate them according to how much alike you are (or would be) in the two situations. Check the column which best expresses your opinion.

The rating columns are headed: *"Degree of Similarity in my Behavior: High, Medium, Low."* The pairs of roles were headed: "Myself," followed by these pairs: As a winner & As an artist, As a cook & As an opponent, On a date & As an activist, When I'm caught doing something illegal & As a participant in a group discussion, As a public speaker & Living at home, As a son (or daughter) & As a patient (when I'm sick), Helping someone & As a dinner companion, As a citizen & As a driver, When reading & At a religious service, When receiving advice & As a housekeeper, As a cook & As a son (or daughter), As an opponent & As a patient (when I'm sick), On a date & Helping someone, As an activist & As a dinner companion, When I'm caught doing something illegal & As a citizen, As a participant in a group discussion & As a driver, As a public speaker & When reading, Living at home & At a religious service, As a winner & When receiving advice, As an artist & As a housekeeper.

The second page requires the respondent to rate himself in each of the 20 roles, according to the same instructions used in *Most Similar Pairs of Self-Roles* (p. 240).

CONSTRUCTING SETS OF OBJECTS

CONSTRUCTING SETS OF FAMILY SITUATIONS (first page)

For each group of family situations listed below, please think of what they are like in your family. On this basis, cross out the number beside any situation that you feel doesn't belong with the rest of the group. You may cross out as many of them as you wish, including all of them or none of them. To the right of each group, please give the main reason why you feel the remaining situations belong together. (If you no longer live with your parents and siblings, please answer as you recall these situations from your youth.)

Family situations in the 10 groups are identified by both number and description in the rating list, which appears on the last page. The groups consist of the same list numbers as shown for *Constructing Sets of Acquaintances* (p. 99).

Finally, respondents rate each family situation in this list according to the same instructions used in *Most Similar Pairs of Family Situations* (p. 000): (1) Going to a family reunion, (2) Being away from home, (3) Being caught in a lie by my parents, (4) Being nagged by my mother, (5) Celebrating my birthday, (6) Discussing career plans with my parents, (7) Having my parents lie to me, (8) Engaging in sports with my family, (9) Going to church with my family, (10) Asking a favor of my father, (11) Discussing politics with my parents, (12) Lending money to my brother or sister, (13) Lying to my parents, (14) Doing household chores, (15) Performing for my parents and their friends, (16) Showing affection toward my parents, (17) Spending my leisure time with my family, (18) Spending time alone with my mother, (19) Talking with my parents about sex, (20) Working for a parent.

CONSTRUCTING SETS OF NATIONS (first page)

For each group of nations listed below, please think of which nations in that group are alike. On this basis, cross out the number of any nation that you feel *doesn't belong* with the rest of the group. You may cross out as many numbers in each group as you wish, including all of them or none of them. To the right of each group, please give the main reason why you feel the remaining nations belong together.

Nations in the 10 groups are identified by both number and name in the rating list, which appears on the last page. The groups consist of the same list numbers as shown for *Constructing Sets of Acquaintances* (p. 99).

Finally, respondents rate each nation in this list according to the same instructions used in *Most Similar Pairs of Nations* (p. 240): (1) Malaysia, (2) Albania, (3) Belgium, (4) Congo, (5) Chile, (6) Czechoslovakia, (7) Dominican Republic, (8) Ethiopia, (9) Ghana, (10) Greece, (11) Guatemala, (12) Taiwan (Nationalist China), (13) Indonesia, (14) Iran, (15) Iraq, (16) Kenya, (17) New Zealand (replaced with United States of America for respondents in New Zealand), (18) Nigeria, (19) Norway, (20) Panama.

CONSTRUCTING SETS OF SELF-ROLES

For each group of roles listed below, please think of yourself and what you are like in the roles listed. On this basis, please cross out the *numbers* of any role in which you are different from the way you are in the rest of the roles in the group. You may cross out as many numbers in each group as you wish, leaving all of them or none of them. To the right of each group, please give the main reason why you feel the remaining roles belong together—that is, the main way in which you react similarly in all of them.

Roles in the 10 groups are identified by both number and description in the rating list, which appears on the last page. The groups consist of the same list numbers as shown for *Constructing Sets of Acquaintances* (p. 99).

Finally, respondents rate themselves in each role of this list, according to the same instructions used in *Most Similar Pairs of Self-Roles* (p. 240): (1) Myself as a casual acquaintance, (2) Myself as a conversationalist, (3) Myself as an artist, (4) Myself at a party, (5) Myself alone, (6) Myself as a worker, (7) Myself as a collector, (8) Myself on a date, (9) Myself when reading, (10) Myself as a shopper, (11) Myself as a work supervisor, (12) Myself as a lover, (13) Myself as an ex-friend to someone of the opposite sex, (14) Myself in an emergency, (15) Myself as a weekend guest, (16) Myself as an ex-friend to someone of the same sex, (17) Myself when I can't have what I want, (18) Myself as a repairman, (19) Myself helping someone, (20) Myself as a loser.

RATING OF OBJECTS

RATING OF FAMILY SITUATIONS

An introduction similar to that used in *Ratings of Acquaintances* appears on a cover page. Twenty subsequent pages are headed by one of the following situations: Arguing with my mother, Being away from my parents, Going on holiday with my family, Being shown off to my parents' acquaintances, Confiding in my mother, Discussing politics with my parents, Eating meals with my family, Getting in a family fight, Lying to my family, Going on a drive with my family, Having a dinner guest at home, Showing affection toward my parents, Showing my parents my school reports, Spending time alone with my father, Telling my family about school, Having my parents lie to me, Visiting friends with my family, Watching television with my family, Writing a letter to my parents, Telling my parents that I'm in trouble.

Below the designations appear 10 bipolar attributes, identified by the following pairs of antonyms, each separated by 7 numbered spaces: enjoyable—unenjoyable, safe—dangerous, fair—unfair, embarassing—comfortable, disruptive—unifying, frequent—infrequent, educational—unenlightening, respectable—demeaning, intimate—impersonal, easy—difficult. At the top of the page the numbered spaces are designated by adverbs as in *Rating of Acquaintances* (p. 101).

RATING OF NATIONS

An introduction similar to that used in *Ratings of Acquaintances* appears on a cover page. Twenty subsequent pages are each headed by one of the following nations: Algeria, Australia, Cambodia, China, Cuba, Japan (replaced by United States of America for subjects in Japan and New Zealand), Denmark, Ethiopia, Finland, France, India, Ireland, Thailand, North Korea, Philippines, Soviet Union (Russia), South Korea, Sweden, United Kingdom (Britain), Yugoslavia.

Below the names of nations appear 10 bipolar attributes identified by the following pairs of antonyms, each separated by 7 numbered spaces: beautiful—ugly, democratic—undemocratic, efficient—inefficient, likable—not likable, neutralist—partisan, planned economy—market economy, progressive—reactionary, rich natural resources—poor natural resources, rural—urban, well educated—poorly educated. At the top of the page, the numbered spaces are designated by adverbs as in *Rating of Acquaintances* (p. 101).

RATING OF SELF-ROLES

An introduction similar to that used in *Rating of Acquaintances* appears on a cover page. Twenty subsequent pages are each headed by one of the following roles: Myself in an emergency, as a sports participant, as a club member, as an activist or crusader, as a dancer, as an entertainer, as a fighter, as a friend to someone of the same sex, as a host (or hostess), as a driver, as a leader, as a neighbor, as a newcomer in a group, Myself when receiving advice, Myself at a party, Myself when I have failed, Myself as a housekeeper, as a student, as a teacher, as a worker.

Below the role designations appear 10 bipolar attributes identified by the following pairs of antonyms, each separated by 7 numbered spaces: imaginative—unimaginative, self-confident—insecure, hardworking—lazy, likable—not likable, calm—distressed, considerate—inconsiderate, skilled—unskilled, serious—light hearted, happy—unhappy, emotional—unemotional. At the top of the page, the numbered spaces are designated by adverbs as in *Rating of Acquaintances* (p. 101).

INDEX